# LYRIC PROVINCES
# IN THE ENGLISH RENAISSANCE

# Lyric Provinces in the English Renaissance

HAROLD TOLIVER

Ohio State University Press: Columbus

Copyright © 1985 by the Ohio State University Press
*All Rights Reserved*

**Library of Congress Cataloging in Publication Data**
Toliver, Harold E.
Lyric provinces in the English Renaissance.

Includes index.
1. English poetry—Early modern, 1500–1700—History and criticism.   I. Title.
PR541.T64   1985        821'.3'09        85–10569
ISBN 0-8142-0391-4

# Contents

Preface — vii

PART ONE: Lyric Locality
1 The Objects of Lyric Address — 3
2 Between Chaos and Cosmos — 35

PART TWO: Social Placement
3 Local Habitation and Its Genius — 53
4 Jonson and the Poet's Circle — 71
5 Donne's Silhouettes and Absences — 95

PART THREE: Natural and Supernatural Provinces
6 Herbert's Interim and Final Places — 125
7 Herrick's Book of Realms and Moments — 147
8 Milton and Others Walking, Soaring, and Falling — 167
9 Momentum and the Spirit's Passage in Vaughan — 185
10 Marvell's Flies in Crystal — 207
Notes — 233
Index — 245

# PREFACE

Poets are not alone in being prepared to see new places in settled ways and describe them in received images. When Henry VII commissioned John Cabot and his sons as representatives to new western lands, he imagined his deputies primarily imposing a transplanted order rather than discovering a new one. The attitude is more important than any specific transplants he had in mind in this westward march of empire: "We have granted to them, and also to every of them, the heires of them, and every of them, and their deputies, and have given them licence to set up our banners and ensignes in every village, towne, castle, isle, or maine land of them newly found."[1] This grandly presumptuous conquest that expects castles in a wilderness and the perpetuity of English law until the end of time aims to encompass all contingencies in its legalistic framework. Outer regions will be assimilated into dynasties, never mind the hostility of natives. In a similar manner, the ancient deserts of the Mediterranean and certain biblical expectations of what burning bushes, what gods, or what shepherds shall exist everywhere encroach upon the deserts of Utah and California: those who travel see these and other new landscapes in terms of old myths of place and descriptive topoi. Their perceptions take on the structure, tonality, and nomenclature of the past; their language becomes as much recollection as greeting.

Modern cultural carryalongs continue to operate much like Henry's, but with perhaps less obvious imperiousness and more bureaucratic efficiency. The motel one arrives at after a long drive, as Richard Wilbur observes, has the usual parking lot "hacked out of a stand of trees" and the usual swimming pool. The uniformity that Henry's agents sought to impose on the wilderness modern technology achieves by erasing traces of locality. As Wilbur speculates, "We Americans might be becoming a race which, for all its restless motion, moves by preference through a repetitive labyrinth of highway, ramp, lobby, snack bar, escalator, and concourse—an anaesthetic modular world in which we are at home only because things are everywhere the same."[2]

When colonizers bring their cargo of cultural expectations to a new time and place, however, they never achieve an unequivocal victory, any more than the Old Testament was ever able to dominate the New; they usually settle for assimilating one thing to another and in the journey of cultural forms end up leaving behind a trail of discards. We tend to forget that much of any given culture was once marginal and had to be nurtured on foreign soil. More often than not, an old empire fails until it changes, as the Cabots failed.

The concern of the literary historian is in part that ever-renewed past being introduced under the new conditions that poets confront and thus the parallel movement of literary and social history. Literature is inseparable from the rest of discourse, as the study of signs the past decade has made clearer; but it also remains distinct from social history, since poets look less to common discourse than to specific literary predecessors as their models. Like explorers and colonizers, they are often careful observers of place, but if they stake claims, they do so not in order to "subdue, occupy, and possess" or to seize "rule, title, and jurisdiction,"[3] but to bring what is distinct and valuable within some sort of verbal compass and relationship with the speaker. They know that muses tend to favor genii loci and that to address the objects of a place they cannot be too arbitrary with them.

It is also true that they bring formulas and loyalty to a cultural heritage with them, which complicates the nature of the lyric address. T. S. Eliot, for instance, would have us apply Latin poetry generally as a standard for the various Western poetries that followed it and measure Milton's provincial eccentricity by its departure from that norm. Renaissance writers as a rule would have agreed. They saw their own localities and historical moments in the figures and kinds of Homer, Theocritus, Virgil, and the Bible. Those who worked their way from pastoral to epic were taking what they understood to be a Virgilian course; others followed

Martial or Horace or Ovid as a given genre and decorum suggested. However, any imaginative excursion or new insight carries the poet away from such points of departure. He cannot know ahead of time what he will find salvageable, any more than wagon trains going westward knew what the terrain and the weather would force them to discard. He can only predict with some certainty that the collisions of received topoi and new conditions will be unsettling.

My more specific concern is not poetry's encounters with new places in general but those of major seventeenth-century poets "on the margin," deciding what to discard as they learn to be new regionalists. I emphasize the displacement and the new because of the remoteness of so many of their lyric sites. A restlessness similar to that of westward exploration is detectable in the wandering of lyric personas and in their new terms of address. If the chronological story of literature in English has been generally one of abandoned centers and styles, abandoned neoclassicism, romanticism, modernism, it was dramatically so in Donne, Herbert, Marvell, Vaughan, and Milton. Literary history as they enacted it was not smoothly evolving but highly reactive,[4] albeit with important retrenchments. The first major shift in the Renaissance was led by Donne and cuts lyric more or less in half at a divide that fell roughly at the death of Queen Elizabeth, the Renaissance being not a single period but a group of overlapping movements. In the earlier Renaissance, courtly poetry broke loose from the comparative anonymity of lyric and took up an acquaintance with continental love poetry. Its commitment to secular affairs and to the educational reforms of humanism placed a good many constraints on the poet. The mid-Renaissance change came as a discarding or modifying of those constrictions, especially their courtly and social obligations, antagonism to which Donne dramatized again and again. George Herbert could not have become the poet he did had he ignored Donne's challenges to courtly love poetry or tried to carry forward Spenser's or Sidney's version of the poetic vocation. Neither could he pretend to be a medievalist, of course, although he took up many of the types, iconic commonplaces, and symbolic uses of sacraments and doctrines from medieval poetry. Instead, he generated a new set of complaints about service (new from a courtly perspective) and a different concept of the obligations of love, to cite just two matters. The service he chose in lieu of service to a patron or Petrarchan lady not only tested his patience and discipline quite differently from the way Wyatt and Sidney were tested but encouraged self-consciousness about the location and the nature of poetry itself.

Sidney and Spenser among the earlier group devote the most attention in poetry itself to the ins and outs of a poetic career, thanks in part to their own on-again, off-again relations to the court. The difference between them and Donne or Herbert is that they either try to remain "in" or explain why it is impossible to do so. Spenser regards fairyland as an equivalent to a new world and departs from predecessors; but he also tends to think of English institutions as renewals of something like a Roman tradition carried through the earlier Renaissance. Seventeenth-century poets for the most part move quite literally outside—into solitary meadows, woodlands, and gardens—or inside to enclosures such as private chambers or the temple. Some of them take leave of the residue of Tudor absolutism they find in James and Charles—the sort of absolutism that commissioned the explorations (and raids) not only of the Cabots but Hawkins, Raleigh, Drake, and others, and subordinated commerce, the church, the educational system, and the arts to its sovereignty. If for explorers, breaking loose began when they discovered the attractions and perils of new places, for Donne it began when he discovered new relations-of-two, not only outside the court but openly distrustful of it. A network of new access roads back to society then had to be constructed and new forms of address worked out that could position the lovers with respect to it and publish them to it.

In the matter of reformation, the seventeenth-century sometimes considered its radicalism a conservative return to origins, as Milton in breaking with kings and prelates believes himself to be returning to scriptural authority and an earlier church. But of course it was a scripture interpreted by the individual reader largely without sanctions other than the ones he found in the better authorities and in his own reason and inner light. That sort of departure also demanded new routes of access, in this case between an audience and the poet deploying scriptural types or framing his own versions of scriptural topics. Such departures from what poets perceived to be the poetic orthodoxies are indeed provincial, not just in Eliot's sense of their requiring deviations from Latin traditions but in the poet's identification with places not at a cultural center. Milton subsequently became something of an establishment himself, but initially his imaginative commitment to Eden and elsewhere was a sign of independence. In his way he voyaged as intrepidly as Satan and ventured as ambitiously as Eve.

I assume in these remarks that such changes in setting help the literary historian assess the poet's relations to predecessors and to what the poet has perceived to be reigning practice. Cutting across such generic divisions as cavalier, metaphysical, devotional, amorous, and odic kinds, the representation of "places" conducts us along the path that lyric and other forms took from Wyatt to Marvell and Milton. Although an examination of actual social institutions and the office-holding situations of poets and their patrons and associates would help us appreciate more fully the connections between history, biography, and symbolic landscape, it would also force extensive digressions. Hence I plan to pursue only the accepted canonical literature, not to explore pictorial traditions, emblem literature, typology, or other features of renaissance imagery. These have received a fair amount of attention, as have the history of ideas, renaissance training in rhetoric and humanism generally, and such matters of intellectual history as Platonism and Hermeticism. My concern is also restricted primarily to lyric address rather than description, together with its implications for the career-mindedness of poets seeking new terrain.

Although I have concentrated on these limited aspects of familiar texts, I have had to make some difficult choices even so to stay within decent compass. One might argue, for instance, for Crashaw and some of the lesser cavaliers and metaphysicals if Herrick is to be here. But I require a follow-up to Jonson and a contrast to the metaphysicals, and the intrinsic worth of the poems argues for Herrick; I've not been convinced of a comparable worth in the several others who might be considered on strictly historical grounds. In Marvell's case something beyond "Upon Appleton House" and the Horatian Ode could easily be justified, but I have not wanted to duplicate an already extensive commentary on the other poems, and these particular ones make the main point.

One could also justify a good deal more on such predecessors as Spenser, Sidney, and Shakespeare. But the current scholarship on Spenser and Sidney seems essentially correct, fairly full, and relevant to my purpose in its demonstrations of the poet's laureate functions and courtly orientation. For Shakespeare the terms need to be set up a little differently and developed extensively. To avoid fattening an already bulky study, I've decided on a separate project devoted to the later plays and to getting a run at Milton. Hence though the passage from those plays to "L'Allegro," "Il Penseroso," and "Comus" suggests a good deal about the renaissance literary "story" and about the relation of dramatic and lyric kinds, I've not tried to do more with these here than is absolutely necessary.

The selection of framing theorists and modern lyricists in the opening chapter is more open to the charge of capriciousness. Though poststructuralism has been on my mind as on everyone else's, I've detoured around the main skirmishes in order to keep theory within limits. Had I been more hospitable toward a number of modern poets, too, they would have taken over. The result would have been far less commentary on the main body of poems I wanted to consider, in a book that submarined into that great sea of discourse on postmodernism still unbottomed after several decades of soundings. The case for "substance" in the seventeenth-century lyricists could only be made finally by prolonged stays in their company. The practical matter too is that one who reads "To Penshurst" or "Lycidas" is not for the moment conscious of much not cited in some way by Jonson or Milton, the unavoidable questions of genre and influence being complication enough.

If this suggests one of those drivers who leave a wake of honking motorists in their wake as they run obliviously through one red light after another, I counter with an alternative figure: finding the main routes clogged, one goes around. And so, for instance, by way of general definition-making, I've drawn upon a small piece of Heidegger and ignored now more traveled routes. That such a bypass is legitimate is suggested by Heidegger's service as a connecting route between seventeenth-century ontology and twentieth-century perspectives. But such choices are no more than convenient, obviously not inevitable, like the selection of one of a dozen models of cars or computers any of which works. We can use, and can afford, only one model at a time. On with the drive itself.

The essays on Herbert and Herrick were published in slightly different versions in *SEL* and *ELH*. Debts to scholars and critics herein are usually specific and are indicated where appropriate, but I have drawn more frequently upon Arnold Stein's Milton than citations might suggest and have kept Earl Miner's view of metaphysical, cavalier, and restoration modes in mind on occasions that may not be evident.

PART ONE

LYRIC LOCALITY

*The twilight song of the wood pewee appears to have no territorial function and is said to be independent of the breeding cycle, and the daytime song also continues long after the end of the breeding season. . . . Similarly, in many species of American song birds, the lengthening, elaboration, and sometimes complete change in the song after the end of the nesting period is noteworthy, and these changes often seem, to our ears, to take the form of aesthetic improvement.—W. W. Thorpe,* Bird Song

> *Forests spread*
> *Brooks plunge*
> *Rocks persist*
> *Mist diffuses*
>
> *Meadows wait*
> *Springs well*
> *Winds dwell*
> *Blessing muses*
> *Martin Heidegger,* The Thinker as Poet

*Nature may be cooked into all shapes, and not recognized. Mountains and oceans we think we understand;—yes, so long as they are contented to be such, and are safe with the geologist; but when they are melted in Promethean alembics, and come out men; and then, melted again, come out words, without any abatement but with an exaltation of power—!—Emerson, Journal "O," for April 1846*

*The Poet should instal himself and shove all usurpers from their chairs by electrifying mankind with the right tone, long wished for, never heard. The true centre thus appearing, all false centres are suddenly superseded, and grass grows in the Capitol.—Emerson, Journal for 27 June 1846*

# THE OBJECTS OF LYRIC ADDRESS

CHAPTER ONE

POSSESSION AND CELEBRATION

We are told that some birds sing with special enthusiasm mornings and evenings to confirm their territories. One would like to believe that their songs do more than assert squatter's rights, however—that they commemorate a locality, for instance, with its particular sunrises, shelter, delectable seeds, or insect provisions. In any case when such virtuoso performers as nightingales, skylarks, cuckoos, oven birds, and gold-feathered birds of mere being get likened to lyricists, it is not merely for command of territory but also for vocal brilliance. As a way into topical mappings of poetry and their word-thing relations, I want to explore that mixture of possession and celebration that human singers find in the twofold nature of lyric as it appropriates and commemorates.

Let us begin with an example, A. R. Ammons's "Plunder," which in its anxiety over the possession it seizes and perhaps the changes it works on its landscape avoids outright rapture over what may be truly there. Its plundering would not get underway at all were it not for meaning and beauty somehow inherent in its scene:

> I have appropriated the windy twittering of aspen leaves
> into language, stealing something from reality like a
> silverness: drop-scapes of ice from peak sheers:
>
> much of the rise in brooks over slow-rolled glacial stones:
> the loop of reeds over the shallow's edge when birds
> feed on the rafts of algae: I have taken right out of the

> air the clear streaks of bird music and held them in my
> head like shifts of sculpture glint: I have sent language
> through the mud roils of a raccoon's paws like a net,
>
> netting the roils: made my own uses of the downwind's
> urgency on a downward stream: held with a large scape
> of numbness the black distance upstream to the mountains
>
> flashing and bursting: meanwhile, everything else, frog,
> fish, bear, gnat has turned in its provinces and made off
> with its uses: My mind's indicted by all I've taken.[1]

Whether or not Ammons had read Jacquetta Hawkes's *A Land* or Paul Shepard's *Man in the Landscape*,[2] he suggests the residual faculties of our ancestors that the environment slowly molded. Though birds and the ancient inscriptions of the ice have no language of their own, the poet finds attractions and repulsions in them, finds something like kinship that could be said to derive from experience of long standing with the planet. What he offers, however, is not the detailed notation of a long-term environmentalism or of the naturalist. Nor does he look for much assistance from previous observers or from demonic or divine beings who might have left their signatures on the landscape. (He does not, for instance, turn noticeably to romantics or to Robert Frost's kind of explicit fabling to capitalize on description or convert analysis into epigram.) Instead he itemizes apparently actual objects reconstituted in his own second world knowing that he cannot help changing things or selecting just the "silverness" he wants. Catching things on the move, he arrests them in icons, tropes, rhetorical devices, twists of individual vision. And so catching itself plundering, the mind is self-indicted—choosing even that word knowingly from the root (*dicere*) that also gives us "diction," "dictator," "dictates," and other staples of naming, ruling over, and accusing.

When parts of the landscape insist upon a greater wildness, the poet discovers the limits of his power. Even the words with which he packages his thefts are not exclusively the mind's or tradition's: some of them suggest primal relations imposed on phonetics by the sounds of leaves, brooks, and birds—sounds that words recapture even as they nudge them toward intelligibility. Without some such independence in the scene, the poet would need less force to subdue it; he would perhaps come closer to mere recording. But nature is both desirable and alien, the poet both observer and raider. Moreover, despite his having taken over the locality, his version of the Promethean alembic leaves the landscape relatively unharmed, and he refrains from touching some of it. In that re-

## THE OBJECTS OF LYRIC ADDRESS    5

spect his appropriation differs from the plunderings of industrialization and other extensions of colonizing, as an odic address to a tree obviously differs from druidic worship of it or an ax's assault upon it. Ammons remarks in "Extremes and Moderations," that the

> artificial has taken on the complication of the natural and where to take hold, how to let go, perplexes individual action: ruin and gloom are falling off the shoulders of progress: blue-green
>
> globe, we have tripped your balance and gone into exaggerated possession: this seems to me the last poem written to the world before its freshness capsizes and sinks into the slush: the rampaging industrialists, the chemical devisers and manipulators
>
> are forging tanks, filling vats of smoky horrors because of dollar lust, so as to live in long white houses on the summits of lengthy slopes, for the pleasures of making others spur and turn: but common air moves over the slopes, and common rain's
>
> losing its heavenly clarity. (*CP*, p. 340)

He is not the first to lament the varieties of exploitation men have invented—religious, scientific, industrial—nor the first to resort to prosy accusations to wedge opinions into the songlike inclinations of lyric. But lyric's mode of perception, which takes "right out of the / air the clear streaks of bird music," also appreciates natural wonders and atones for its intrusion even as it intrudes. The result is the settling in of a local genius who stakes out a territory while commemorating it or rather *as* his commemoration of it.

The parallel between poets and birds, however, also stresses often an instinctive and spontaneous accord of singer and setting, or the desirability of such. Its appeal to several poets has been a suggestion of superior consciousness in that effortlessness, which underscores by contrast the labors of poetry. Even transcendentalized birds have no need to use force and so can escape the ambivalence of poets who are alienated from what they name even as they are attracted to it. John Crowe Ransom's prosaic ducks, for instance, model an entirely guiltless, though in this case also songless, accord with place. Because they need very little to take up residence wherever they touch down, they forestall competition between possessor and site. Though local while they nest, before and after that they make the entire domain of water and shore theirs without leaving marks upon it:

> Ducks require no ship and sail
> Bellied on the foamy skies,
> Who scud north. Male and female

> Make a slight nest to arise
> Where they overtake the spring,
> Which clogs with muddy going.
>
> The zone unready. But the pond,
> Eye of a bleak Cyclops visage, catches
> Such glints of hyacinth and bland
> As bloom in aquarelles of ditches
> On a cold spring ground, a freak,
> A weathering chance even in the wrack.
>
> The half-householders for estate
> Beam their floor with ribs of grass,
> Disdain your mortises and slate
> And Lar who invalided lies,
> The marsh quakes dangerous, the port
> Where wet and dry precisely start.[3]

Ducks need no property, permanence, separation from the elements, storable food, or navigational help. They go

> where the winds and waters blow
> On raveling banks of fissured seas
> In reeds nestles, or will rise and go
> Where Capicornus dips his hooves
> In the blue chasm of no wharves.

As Ransom realizes, ducks in themselves are of no great concern of poets or their interpreters and are not likely to be allegorized as visitant seers. But they nonetheless contrast meaningfully to poets, who need a great deal. Ideally, in Ransom's view, poets should also be adaptable and beyond questing for subjugating ideas. They should live at one with seascape or landscape and carry fewer houseplans and Platonist schemes about with them. But it is inhuman to disdain mortises and to leave without packing or remembering. Although ducks are a remonstrance, almost an ideal, no mere human can hope to emulate them.

The birds of the romantics in contrast are beyond rather than below the human. More wandering voice and mystery than definable thing, Wordsworth's cuckoo, for instance, is what the visionary poet would like to be. Its very presence "at once far off and near" transforms the ordinary earth into a golden place recalled from the poet's youth. Wordsworth addresses it as an "invisible thing, / A voice, a mystery," with an enthusiasm quickly aroused, the lyric crossing well underway from the outset:

> O blithe New-comer! I have heard,
> I hear thee rejoice.
> O Cuckoo! shall I call thee Bird,
> Or but a wandering Voice?

But the speaker is also held off and realizes that the cuckoo as mere bird babbles and belongs to the same earth as he does. Its twofold nature reveals a like discrepancy between two levels of the scene, one naturalistic and the other transcendent. "Fit home" for such a bird, earth follows it into mystery, as the bird becomes half absence, half presence, the lyric crossing it entices half commemoration, half elegy.

In using the word *crossing,* I am planing down a word from Harold Bloom to fit a more limited purpose. By it I mean primarily bridge-building between the poet and an other that may seem to come to meet him. He can achieve no possession and make no lyric address without closing with it in some way. But even so prepared for lamination into the context I want for it, the term raises problems. It is difference in the object that makes it stand out—stand out from other objects, stand outward from the consciousness that seeks to master it—yet the poet's vocabulary is the common one, entangled in his other moments and in culture generally. Any good poem has to twist words almost loose from those connections to make any difficult crossing possible. Thus when Cleopatra, one of Shakespeare's most prolific myth-makers, says of Anthony, "His legs bestrid the ocean, his rear'd arm / Crested the world: his voice was propertied / As all the tuned spheres" (*Antony and Cleopatra* 5.2.82–84), she forces us to pause not only on the outmoded "bestrid" but on what are ordinarily the familiar "reared" (raised up, bred, threatening, mastering), "crested" (heraldic, topped, making the world a shield), and "propertied" (made properly his own, took over the characteristics of, cosmic in size and balanced in proportion). In their combinations these modifications of common language sustain a hyperbole unusual in its visual concreteness and sense of muscularity even for Cleopatra—frequently aware of Antony's great weight. A colossus is thus placed by her swerves from the common track, and the crossing she makes is doubled: the word-user gets from unvoiced (perhaps unrealized, inert) feeling to the satisfactions of a grand gesture that sweeps Antony into her mythic empire, and as rhetorician she carries with her such listeners as are of a mind to follow, so that they too take leave of their apathy and join her enthusiasm. Any deviation from ordinary language may achieve something similar, but only in collaboration with our sense of supportive common meanings of legs, arms, voices.

If enough valedictory substance survives such verbal leaps, the crossing tends to be lyric, as the Antony of this perception, whether formally addressed or not, is made a verbal presence over and above the real presence we have seen enacted up to this point. But he is also in a sense *merely* her verbal presence, and such praise can be generated only after he has taken his stoic Roman exit. Indeed, it is precisely his absence as a real creature, a limited personality after all, that makes Cleopatra's bridge-building possible. Subject and object are not really woven together; both remain in their places. Yet the attraction is strong enough to call Cleopatra after him, not merely with words of course but with quite poisonous asps.

We clearly need a metaphor for such verbal possessions and repossessions that will suggest the traffic back and forth. Yet several sorts of confusion are possible in the choice of "crossings," if we take it to mean contact with exclusively personal objects. Even an artfully prepared context may not effectively trim off all the dangling references that words and images carry with them. Ransom puts some of the leftovers of "estate" to ironic use, for instance, in mocking simultaneously the pretensions of human households and the lowliness of ducks. It isn't clear that Wordsworth gets rid of the trailing associations a cuckoo brings with it. He leaves us wondering if a better visionary emblem couldn't have been found than the one that pops out of clocks and reminds us of simpletons and cuckholds. Dolabella and about half the readership of *Antony and Cleopatra* have reservations about the reconstructed Antony as well.

For Shelley likenesses between the poet and the skylark generate a slightly different ambivalence. Like the cuckoo the skylark eludes definition, not because of obscurity but because of its transcendence and the simplicity of its joy, which serves as a reproach to men who "look before and after / And pine for what is not." Describing it is simultaneously the poet's calling and a distortion of its nature. Its reality is less at issue than the poet's perceptions and the inadequacy of human song, which becomes doubly painful beside the skylark's "clear keen joyance":

> Better than all measures
>   Of delightful sound,
> Better than all treasures
>   That in books are found,
> Thy skill to poet were, thou scorner of the ground.
>
> Teach me half the gladness
>   That thy brain must know,
> Such harmonious madness
>   From my lips would flow
> The world should listen then—as I am listening now.

Translating the relationship of bird to poet into that of instructor to ingenue enables Shelley to imagine a future closing of the gap between them: what the bird knows and can do, it will teach the bard. But the discrepancy between them can never be totally erased as long as metaphor imposes an alien materiality on the bird. The chief declared nay-sayer in this case is Thomas Hardy, who in looking for Shelley's emblem of transcendence finds instead merely common dust:

> Somewhere afield here something lies
> In Earth's oblivious eyeless trust
> That moved a poet to prophecies—
> A pinch of unseen, unguarded dust:
>
> The dust of the lark that Shelley heard.[4]

The lack of location in "somewhere" and earth's unseeing indifference preclude any but fanciful connections with such a once-etherial creature; and so faeries are commissioned to find it and bring it back in a silver-lined casket—it has taken so little to inspire a bard to such "Ecstatic heights in thought and rhyme."

The aim of the better song Shelley requests is not merely celebration: it is also instruction, as transactions between singer and place are again complicated by the world that listens and implicitly by predecessors who condition both singer and audience. Obviously no poet possesses or commemorates in a vacuum, and that conditioning of song by tradition adds dimensions to the "indictment" that Ammons, Wordsworth, and Shelley acknowledge in their different ways. As Emerson writes in completing the second journal entry at the head of this chapter, "Now and then we hear rarely a true tone, a single strain of the right ode; but the Poet does not know his place, he defers to these old conventions" (Journal for 27 June 1846).

In pastoral lyricism, to take an extreme case of that dependence on conventions, the poet adopts a set of artifices and wears a well-used mask. The metropolis to which he and his readers normally belong lies at some distance from the Arcadian rusticity to which he goes to get a vantage point back on the metropolis. Both the taking up of the convention and its perspective on the capital are public acts. Virgil's first eclogue, for instance, is acutely aware of its cultural center and dramatizes the relationship between shepherdom and Rome, or more broadly, between shepherds and several territories. While Tityrus remains at ease in pleasant fields, pastures, and orchards, Meliboeus heads into exile toward what he considers the ends of earth, as impious soldiers and barbarians take over his fields. The "god" that gives Tityrus his ease is none other than the city itself ("urbem quam dicunt Romam"). The central authority of empire and its patronage of shepherd-poets stand behind him, whereas for Meliboeus just enough rural pleasantry remains to remind him of what he has lost: rest on green boughs, a supper of mellow apples and cheese, and friendship for an evening. In less identifiable locations such as Frost's New England and Spenser's faery land, the poet proceeds to a personal "elsewhere" but is still likely to use it to size up a familiar world. Like all poets however isolated, he must negotiate between his and tradition's landscapes if only, again, because the vocabulary he uses is the common one, refashioned.

Cultural recollection, then, is always part of the crossing, or perhaps "knitting" would be better in such cases, since a wealth of implications and intersections gives any poet working within a recognizable tradition a tissue of references to work with. Despite the relative privacy of lyric and the singularity of its voicing, relations to such traditions and to the listening world wedge between poet and object and make any reading of a poem a retrospective act, embedded in the diachronicity of influences. Songs come by the promptings of species and book placements or "topics," not solely by individual virtuosity. I raise that complicating of the poet's verbal plundering only in a preliminary way, since it is best considered in specific cases, as a matter of period styles and influences. But it should be noted that the self-orientation of lyric is often at odds with its public dimensions, its orphic ambitions with its laureate ones. Whereas celebrations of place and descriptive amplitude underscore lyric's referential interests and whereas the orphic poet—the enchanting son of the muse Calliope—seeks to tame a wild nature, the listening world demands its place. The lyricist need not acknowledge that as explicitly as Shelley does; Ammons and Wordsworth are not exceptional, for instance, in ignoring both the conventions they use and the listener, and even Shelley thinks of the listening world primarily as proof of the poet's authority. The ambitious bard feels himself the true center, legislating for mankind, "all false centres" else superseding. But if the poet adjusts to the authority of the capital, as Tityrus does, he applies it to the setting, superintending in its name, less an orphic figure than agriculturalist in an economy centered elsewhere.

Whether the authority he applies is personal or is sanctioned by convention, fastening the object in words is an authoritative act that seizes possession by a certain means that informed readers are expected to recognize. But seizes possession of what? The balancing of rhetorical, mimetic, and expressive elements, like questions of substance, are sufficiently sensitive and debatable in lyric to require some further elaboration. Hence before taking up specific renaissance variants, I want to offer a minimal theoretical framework for them. First in passing and later with some explicit attention, I will also suggest reasons for lyric address being crucially periodized.

## TO POSSESS IS TO IMPOSE DESIGN AND TO CLAIM REAL SUBSTANCE

In what sense does a lyric address incorporate the topographical features of an actual place? Does a poem in some way recover reality or merely create stage settings for self-expression, claiming exemption from the rules that ordinarily judge an Antony and install entries for "cuckoo" in the dictionary? If the nature of the real, even apart from our attempts to formulate it, is problematic, it is surely more so in a poem that does not claim to mirror nature exactly or collect its particulars one by one like so many potatoes brought to the cellar. Such directives and temporal indicators as "here," "there," "now," and "then," and features of direct address become special conventions and discourse labels in poetry. They do not carry the precise meanings that the same words would have in direction-giving on a London street corner. Pointers in lyric set a tone, bridge elements, and establish grammatical relations. Thus when "On a Drop of Dew" begins "See how the Orient Dew, / Shed from the Bosom of the Morn," we are introduced not to an actual but to a composed scene mapped as a set of progressing signals to the reader.

More answerable than simple mimetic theory to that dissolving and recombining of borrowed parts is Sidney's notion that the poet's invented or second world is more perfect than the one we normally inhabit and more responsive to the poet's desire. In Sidney's implicit analogy, an idea or foreconceit is to a poem what the creator's plan is to the cosmos: it deals with a real world and prevents images from becoming private castles in air without bearing on the moral decisions we have to make. However, Sidney does not explore differences between the way objects appear in language and the ways we encounter them through the senses. For him the poet's reformulation of reality is primarily for instructional purposes, as in its presenting of princes and heroes better than life's. Unfortunately, not all fictions create an improved—merely an altered and more coherent—nature. Also, unlike rearrangement of actual objects such as a gardener makes, the poet's materials are merely verbal. They rearrange our ideas. Poetics must therefore consider specifically verbal topical mappings: whereas in the daily world we approach objects as ontological things, the poet's invented heterocosm gives us pageants and performances; and whereas real sea lions and serpents are not obliged to illustrate anything except natural laws, hermeneutic practice teaches us to expect objects-as-images to be revealing.

For instance, since the grounds of a likeness cannot at the same time be exclusively topographical and meaningful, the poet usually gives objects lying in the same vicinity metaphoric and synecdochial connection. Compression and epitomizing are especially vital to the renaissance enterprise of preparing objects for inclusion in what Sidney considers the golden world. Indeed, synecdoche, the seizing of the whole by a representative part, is made to assimilate a good deal, its value being a kind of logical governance. What counts in it is the power that control of the part gives its user—power to represent in a compressed form without sacrificing scope, for instance, as in Donne's claims to be able to recapture the entire world by his mastery of love's chambers, or as in Marvell's reduction of all that's made to green thought in the garden's containment of the world's best resources. As Blake realized in "Auguries of Innocence," an important and quite special power of symbolic thought and especially of poetry is "To see a World in a Grain of Sand." At the same time, the user of synecdoche cannot automatically claim that nothing counts *except* the part he cites. On the contrary renaissance poets are likely to maintain that possession of the whole would be better if one had the means. Thus in "On a Drop of Dew," Marvell's central demonstrator is metaphorically like the soul, which in turn is a small part of the whole to which the poem conducts our attention; but neither likeness nor dew-drop compression is as good as reincorporation of the soul into its source: it is better to be dissolved into the Almighty Sun and be possessed by it. No coy figure makes that crossing for us.

That the various rhetorical, figural, and logical devices of language appropriate reality is the main cause of the poet's indictment, then, and from a modern perspective it is grammatical relation and other tools of language that Sidney should have credited with the poet's remaking of nature rather than witty reinvention of a golden world. Indeed, Michael Riffaterre suggests on behalf of a sizeable body of recent theorists that as soon as poet and reader get involved in poetic signs they leave the so-called real world behind as merely a first level.[5] The second of two levels or stages of reading is a manifestation of *semiosis,* an especially systematic use of signs that often comes equipped with a metalanguage to fend off naive referentiality. That notion is more valuable to account for Ammons's kind of poem than Sidney's "foreconceit," translated into a second nature; but one is nonetheless hesitant to sacrifice the signified world entirely to the play of signs. Maintaining the necessity and virtual independence of a second level of discourse is tantamount to making the poet's inventions both different in kind from and better than the experienced world. It is true that a good many renaissance readers also expected serious texts to proceed to some such higher level. But even the didactic poetry they called for did not completely sever words from things or lose concretion in systematic ideas. Sidney's view of poetry is reinforced by the assumption that history and philosophy—servants of truth in its concrete and abstract forms—are not so far apart that it cannot combine them in its pleasurable fictions and metaphors. In uniting them not all poems lean toward symbolism or allegory, which sacrifice real lions to the courage or the wrath they signify and depopulate settings to make trophies. Sidney insists on some level of literal imitation, as Dante on the allegory of theologians, to discourage hasty flights from locality.

Another reason not to sever texts from their references is that literary periods and trails of influence get obscured when we do so, as under new criticism's more extreme versions of formalism, which are usually applied more to lyric than to other forms. My assumption is that significant lyrics always respond in some way to historical circumstances and that the term *imitation* is useful to describe that response, provided that we are aware of the special workings of language in them.

One instrument of such awareness if we choose to draw upon it is Heidegger's word *gestell,* or "placement."[6] The English equivalent carries traces of "locus" while pointing up the poet's resituating of objects in imagistic and metrical settings for purposes that we detect primarily in the poem itself. That trace of topography makes "placement" particularly useful for topical mappings and salvages some of the ambiguity of "topoi." Two other Heideggeian concepts make convenient accompaniment for that "framing" and draw us a little further in the direction of mimesis—the poem's capacity to "let things dwell" and its "lighting up" of objects or bidding them come to light (p. xvii). I include them incidentally here, more or less uprooted from their contexts, because they suggest the celebrational aura of lyric. What Wordsworth, Keats, and Shelley see in their respective bird-singers is some such special illumination, which in a toned-down version is also what Stevens discovers in the bird singing from its palm at the end of the mind. Neither phrase is quite identical with "mimesis," nor is either very hospitable to the romantic preoccupation with the self and the transcendent Idea in which the self is sometimes immersed in the Hegelian view of lyric.

Rather, they find the emergence of the poem only in negotiations with a setting, while also acknowledging implicitly the threefold interactions of language, reality, and poet-as-such (whatever his identity may be on occasions when he is not writing). What "placement," "letting dwell," and "lighting up" collectively point to—with some tension among them—is the fitting of objects into interpretive schemes in such ways that reading can engage them on analytic grounds—as images of the real and expressions of attitudes toward it. To be appreciated in its own light, the object must be allowed to dwell where and as it is; yet paradoxically poetic framing also unfailingly pulls it from whatever primary settings experience may have provided for it. The strength of the pull is a measure not merely of the poet's personal strength but of a chosen language, selected from the cultural stock and altered more or less as intent and a given regionality dictate. The appropriated object-image must carry some fragment of a first world with it but carry it into an illuminated state that is the poet's version of empire, now more likely a personal empire like Ammons's than a collective one like Virgil's or Ben Jonson's.

However, we must take any poetic empire, private or public, to mean not placement merely but placement with something of what Morse Peckham thinks of as a perilous or chaotic relation of parts or that Herrick in a more genteel way talks of as a "delight in disorder."[7] Every act of placement in a good poem is also an act of displacement in which received tropes, and reality itself, are shown to resist. Ammons's "Plunder," to return to it, assumes that however commanding the poet, his language sometimes proceeds through mud roils, combing from a thick and murky substance. Since he makes no claim upon them, frog, fish, bear, and gnat turn away and make off. The physical world adds up to too much for any one act of lighting and placing to handle it. A resilient poet may retaliate by means of whatever vocabulary he employs for bears and gnats escaping, but he knows limits. He balances the language we know, in the rhythms we expect, against surprising departures in both and may balance images brought forward with rebelling things and their qualities.

This disorder is the other side of presence in worthwhile lyrics, as some degree of social disorder is the proof of order. Heidegger's brief list of natural phenomena at the head of this chapter is a case in point. Forests spread, as is their wont; brooks plunge; mist diffuses: the poet has an exact word for what each does and a way of lining them up in orderly parallels that do not appear to be confusing. But words and phenomena also draw apart and do not quite form a closed system. The poet's preemptory way with both is as evident as the gardener's work from a severely pruned tree. Now forests do of course exist and may even logically be said to spread, but saying that also applies a human scale and a panoramic eye to them and rules out all the other things forests do and are. *Plunge* as a word for what brooks do moves further out of language's neutral zone into animation; it is as much dramatic as it is descriptive. Rocks do not really persist; they lie quietly without an effort of will. *Blessing* breaks such parallels even as it submits to the same grammatical construction; it muses and is implicitly hospitable to muses, but the other things in Heidegger's list may not be blessings, and all of them pull in their own directions against regulation. Their claim to our attention is partly that they exist and act as we perceive them, and this causes the poet to muse—perhaps to muse the obscure even as he excludes complications. Unlike Browning's lark on the wing and snail on the thorn, these behaving things do not capitulate to Pippa's optimism: they can be said on second glance to insist on a degree of confusion, which the poet controls by the brevity of his list and scarcity of detail. To appropriate and to be appropriate are two sides of the same thing.

Disorder by its nature is multifaceted and resourceful. It can inhere in the object or the observer, or in language, or in a collision between these and the audience's tradition-shaped expectations. Emily Dickinson's cryptic notation of an invisible choir celebrating its summer mass combines something of all of these:

> Further in Summer than the Birds
> Pathetic from the Grass
> A minor Nation celebrates
> Its unobtrusive Mass.
>
> No Ordinance be seen
> So gradual the Grace

> A pensive Custom it becomes
> Enlarging Loneliness.
>
> Antiquest felt at Noon
> When August burning low
> Arise this spectral Canticle
> Repose to typify
>
> Remit as yet no Grace
> No Furrow on the Glow
> Yet a Druidic Difference
> Enhances Nature now.[8]

The insect nation is comfortably at home; yet to human listeners it makes a foreign sound. Its voices and its residences are not ours; it remains invisible and intensifies loneliness. It may remind us of the way in which romantic birds disappear or send their songs from the borders of other worlds, but it is less grand. As in Heidegger's compressed poem, the abandoning of copia and an eliptical entrapment of meaning put off full possession. So compressed and unusual are Dickinson's "pathetic," "antiquest," and "furrow on the Glow," in fact, that one cannot be sure the text is right, as elsewhere it is a slant of light or a tone that introduces a similar estrangement.

Reality lends itself to different measurements and formulations, each but a provisional rendering, none a complete conquest. As one such formulation, lyric retains more of a speaker's affective response and more of the physical object's particularity than most others, which is part of its acknowledgment of disorder. Its conversion of things into images is often vivid, as it pinpoints something we have heretofore not noticed. As Wallace Stevens writes in *Adagia*, "The final poem will be the poem of fact in the language of fact. But it will be the poem of fact not realized before." Or again, "Perhaps there is a degree of perception at which what is real and what is imagined are one: a state of clairvoyant observation, accessible or possibly accessible to the poet or, say, the acutest poet." Or still again, "To be at the end of fact is not to be at the beginning of imagination but . . . to be at the end of both."[9] Certainly not avoidance of fact but distrust of commonplaces and universals characterizes the modern retreat from an earlier mimesis. Thus John Crowe Ransom's assault on the poetry of ideas is adamant against Platonist verities but quite comfortable with the properties of things. Objects have a built-in resistance not to poetic imagery but to structure and unified designs. As discrete entities they have a good many more sensory properties than any statement can render, but when they are converted into metaphors or images, they pull a respectable portion of thingness along, "presenting images so whole and clean that they resist the catalysis of thought." Despite the somewhat shadowy existence of a poem's simulacra, the citation of surfaces, in collaboration with meaning, gives things a presence, a sentiment that gets repeated over and over again among twentieth century anglo-American poets and critics.[10] The key matter for Ransom, one of our better spokesmen in this particular matter, is equilibrium: one must resist the temptation to pursue ideas at the expense of concretion but also the pursuit of *dinglichkeit* for its own sake. Substance and design are on a teeter-totter: where one prevails, the other falters. Thus neither the random surfaces of things nor the mind's order should be allowed to dominate: "Things as things do not necessarily interest us," and overly ranked and arranged objects certainly do not—where "things are on their good behavior, looking rather well, and arranged by lines into something approaching a military formation" (p. 872).

In terms of texture, the *qualities* of objects are not to be sacrificed to ideas. For Ransom, they are like those that Heidegger finds in *Physis,* which he translates not as "nature" but as the "emerging and arising, the spontaneous unfolding that lingers."[11] Qualities must be stable enough to be named, but our attention is directed more to the subject identifying them and to their arising than to their standing. Nothing nameable can be totally unique or subjective; the spontaneous unfolding must linger. But neither is its being or its naming ever quite finished. Anticipation and memory are part of a very tentative present. Thus in Ransom's words, too, "The aesthetic moment appears as a curious moment of suspension; between the Platonism in us, which is militant, always sciencing and devouring, and a starved inhibited aspiration towards innocence which . . . would like to respect and know the object as it might of its own accord reveal itself" (p. 877). If the poet squeezes objects tightly or yokes them firmly to a conceptual scheme, they become allegorical or rhetorical. Whether he tries to honor the thing itself without ideas or exploits it for illustrative purposes, however, he can neither cancel its properties entirely nor avoid some degree of exploitation.

SOME RENAISSANCE PREFERENCES IN DESIGN:
IDEA, EMBLEM, AND MUSIC

Renaissance poets and apologists normally say that they prefer the educative, bound image to the rebel image. Sidney, for instance, expects poetry to bind whatever historical concretion it uses to philosophy or to moral example. In the terms of Graham Hough's wheel of literary types in *A Preface to The Faerie Queene*, not only Sidney but other contemporaries of Spenser lean toward thesis-dominated forms and prefer emblems and hieroglyphic symbols to an image-dominated realism or an "image complex" incarnation of themes.[12] The rhetorical figures and structural patterns of renaissance manuals on good speaking and writing are other forms of that thesis dominance, and more relevant to lyric's musical alliances, so are the sound systems of meter and rhyme. Indeed, what imagery does with objects in putting them into such formulas as renaissance schoolmasters called *topographia, chronographia,* and *apostrophe,* musical settings and voicing do with phonetic design and stanzaic pattern, which are less talked about in renaissance advice-giving manuals. In songs proper, melodic sequence is usually accompanied by conventional and illustrative statement, which doubles up on the dominance. Compared with narrative and dramatic forms, such statement is attitudinal in lyric. Despite irregularities and the subversions of wit in some hands, they are parceled out in well-ordered cantabile elements. Their progression offers formal satisfaction after very brief, measured withholdings; synchronized with abstract statement or set within narrative, songs tend to suggest that the poet thinks first of closing the unit even when he has further meanings and perhaps a story to get on with. Sooner or later, however, statement, story, and musical unit wind up together. The range of disciplinary orders that renaissance lyricists impose on mimetic substance is thus considerable. Lyric is made to support social functions (educational or profitable, entertainment or pleasure), formal functions, and private functions having to do with plangent, confessional, and celebrational motives. Its means of presentation range all the way from the analytic (in argument, definition, and meditation) to the dominantly melodic, and include in between narative, dramatic, and pictorial or iconic modes. The latter in itself includes emblematic, hieroglyphic, allegorical, symbolic, and many another figural use of imagery.

Given all these formal and conventional resources for a poet to choose among, it is difficult to cross them with thematic interests and come up with anything like a clear historical pattern of developments. But as Jerome Mazzaro points out,[13] renaissance lyric does move generally from formula-governed cantabile-lyric mixtures in the sixteenth century to separations of statement from music in the last decade of the century and thereafter. I take that to be symptomatic of a broader shift in poetic location and voice, from relatively social to relatively private functions, and from a reliance on formal conventions to individual eccentricities. Where stress in the courtly lyric falls on grace of movement and humanist service in both educational and entertaining ways, seventeenth-century emphasis falls on the individual voice in dramatic situations, often reinforced by a striking use of iconic figures and paradoxical wit. This is an over-simplification, and any of the features of lyric can be mixed with any other at any time, as in the complex musical-dramatic settings of Wyatt. But it has more than a grain of truth. If in the modes of the earlier renaissance musical lyrics are basically public performances, later lyrics seek to convince or cajole. They do so sometimes by a jarring of wits in conceits and images, sometimes by an argument set in dialogue exchanges that bear upon its progress, as Donne's intimate settings bear upon definitions of love. Where earlier modes are artful or conceal artfulness behind an easy surface, later ones expend an obvious energy in arguing positions and presuppose social and intellectual differences to be overcome in the audience.

But let us descend to examples, some of which will qualify theme dominance—one kind of possession-seizing—with something akin to "Shakespearean" incarnation, which allows objects recognition in their own right and sometimes makes them stand off as though ready to escape whatever order the poet would impose upon them. In the Coleridgean terms that Hough draws upon, that incarnation makes an image partake of the reality it renders intelligible; it may also risk the unintelligible or unmanageable. Like its companion pieces in the anthology *England's Helicon* (1600, 1614), "The unknowne Sheepheardes complaint" contrives its general statements in madrigal form and dresses them up in elaborate rhetorical patterns. It is clear from it that not merely thematic precept but felicities of diction and image govern the selection of its well-manicured details:

> My Flocks feede not, my Ewes breede not
> My Rammes speede not, all is amisse:
> Love is denying, Faith is defying,
> Harts renying, causer of this.
> All my merry Jiggs are quite forgot,
> All my Ladies love is lost God wot.
> Where her faith was firmely fixt in love,
> There a nay is plac'd without remove.
>    One silly crosse, wrought all my losse,
>    O frowning Fortune, cursed fickle Dame:

> For now I see, inconstancie
> More in women than in men remaine.[14]

Such complaints about inconstancy in *England's Helicon* are similar to Wyatt's bitterly voiced ones, and the language is similar to Spenser's. But the identifying features of the poem are more periodized than personal. Usually attributed to Richard Barnfield, the stanza could have been written by any number of talented versifiers among the Edmund Boltons, Nicholas Bretons, Robert Greenes, Antony Mundays, Michael Draytons, Sidneys, or Spensers of the later sixteenth century. Praise of Eliza or Beta turns up among them frequently and masks praise of authority behind shepherd conventions, just as love sonnets of the period suggest parallels between unsuccess at court and unfruitful love. One finds very little in such works that Donne or Herbert could have written, though they too knew the attractions of song. The difference is partly in the sixteenth-century use of conventional topoi and mythology and the posed attitudes of the personas, hence the avoidance of the dramatized course that mediation or felt thought might take. Despite a somewhat stretched-out parallel between what love, faith, and hearts do and how flocks, ewes, and rams react, poetic movement for the unknown shepherd is choreographed not by witty or unexpected connections but by a careful measuring of phrases and syllables. Meaning is secondary to musicality and rhetoric, with their antitheses, incremental addition of one illustration to another, and softened and sweetened paradoxes. The poem is spoken or sung in first person, but the character of the performer is submerged in that rhetorical and metrical patterning, which is repeated until it needs variation and then complicates the stanzaic scheme with an equally exact second formula. Adjectives are obliged to wear stage costume, as in "merry," "frowning," "fickle." Committing his effort to attitudinizing and sound system, the poet requires of theme and image only enough material to embroider the design, just as all he requires of psychology and drama are pretexts for movement.

It may seem to stretch definitions to call both this poem and Ammons's "Plunder" or Dickinson's "Further in Summer" by the same name; and the historical distance is as great as the generic distance. But personal feeling, pretended or real, establishes the kinship between them, and perhaps a sense of wonder also, since all three poems make impassioned crossings of a speaker to something resistant. They juggle desired possession with a sense of the escaping prize. Here it is musicality that catches up the pictorial pieces; in Ammons it is less the regularities of argument or phrasing and more the will of a speaker that governs choice. One is set in a conventional Arcadia of course, the other in a landscape never conceived in quite that way before. The possession of materials that the song claims is more or less in the public name; Ammons plunders in his own name.

Closer to *England's Helicon* historically but also quite distant stylistically, Donne engineers a deflection from courtly lyrics of "The complaint's" kind early in his career in such poems as "Song: Goe and catche a falling starre." His songs are as musical as the complaint, but the wit that links various strange sights to constancy in "Goe and catche" is more daring than the wit that associates fickle women with sheep:

> If thou beest borne to strange sights,
> > Things invisible to see,
> Ride ten thousand daies and nights,
> > Till age snow white haires on thee,
> Thou, when thou retorn'st, wilt tell mee
> All strange wonders that befell thee,
> > And sweare
> > No where
> Lives a woman true, and faire.[15]

Much of Donne could be set to music and several of the *Songs and Sonnets* were. But the effects of such a song are less accountable to music or rhetoric than are the enumerations of pleasures and pains and general accounts of time and fortune that fill English verse through the 1590s. The disturbed courtier in Wyatt heralds Donne, as Spenser heralds the professional poet's concern with his career; but Donne complicates both. Not incidentally he commits himself to private settings and small dramas or unfolding arguments within them. However, he is as thematic and as concerned with universally valid propositions as his predecessors. The difference lies partly in the paradoxical nature of those propositions and their dramatic impact.

The musicality of earlier renaissance songs and sonnets distinguishes them not only from the personal verse of the metaphysicals but from verse whose design is governed by allegory, argument, or fable. Definition and moral precept reign in both and also in poems dominated by musical and iconic design. The emblem with its inscribed messages and equating of pictures and precepts is perhaps lyric's most demonstrative form of moral statement. In its sacramental and mystical variants, it virtually equates poet and theologian and as part of a doctrinal system depicts nothing merely for its own sake or for decorative purposes. For the reader to enter such written-out pictures is to leave behind the textured world for an expressive field given entirely to message bearing. Though in more sophisticated variants the emblem book may exploit discrepancies between picture and word and become self-conscious about the arbitrary nature of the connection,[16] the attraction of simpler emblems is precisely their point-by-point assignment of significance to conquered objects.

Pictorial and musical design both collaborate well enough with thematic illustration; lyric after all is not foreign to either logic or judgment, and the lyricist can be as concerned with concepts and definitions as the philosopher. For both, the word *substance* and its synonyms can apply either to the material world that Ransom likes to see given its due or to essence. But with respect to the latter, poets are not likely to be as rigorous as philosophers in holding to their *substantia, ousia,* or *essentia*.[17] The objects they address will sometimes be found fighting the harness even in highly manipulated atmospheres such as those of *England's Helicon*. Rather than extracting what evidence flocks and fickle dames afford, however (though the interplay of "feed," "breed," and "speed" would give us a foothold), we will fare better in demonstrating that with a more complex imagery and less conventional topography, or simply with a stronger poetry. In such a poetry, celebration and possession, like texture and design, often wage an indecisive struggle. Objects require recognition where they stand, at a distance; yet the patterns of lyric, the statements it makes, and the self seeking to cross over to possess them struggle to fasten them down.

### RENAISSANCE POSSESSION AND LOVE

Although they are not totally adequate by themselves to explain lyric's blend of celebration and possession, moral consciousness and language provide the chief means of crossing. Design and the act of placement fall under the technology that poets apply to subjects. If much of renaissance lyricism favors illustrative images, musical regularity, and moral or philosophical abstraction—and thus the dominance of design over rebellious substance—love poets, a sizeable portion of the whole, frequently find the beloved to be out of reach; celebration and possession come unbalanced in elegiac frustration. The value of the object is clear; how to approach it is not. Like the unknown shepherd complaining, the poet may convert his longing into thematic universals and allay it with philosophy, but that strategy only disciplines the subject and leaves the object "wyld," to use Wyatt's well-chosen word in "They Flee From Me" and "Whoso List to Hunt." If love poetry receives less emphasis here than it deserves, it is because I do not want to stray too far from topographical keys, which are stronger in other kinds of lyric. However, concern for place and for language intrudes into courtship, and so examples that will do some justice in passing to the sonnet tradition are not very far out of our way. At the same time, they allow us to mark differences between the court-oriented lyric and later verse—and thus put us in a position to follow the progress of love eventually into such places as Milton's Eden and Marvell's green world. The path from the courtly love lyric to Donne is more direct.

Herbert's "Vertue" suggests itself as an initial example, first because it concerns a setting rather than a specific beloved, but also because it addresses its objects with something very like a lover's longing, and then for moral and other reasons veers away from them:

> Sweet day, so cool, so calm, so bright,
> The bridall of the earth and skie;
> The dew shall weep thy fall tonight;
>     For thou must die.
>
> Sweet rose, whose hue angrie and brave
> Bids the rash gazer wipe his eye:
> Thy root is ever in its grave,
>     And thou must die.
>
> Sweet spring, full of sweet dayes and roses,
> A box where sweets compacted lie;
> My musick shows ye have your closes,
>     And all must die.
>
> Onely a sweet and vertuous soul,
> Like season'd timber, never gives;
> But though the whole world turn to coal,
>     Then chiefly lives.[18]

The musical design, particularly the refrain, allows Herbert to exploit parallels for cumulative elegiac effects. But ultimately the poem explores a quite different lyric impulse. If the first movement offers a restrained but mounting elegy, the second comes to the virtuous soul's imperishable life as the one that counts. Since only paradise fulfills the self completely, only the virtue that achieves it can lift the poem to a higher celebrational plane. As a moral abstraction, virtue thus governs the reception of place and provides the crossing force that carries lyric into its visionary phase.

Whereas in Milton's Eden, Adam and Eve fashion morning and evening songs out of such things as the day's opening and the night's coming on, here transition and slippage from the golden age undo our sympathies. The last stanza does not address, then, but declares, widening its vision beyond things close by to things unapproachable by normal means. All told, "Vertue" strikes an unusual balance between celebration and dispossession. Its iconic and melodic combination makes splendid use of remodeled Elizabethan resources. In the context of *The Temple,* it also suggests the seriousness of Herbert's relocation of lyric in sacred precincts, but that is a matter for later.

Although Shakespeare may not seem to offer inevitable choices to put beside "Vertue," two of the better known sonnets, 116 and 129, carry further the age-old matter of possession and dispossession and suggest modifications of the historical observation I made earlier concerning the dominance of illustrative imagery and rhetorical patterns. Ordinarily, courtly love offers little opportunity for the fulfillment of lovers, who are suspended between desire and idealism. Shakespeare momentarily separates these two components into lust and pure love, love being his term for the marriage of true minds, lust for illusory enticements of flesh, one idea dominated, the other thoroughly incarnate, yet paradoxically beyond possession. Sonnet 116 defines a purified version of personal attraction as a union of minds standing free of all occasions and phases; sonnet 129 makes passion the opposite of that platonic union in every respect. But each implies the other and keeps lyric from drawing entirely into their extremes—keeps it somewhere in view of both. The difficulty is that what is momentarily seizable physically, in lust, is neither lasting nor praiseworthy; what is praiseworthy in love is immaterial and not possessable in a worldly way.

The negative case first:

> The expense of spirit in a waste of shame
> Is lust in action, and till action, lust
> Is perjured, murderous, bloody, full of blame,
> Savage, extreme, rude, cruel, not to trust,
> Enjoyed no sooner but despised straight,
> Past reason hunted, and no sooner had,
> Past reason hated, as a swallowed bait,
> On purpose laid to make the taker mad.
> Mad in pursuit, and in possession so,
> Had, having, and in quest to have, extreme,
> A bliss in proof, and proved, a very woe.
> Before, a joy proposed, behind a dream.
>     All this the world well knows, yet none knows well
>     To shun the Heaven that leads men to this Hell.[19]

Although this compact and hurried course through passion's phases looks like a definition and offers enough of one for the poet to reveal lust as the familiar thing we recognize, from another angle no complete definition actually develops or can develop. The poem silently acknowledges the failure of rational statement-making in the face of lust's contradictory moments. It will not stand still for its portrait. The third and fourth lines disrupt the movement we come to expect of Shakespearean quatrains, stumbling over a list of distressful adjectives as though picking a course through rubble. They present the opposite of love in its courtly varieties, "perjured" recalling the oath-swearing that honest love depends upon, savagery removing lust from the polite world to the animal world and placing it beyond moral codes. In that context the lines are implicitly dialectical and historical: they turn against a host of courtly ideals as a social background and against the sonnet tradition as a literary background.

The second quatrain builds upon this acknowledgement of lust's uncivilized extremity. Not merely rational faculties but the feelings are put off by lust. But a more telling mark against its definability comes in the third quatrain's antithetical view, which contradicts the opening sections, "bliss in proof" being opposite to an "expense of spirit" as lust's consumption. The privileged word in the abortive definition is "dream," which suggests that lust recedes into vagueness whenever one tries to sum it up. Despite dream's resumption of a hindered lyricism that has flashed momentarily in "Bliss in proof" and "a joy proposed" and despite its being confusable enough with love's visions to lead lovers on again and again, its hold on reality is even weaker than madness might claim. Its vagueness would drop the sonnet into skepticism were it not for the final couplet, whose epigrammatic summary performs a rescue mission of sorts. We know well enough the experience of lust, and we know the several faces it presents. What we do not know is how to put it under verbal arrest. Paradoxically, the certainty of the sonnet lies in its defining of that uncertainty; its possession is knowledge of lust's dispossession. Shakespeare's saying this amounts to a final displacement of topics that usually support renaissance love, since courtship should sublimate passion and convert it into the codified social graces that make up a middle ground between Platonist idealism and lust. We know from previous sonnets in the sequence approximately what Shakespeare thinks love should be: certain commonplaces and images should march in support of two parties whose union is a high cause and a powerful symbol of social achievement and status. Here all that ought to be substantial escapes, and lyricism is stifled at its source, in the very attractions of the object. The only way to avoid that stifling and lyric's diversion into satire and anatomy is to avoid lust itself.

Problems with definition and possession come with authentic love too, but obviously not of the same kind. As Sonnet 116 conceives of that sort of love, it transcends pursuit and requires statements first about what it is not. Whatever alters or bends or is subject to time, for instance, is not what the poet means. An outbreak of positive feeling comes only when Shakespeare is ready to put a lyric stamp on the emerging definition:

> Oh no! It is an ever-fixed mark
> That looks on tempests and is never shaken.
> It is the star to every wandering bark,
> Whose worth's unknown, although his height be taken.

So transcendent is this love and so certain its definition—once we cease to look in the wrong places for it—that feeling can be confidently based upon it. The expansion of love's horizon climaxes in the third quatrain with a glimpse of apocalypse and the sturdiness of a love that "bears it out even to the edge of doom." "Doom" is placed comparably to "dream" in Sonnet 129 and has a similar function in carrying beyond definable experience. But where "dream" moves toward vagueness as though looking backward toward a vanishing entity, "doom" lies ahead at the borderline between the defined world and another world to come, where love will cease to be tested by vicissitude and like Herbert's seasoned soul will be definitively placed. In the certainty of that placement, one almost fails to notice how negatives continue to function in it. Love is that which is not shaken; its true worth is unknown. Even bearing it out is a kind of passive resistance to motions that might accompany it. Love may stir us but is not itself moved; it may exist, but we cannot possess it now sufficiently to put it into action.

The commonplace contrast to Shakespeare's "doom" is the ever-shifting region from which Wyatt singles out woman's fickleness and the intrigues of court as most destructive to love's satisfaction. Indeed, instability fills not only Shakespeare's and Wyatt's sonnets on time and infidelity but practically all renaissance love poetry in one way or another, which seldom allows possession of what it cherishes in either its English or its continental versions. Instead, it uses love, as Arthur Marotti points out, to encode a complex set of social attitudes toward failure.[20] In Fulke Greville's *Caelica*, the setting for Myra's constancy is the entire mutable nature of things created from the four elements:

> The World, that all containes, is ever moving,
> The Starres within their spheres for ever turned,
> Nature (*the Queene of Change*) to change is loving,
> And Forme to matter new, is still adjourned.
>
> Fortune our *phantasie-God,* to varie liketh,
> Place is not bound to things within it placed,
> The Present time upon time passed striketh,
> With *Phoebus* wandring course the earth is graced.
>
> The Ayre still moves, and by its moving cleareth,
> The Fire up ascends, and planets feedeth,
> The Water passeth on, and all lets weareth,
> The Earth stands still, yet change of changes breedeth;
>
> Her plants, which Summer ripes, in Winter fade,
> Each creature in unconstant mother lyeth,
> Man made of earth, and for whom earth is made,
> Still dying lives, and living ever dyeth;
>    Onely like fate sweet *Myra* never varies,
>    Yet in her eyes the doome of all Change carries.[21]

To that list of forces with which love contends, Greville adds "faction, that ever dwells / In Courts where Wit excells" in Sonnet 19. The lover, like Wyatt's in "The Long Love," must flee to the woods "With *Love* to live and dye," preferring exile and solitary constancy to still more of fortune's vicissitudes. Or as Wyatt concludes (quoting Petrarch), "Good is the life ending faithfully"—faithfully and fulfilled only as distant devotion. Governing many of these resignations of the lover is the figure of Fortune, which rules over Venus, Mars, and Cupid. Working hand in hand with faithfulness, fortune denies completion and fosters bitterness over the inability of courtly games to produce winners.

Love's losses, then, fall into a familiar pattern of universal ones like those of "Vertue" and often reflect an accompanying social slippage. That mind and heart find their satisfaction only in permanent bonds makes those losses inevitable. Wyatt's "In Eternum I was Once Determed," for instance, entertains assumptions about true love similar to Shakespeare's and Greville's. Idealizing codes do not find expression in the eyes' quaint games:

> In eternum I was once determed
> For to have loved, and my mind affirmed
> That with my heart it should be confirmed
>    In eternum.
>
> Forthwith I found the thing that I might like,
> And sought with love to warm her heart alike,
> For as me thought I should not see the like
>    In eternum.

> To trace this dance I put myself in press;
> Vain hope did lead, and bade I should not cease
> To serve, to suffer, and still to hold my peace
>     In eternum.
>
> With this first rule I furthered me apace,
> That as me thought my truth had taken place
> With full assurance to stand in her grace
>     In eternum.
>
> It was not long ere I by proof had found
> That feeble building is on feeble ground,
> For in her heart this word did never sound—
>     In eternum.
>
> In eternum then from my heart I kest
> That I had first determed for the best:
> Now in the place another thought doth rest
>     In eternum.[22]

The lover's initial search is for the right person to fill a form already implanted in the mind. Should such a person turn up, the gap between eternity and the temporal world might be crossed and lyric find a definitive object of praise. The poem implicitly concedes that one's expecting to love for always is unrealistic, but one should not be so readily disappointed. What the lover seeks apparently are some of the satisfactions that a Beatrice or Laura promise or that the lady of *Amoretti* will later extend to Spenser, supplemented by what he would gain in personal affection if the game were played by the rules (the purpose of courtship being to "warm her heart alike"). Having held up his end, suffered quietly as he is supposed to, and come to the edge of realization—close enough to think truth embodied and grace granted—the lover finds his expectations in error. Concrete proof topples the superstructure of procedures and beliefs.

Awareness that individual cases undo ideals is perhaps what leads Shakespeare to use the similar term "proved" in Sonnet 116. If true minds are not united in eternity beyond error, all love's language is poisoned at the root and the lyricist possesses nothing. Content then slips out of the poet's best words, and we should not be surprised to find him saying that if he is wrong about this he must be wrong about everything and has never truly written, no one ever loved. Where Sonnet 129 breaks all ties between emotion and intellect, Sonnet 116 goes beyond feeling to an extreme Platonist assertion. In both cases the poet will have nothing further to do with courtship as Wyatt, Sidney, and the Petrarchans codify it: love belongs to the poet's ideal realm, or possibly to his and the philosopher's. It does not belong to historians, to rhetoric, or to manners; it permits no half-way measures. When Donne in "A Lecture upon the Shadow" fears love's instant decline after the high noon of its realization and when Marvell later adds that love is a conjunction of minds and an opposition of stars, they too fear that it is too good for this world. Wyatt's less categorical notion is that what can be won can also be lost. The pursuit of love among the factions of Caesar's court is a dance, a hunt, a press, a quaint game in his recurrent metaphors. He is realist enough to know that, if not accept it. What makes him aghast, however, is not merely change but sudden change. As "It May Be Good" summarizes, love's recurrent unsuccess brings a failure of confidence: "For dread to fall I stand not fast."

That courtship is often unproductive in renaissance love poetry is not due, as Wyatt might seem to imply, solely to violations of its rules, nor are its analogues strictly social and political. Lyric in the view I am proposing always withholds its objects in some way. As both "Vertue" and a good many love sonnets illustrate, a lyric can be fairly sure of its commitments and finished in its definitions—hence be relatively closed as a form—and still not consumate a union of subject and object. If love "bears it out" to the edge of doom, for instance, it must require a good deal of patience and endurance up to that point; lovers must be alert to its perils and therefore a little uneasy with its conditions, if not its essence. In the light of Shakespeare's other sonnets, Wyatt, Sidney, and the sonnet company, bearing it out cannot be an easy task. Likewise, if the soul "chiefly" lives only after doomsday, it must spend its probationary period getting seasoned in a lesser life. Foreshadowings of end things are beleaguered by an all-to-human fondness for sweet days and roses. Such ambitious lyrics, in looking to the complete possession that love or paradise promises, seek something akin to the equilibrium of Milton's exiled Adam and Eve—possessed of sure vision and perhaps happier far within because of it but nonetheless proceeding into the main trials of faith. With some caution, we can use Milton's example as reasonably binding in establishing one prominent renaissance sense of the lyricist's territorial situation. However, before doing so, I want to examine a final central ingredient in lyric address—its dramatic passage and sense of the coming on of the object.

### THE POET CALLED FORTH

Address or apostrophe is to lyric roughly what motives or animation are to drama or narrative and as more distant address is to epistle: in place of agents and actions, lyric is moved by perceptions of the object in rising or subsiding phases in which the object is not fully seized. Awakenings to presence and realizations of loss are typical of its "plots" or movements. If a thing may "solicit us by its looks" (*eidos*) as Heidegger remarks—including its texture, form, and composite appeal[23]—the critical matter for the lyricist, thus summoned forth, is how and to what end to make his address and what those looks signify. Reading them is, of course, one phase of possession and celebration. Objects and callings thus seem to come always in tandem, though poets are usually less successful when they stand squarely before something: like lovers inspired by the Atlantic ocean between them, they are often more at home with less than full presences, with promising texts of predecessors, for instance, or simply with fictions that allow imagination and convention room to operate and thus to amplify significance.

Whether or not awakenings can be said to be quintessentially lyric, they make a useful index to the mix of possession and celebration. They also provide some assistance in marking period distinctions. They provide telling moments for gauging the nature of the object's solicitation and the onset of meeting consciousness and of language, since as Heidegger also remarks, "The beautiful belongs to the advent of truth, truth's taking of its place."[24] A variety of poets could be called upon to provide examples, but I will suggest only minimal cases here, from Stevens, Donne, and Milton, in order simply to conclude the case for topographical withholding-and-possession and frame a more complete discussion of poetic vocation in its seventeenth-century differences later. To that end one logical place to begin is the bird's scrawny cry that summons the speaker of Stevens's "Not Ideas about the Thing But the Thing Itself," and one place to settle in for a more thorough exploration of the roots of lyric is Milton's awakening first man and woman. Since the latter is so complex an example in both its setting and its period implications, I will merely glance at it here and devote the next chapter to it.

Stevens's bird call comes to the waking consciousness at the winter-spring juncture of the seasons, always a precarious and exciting moment in Stevens, and at dawn as well. If his title has any truth to it, we have primarily that highly seasonal and timely call to thank for the poem. Next to awakenings in Donne and Milton, the speaker's reactions to it appear particularly modern in their absence of metaphysical certainties and illustrative ideas, but as the "clear streaks of bird music" in Ammons and the calls of the romantic nightingales, skylarks, and cuckoos suggest, we are likely to find self-consciousness in any lyric awakening. Stevens claims not to have appropriated the object, and the speaker tries to remain subject to it despite the same storehouse of expectations that anyone carries. Stevens is clearly not interested in taking the thing as a sign of something other than what it seems and forbids its being subdued by allegory or surrendered totally to definition. Coming from sleep and weakened by a lack of validating coordinates, the speaker concentrates as exclusively as he can on impressions. Failure of the thing either to declare itself or to maintain some distance would abort the lyric effort. The waking mind seeks enlightenment in innocence, as Adam might, then, but without Adam's theology or integration of creaturely fact with the divine plan. Unlike the nightingale, the cuckoo, or the skylark, this bird is not escaping but coming into range.

From earlier creative stalemates, a sense of inertia from the long sleep of intelligence may still linger. In any case the poem concerns itself with the initial movement only and barely glances at subsequent stages, including a crescendo apparently to come in the fullness of "the colossal Sun, / Surrounded by its choral rings." The conviction the bird brings does not depend upon that sun, but it is reasonable to assume that when birds begin carolling, summer's green barbarism is on the way and with it, stronger and stronger summonings to poetic celebration. But Stevens's main point is that growing presence and the simultaneous onset of something like new knowledge do not require elaborate explanations for an appreciative, newly vital consciousness, which puts predecessors behind it. Despite its tentative outset in this early hour, the self gains authenticity just now, well-grounded in the rising season as it is. It flowers from a stored potency both in itself and in its well-met bird, as it has still more tentatively in "The Sun This March."

As the postponing of new knowledge suggests, a calling for Stevens is less prepossessing than it is likely to be in awakenings that suppose the mind's being at home in some totality, which in the Renaissance usually includes something like Marvell's "Glories of th' Almighty Sun"—obviously a different sun than Stevens's. This is a very gradual awakening, and even at the conclusion it is not fully possessed of any greater song the bird may herald with its as yet unsustained and ungraced "C" note. The awakenings of Donne and Milton are to higher realities seen synecdochially in something at hand. But both poets provide a spectrum of solicitations and addresses of varying strengths, from those in which the object is almost fully possessable to those in which the calling fails. Donne offers several examples both of the poet being summoned and of lovers rejoicing in their mutual possession, which in *Songs and Sonnets* is usually both physical and spiritual. He uses the threat of change and a previous history of imperfect affairs to buttress claims for the permanence of that possession. He implicitly contrasts love's dialogue to the pleadings of Petrarchan lovers and knows that the best time to understand the nature of love is as it comes into fruition or is threatened. At those critical moments, being is shaded by absence even as the beloved declares itself. As the awakenings of "The Good-morrow" and "The Sunne Rising" indicate, the soul greets as an ideal mate only one who can be fully known—and because known, fully possessed. The lyric force of the negatives in those instances comes from the surrounding world, busy in its lesser pursuits. Love itself does not alter and finds no alteration; nor is it a dream or mere ideal. Vicissitude and the escape of substance from language are fully overcome, or so the speaker maintains.

The poet's calling is more problematic in the religious poems, which suggest the importance of a transcendent object to one part of Donne and the weakened pursuit of a spotted soul. Where the lover in *Songs and Sonnets* often manages to be either sinless or oblivious to sin, the writer of holy sonnets is neither. As Donne comes to realize in the Anniversaries and "Hymne to God my God, in my sicknesse," the soul must travel extensively. Specifically, it must journey through death's straits to be cleansed, its full consciousness paradoxically requiring a preliminary unconsciousness:

> I joy, that in these straits, I see my West;
>   For, though theire currants yeeld returne to none,
> What shall my West hurt me? As West and East
>   In all flatt Maps (and I am one) are one,
>   So death doth touch the Resurrection.
>
> Is the Pacifique Sea my home? Or are
>   The Easterne riches? Is *Jerusalem*?
> *Anyan,* and *Magellan,* and *Gibraltare,*
>   All streights, and none but streights, are wayes to them,
>   Whether where *Japhet* dwelt, or *Cham,* or *Sem.*[25]

Although Donne plays symbolically with the globe and an expanding sense of place, the geography here is also literal, as again in "Goodfriday, 1613. Riding Westward" and "The Good-morrow." No one place in it is a conclusive destination.

If awakenings do not come to a satisfactory conclusion, it is because God is withheld, or perhaps also because the calling itself is mistaken. To Milton as well as to Donne, a missed calling is parallel to spiritual misguidance and indicates that what prohibits a completed crossing is internal as well as external. The archetype of that failing for Milton is Satan, a figure of strenuous negations who addresses hell, the sun, and Eden each in a state of siege. Continually on the verge of lyric, Satan veers recurrently into self-debate and lament. Although the pattern he sets is adoptable by others, its importance is not merely its influence but its indication of the danger of linking possession too tightly to knowledge. But Milton expects successful callings for the poet normally. Blessed by the logos, he hopes to achieve the same vision and power that once prevailed in the creation. To the extent that paradise is equatable with the divine presence, he repossesses it not merely in the future but in the act of writing, his form of adamic awakening. If Satan wages war to seize empire, unfallen angels and humankind sing of it, mixing possession and celebration appropriately. Indeed, *Paradise Lost* offers a comprehensive set of responses at various distances from the creator. Meet conversation and lyric address, for instance, have their prelapsarian mixes of celebration and dominion. Argument, debate, elegy, and anguished meditation follow in due course and introduce their version of the siege of contraries. Milton's study of the first human makers of language includes everything from horticultural advice-giving to love-making, from philosophical discourse to lyric. It not only underscores the distinctiveness of lyric for us but coming as it does in contradistinction to predecessors, it also provides means to establish period differences. It has the disadvantage of being complex and inexhaustible so that whatever one tries to pull from it leaves the rest somewhat reluctantly; but no mustering of renaissance topographical keys to lyric can exclude it or treat it lightly.

> *So eagerly the fiend*
> *O'er bog or steep, through strait, rough, dense, or rare,*
> *With head, hands, wings, or feet pursues his way,*
> *And swims or sinks, or wades, or creeps, or flies:*
> *At length a universal hubbub wild*
> *Of stunning sounds and voices all confus'd*
> *Borne through the hollow dark assaults his ear*
> *With loudest vehemence.*
> *Paradise Lost, 2.947–54*

> *I saw when at his Word the formless Mass,*
> *This world's material mould, came to a heap:*
> *Confusion heard his voice, and wild uproar*
> *Stood rul'd, stood vast infinitude confin'd;*
> *Till at his second bidding darkness fled,*
> *Light shone, and order from disorder sprung:*
> *Swift to thir several Quarters hasted then*
> *The cumbrous Elements, Earth, Flood, Air, Fire,*
> *And this Ethereal quintessence of Heav'n*
> *Flew upward, spirited with various forms,*
> *That roll'd orbicular, and turn'd to Stars*
> *Numberless, as thou seest, and how they move;*
> *Each had his place appointed, each his course,*
> *The rest in circuit walls this Universe.*
> *Paradise Lost, 3.708–21*

# BETWEEN CHAOS AND COSMOS

## CHAPTER TWO

CROSS-REFERENCED REGIONS

Placement, possession, substance, calling: when we pivot these and related terms around to face the seventeenth century more squarely, they require adjustment to fit texts like Milton's *Christian Doctrine* and *Paradise Lost,* where places are either validated by some degree of divine presence or judged by its lack. To such topics we also need to add, for Milton's extensive epic cosmos, the principle of analogy and epitome by which one region reflects or contains another. With hell, chaos, heaven, Eden, and the wilderness as his chief settings, Milton is an ambitious and contrastive realmist, as Satan is an intrepid and combative voyager who carries those contrasts with him. His regions comparisons are often triple and quadruple, among them allusions to classics and to the present of the narrator.

The analogical stationing of realms is not unique with Milton, of course. When Marvell conceives of the soul in "On a Drop of Dew" as a reflection of "the clear Region where 'twas born," he establishes double regions in an elaborate formal simile. The exiled soul "recollects" one place from another, gathering itself "in its pure and circling thought":

> Every way it turns away:
> So the World excluding round,
> Yet receiving in the Day.
> Dark beneath, but bright above:
> Here disdaining, there in Love.

Undesirable in itself the lower realm is receptive to the upper one only insofar as the soul remains uncontaminated in it. The upper region is often signalled for neoplatonists by a light playing across surfaces or being cast outward from the intellect. The soul here, receiving no aid from its purple flower-body, shines therein with its own "mournful light," carrying entirely in itself the replica of its source.

As Terry Comito has pointed out, it is often fountains, in literary renderings of gardens, that gather the serene rays of paradise in their shimmering and sparkling.[1] But nothing makes an absolutely sure medium through which paradise can be seen. In Vaughan's "Regeneration" the fountain spends its language "on the dumbe shades" as a music of tears, and its cistern has diverse stones, "some bright, and round" but others "ill-shap'd and dull." Water in "The Water-fall" is similarly ambiguous. It is a "useful Element and clear," a "sacred wash and cleanser," and Vaughan exclaims, "What sublime truths, and wholesome themes, / Lodge in thy mystical, deep streams!" The fall of loud brooks "in streaming rings restagnates all" in imitation of eternity's stasis and ring of calm. Yet it is not water but Vaughan's "invisible estate," his "glorious liberty, still late," that conducts him upward finally: "Thou art the Channel my soul seeks, / Not this with Cataracts and Creeks." The analogy holds just long enough to make the regional contrast clear and to measure the limits of likenesses. In less Platonist versions, the heavens may be doubled or at least received in lower realms, as the realm of Neptune in *Comus* is assigned from above and remains hospitable to the Attendant Spirit from Jove's starry court. The ocean is sufficiently established as a duplicating place in "The Garden" for Marvell to think of the mind itself as an ocean wherein each kind finds its resemblance.

Despite such forerunners *Paradise Lost* goes much further with the interactions of complementary and contrasting realms and looks further into extremes in the expressive language of place already rendered into topics by scripture and its commentaries. Milton's two main localities of "hubbub," for instance—hell and chaos—deny analogies except of an ironic sort.[2] As a place of primal disorder, chaos lies outside expression; since the logos has not penetrated it, proportioning and description flounder in it. Between paradise and chaos, the cosmos is intelligible but also bounded by them, so that the poet in defining it must go outward into them by a metaleptic tracing of the same power that set the boundaries.[3]

## SONGS OF GREETING AND ODES TO TREES

The songs and addresses of Adam and Eve, together with the narrator's invocations, are Milton's chief inset lyrics. They warrant our attention both for their establishing of a human center between demonic and celestial extremes in *Paradise Lost* and for their usefulness in outlining other seventeenth-century realm-crossings. As chronologically the first genii loci this side of the creator himself, Adam and Eve have a readable terrain to work with and not surprisingly avoid serious errors in its interpretation.[4]

Among Milton's demonstrations of attunement between intelligence and creation, however, Eve's lyrics are especially sensitive, beginning with her extended address to Adam in Book 4 (635–58). That opening example of her lyricism sets a standard with which Milton measures certain renaissance predecessors in the love lyric and Eve's own developments later. It is dutiful before it lists the objects of paradise that appeal to her and again after she has summed them up:

> My Author and Disposer, what thou bidd'st
> Unargu'd I obey; so God ordains,
> God is thy Law, thou mine: to know no more
> Is woman's happiest knowledge and her praise.
>
> 4.635–38

Eve's attraction to Adam is reinforced by this bracketing assessment of place. Obligations also have something to do with it, but questions of marital authority are diminished for the time being by the interdiction, which overshadows other matters of rule-making and dominion. Eve's speech not only endorses creation's gifts but cherishes them with propriety and due weight, which corrects Sin's earlier version of rhapsody over an imagined Eden to come. Her awareness of disobedience is limited momentarily to a denial of any: she fully repossesses Eden and is in turn possessed by her author and disposer. Although that bow to masculine authority may not fit our ideas of ideal husband-wife relations, it confirms the limits that Milton sets for all intellects. Only through that "happiest knowledge" can one make the crossings of envy-free love to the other, which Satan finds impossible to do. Without it, competition and struggle for empire intrude, and every crossing becomes an intelligence mission or invasion. Thus it is that Eve's other delights must be secondary to her delight in Adam, who brings into focus her native balance of possession and celebration:

> With thee conversing I forget all time,
> All seasons and thir change, all please alike.

> Sweet is the breath of morn, her rising sweet,
> With charm of earliest Birds; pleasant the Sun
> When first on this delightful Land he spreads
> His orient Beams, on herb, tree, fruit, and flow'r,
> Glist'ring with dew . . .
>
> 4.639–45

This rendering of tribute allows no romantic breach between rising appreciation and its object. Neither Adam nor Eve knows a higher paradise as yet or looks for advancement. Even here, however, the reader needs to be wary of negotiations between desire and fulfillment and distinguish carefully between this early expression of marital love and later reachings for transcendence. Milton is simultaneously filling out the contrast with Sin and preparing for realmic contrasts that come in Books 9–12, where heaven and hell find new representation in Eden. Feeling achieves immediate gratification here not as the fulfilling of ambition but as a domestic satisfaction. It can very easily grow more complicated, but when Adam replies to "Daughter of God and Man, accomplisht Eve," he suggests that she is already a finished product, not merely a promising pupil. The title is in fact quite exact for the time being and shuts off access to other realms and other planes of knowledge. The relationship with God is solid and the adjective "accomplished" is a tribute to a generous creation. Eve thus requires no course of discoveries of the sort that might bring uneasiness in their wake, whatever Adam might still have to teach her about the purposes of stars. The possibility of sorrow and early loss and the conversion of tribute into elegy, and of marital dialogue into quarrel may be hinted by Satan's presence, but they lie far off. Eve has no difficulty accommodating herself not only to rapturous speech but to the quiet tone of lesser dialogues. She fulfills the express purpose of her making that God and Adam have collaborated in working out. In the addresses of the first parents to each other, Milton thus establishes a well-met language that ranges from information-giving dialogue to love lyric. Although their speech is limited by its circumstances, it is both ideal in its kind and encompassing. The creator's presence is its underlying substance, as are the connections that make their surroundings part of a created totality.

All this is relatively straightforward, but it is also placed under shadow by Satan's presence and the distance between Eden and the reader. Satan has already challenged the edenic balance of possession and celebration by his vow at the beginning of Book 4 to seek divided empire. He has also substituted embittered self-analysis for the language of thanksgiving and praise and has begotten inappropriate hymns of praise in others. As his helpmate, for instance, Sin upends rhapsodic proprieties in foretelling Eve's version of them (2.864–68). She has her own vision of holy calm that she plans to maintain in Adam's and Eve's place. Those are important acts of misnaming and seized verbal possession, not only because they fill out a set of perspectives by which we gauge Eve's lyric skill but because of the general importance of idolatry in Milton's theory of signs. As a master of icons and tableaus, Satan is always setting scenes, staging speeches, and rearranging the relations of inhabitants to their places. So that he can serve as God there, he makes hell heaven translated; he makes Eden a demonstration of his influence, which requires his changing of Eve's perception of it and translation of the forbidden tree into an object of worship. What Sin will introduce to Eden under his auspices is a will to devour its forms, a will that we do not find in Eve's celebration, of course, but do find in the satanic command over things, always their unmaking. In Sin's praise of her consort is also the marital competition that Adam does not inspire in Eve as we first see her.

Eve does fall into a similar style, however, in her address to the forbidden fruit and revision of her address to Adam, both of which reveal the difference in lyric that satanic language works. Satan has by then of course modeled for her a new ode to place in his own idolatrous address to the tree:

> O Sacred, Wise and Wisdom-giving Plant,
> Mother of Science, Now I feel thy Power
> Within me clear, not only to discern
> Things in thir Causes, but to trace the ways
> Of highest Agents, deem'd however wise.
>
> 9.679–83

As Satan's cursing of the sun and Eden also illustrate, he is never more isolated than when he addresses things close by that press upon him and desert him simultaneously. As a God-substitute, the wisdom-giving plant here assumes a mystical crossing of object to subject and infusion of divine powers from one to the other, distantly like the infusion of Holy Light into the darkened mind of the seer.

But of course no real lyric crossing takes place, here or in any of the satanic apostrophes and rhetorical shows. Indeed, the closer Satan stands to Eden, the more forced his appropriation. Eden is a torture to him precisely as a reminder of his own lost seat:

> O Earth, how like to Heav'n, if not preferr'd
> More justly, Seat worthier of Gods, as built
> With second thoughts, reforming what was old!

> For what God after better worse would build?
> Terrestrial Heav'n, danc't round by other Heav'ns
> That shine, yet bear thir bright officious Lamps,
> Light above Light, for thee alone, as seems,
> In thee concentring all thir precious beams
> Of sacred influence: As God in Heav'n
> Is Centre, yet extends to all, so thou
> Centring receiv'st from all those Orbs.
>
> 9.99–109

His dislocation is permanent as well as multifaceted—geographic, verbal, spiritual. When feigned zeal for humankind culminates in "Queen of this universe," we realize how close rapture is to mere flattery and both are to idolatry, although Eve finds such words "impregn'd / With Reason." We recall that hypocrisy also governs Sin's address to Satan and his to the tree. Indeed, Satan is obsessed with the notion in his soliloquy at the beginning of Book 4 that all show is poisoned by insincerity and that no real bonds of love exist even between angels and their God.

Eve's version of the satanic ode has a hurried list of justifications and apparent analyses of the trees' properties and functions:

> Great are thy Virtues, doubtless, best of Fruits,
> Though kept from Man, and worthy to be admir'd,
> Whose taste, too long forborne, at first assay
> Gave elocution to the mute, and taught
> The Tongue not made for Speech to speak thy praise:
> Thy praise hee also who forbids thy use,
> Conceals not from us, naming thee the Tree
> Of Knowledge, knowledge both of good and evil;
> Forbids us then to taste, but his forbidding
> Commends thee more, while it infers the good
> By thee communicated, and our want:
> For good unknown, sure is not had, or had
> And yet unknown, is as not had at all.
>
> 9. 745–57

If her address does not rise immediately to odic enthusiasm, it is because she must first sidetrack reason and redefine the prohibition. Having tasted the fruit, she becomes convinced of her true calling as knower *and* possessor. She defines the geography of Eden as not a stable and assigned hierarchy of forms but a place for questing minds working toward their highest possession. Rapturous songs of this new sort will follow daily—or so it seems in her first enthusiasm:

> O Sovran, virtuous, precious of all Trees
> In Paradise, of operation blest
> To Sapience, hitherto obscur'd, infam'd,
> And thy fair Fruit let hang, as to no end
> Created; but henceforth my early care,

> Not without Song, each Morning, and due praise
> Shall tend thee, and the fertile burden ease
> Of thy full branches offer'd free to all;
> Till dieted by thee I grow mature
> In knowledge, as the Gods who all things know.
>
> 9. 795–804

Eve is of course confused as to presence and calling and avenues that knowledge opens from one realm to another. God works by analogy and substitutions, putting paradise into lesser figures and accommodating messages through interpreters. His representatives are clearly delegated and have exact commissions. He is thereby imparted from a distance, and between his first appearances to Adam and Eve and the recovery of paradise, he does not presuppose them "mature / In knowledge." In its romantic style, Eve's lyric presumes to bring the invisible nearer than that by removing the intervals that keep the hierarchy vertical and lengthy. Where celebration of an appropriate sort recognizes and cherishes degrees, analogies, and differences, she plans literally to devour what she praises and to be substantially changed by it. Up to this point, she has entertained just one set of presuppositions about paradise; she now introduces a hypothetical set of pre-texts in which what the great interdictor has said is replaced by what a venturesome and subtle interpreter might speculate. Whereas the hermit-seer of "Il Penseroso" plans to explore the secrets of things because he has to—the world having fallen into obscurity for genii loci—Eve plans to look into them because secrets yield power.

Obviously a good deal breaks apart in that redefinition of lyric crossing as magical tie, such as alliances between knowing and possession, perception and feeling, self and other, ego and its acknowledgment of obligations to authority. In the metapoetic dimension of *Paradise Lost,* Eve's revised lyricism constitutes a key phase of Milton's anatomy of fallen language based in pride—if one can assign the cause a single name—or in a kind of narcissism hinted earlier in Eve's pool-gazing. Spontaneous verse needs no such rationalizing as she now applies in this complicated and crafty verse. It is sustained by preliminary recognitions of the source of things and is definitional even while it is rapturous. Here, definition in the sense of acknowledged limitations of substance is circumvented; the tree grows elusive even as it seems to open up vistas. Behind the upsurge of ambition is still a domestic relation, however. Adam is not being by-passed by Eve's quick transcendence but gathered into her train. Among other things the tree-directed rapture is a new kink in the meet conversation that will require him to turn to something like troubadour lyric for a new supply of terms.

That Eve changes so quickly and with so little effort from Satan provides a new cause for complaints in the transition stage of *Paradise Lost* in Books 10 and 11—complaints more able to engage our sympathy than satanic ones and less vulnerable to irony than Sin's raptures but nonetheless troubling. Milton makes a similar conversion of pastoral joy to sorrow in "L'Allegro" and "Il Penseroso" and in the blight of "Lycidas":

> But O the heavy change, now thou art gone,
> Now thou art gone, and never must return!
> Thee Shepherd, thee the Woods, and desert Caves,
> With wild Thyme and the gadding Vine o'ergrown,
> And all their echoes mourn.
>
> 37–41

But *Paradise Lost* is more encompassing. In effect, Eve begets the ambivalent condition of all lyric crossings hereafter. As Adam discovers, Eden so alters in its promptings of song that it becomes a virtual blank and stalls any journey of mind through terrain to the creator:

> This most afflicts me, that departing hence,
> As from his face I shall be hid, depriv'd
> His blessed count'nance; here I could frequent,
> With worship, place by place where he voutsaf'd
> Presence Divine, and to my Sons relate;
> On this Mount he appear'd, under this Tree
> Stood visible, among these Pines his voice
> I heard, here with him at this Fountain talk'd.
>
> 11. 315–22

For Eve, too, visitations to flowers in their ranks and tribes are now to be forbidden, and so for post-edenic poetry topography becomes enigmatic.

Michael eventually remarks that God is still omnipresent in it, merely in less visible ways. He fills

> Land, Sea, and Air, and every kind that lives,
> Fomented by his virtual power and warm'd:
> All th' Earth he gave thee to possess and rule,
> No despicable gift, surmise not then
> His presence to these narrow bounds confin'd
> Of Paradise or *Eden*.
>
> 11. 337–42

However, as history discovers, the divine presence is perturbable in that lower world—enough so to destroy Eden and bring the flood. What Michael postpones saying is that God will show himself not only in providential gifts but in the tormented sea, the pillar of fire, and the parched land—new materials for the interpreter and barriers to lyric enthusiasm. If Satan and his host discover ashes where they expect fruit, in the offing for human genii loci are also the vanity of Babel and philosophical errors that land their followers in the Limbo of Fools.

In its analysis of lyric occasions, *Paradise Lost* is concerned with God's partial retractions in other places as well, or more broadly with the "art of presence," in Arnold Stein's apt phrase, which I take to include half-presence as well.[5] One thing is meant to be separated from another from the outset, the universe having been made by partial, graded expressions of the logos. Although Satan must bear the blame for inventing illusory rapture, difficulties with the full expression of one thing to another begin with that separation. Some formality and estrangement accompany approaches of one creature to another even in the love talk of Adam and Eve. The dusk of heaven is a revealing emblem of that partial knowledge, like the rhythmic "grateful vicissitude" of Eden's own days and nights. More and then less of God is communicated to his realms in the pulsations of light and dark, as in the issuing of his messengers; presence and absence are as twins, each inconceivable without the other, as good and evil are, darkness of course being the inferior twin—even (in Milton's peculiar word) an "obsequious" or "following" one:

> Light issues forth, and at the other door
> Obsequious darkness enters, till her hour
> To veil the Heav'n, though darkness there might well
> Seem twilight here.
>
> 6. 9–12

In the retractions of light, both free will and disobedience become possible. After the fall the rift widens, as grateful vicissitude becomes a sharper seasonal vicissitude and the round of complementary opposites comes to resemble Satan's seige of contraries.

## SATAN BRINGS HIS ROAD SHOW HOME

The most extreme examples of the erosion of divine presence and dispossession come in Satan's travels, which have lyric pauses and apostrophes. Satan's attempt to stage an analogue to Christ's post-creation return to heaven points up forcefully the absence, in both chaos and hell, of positive recollections of other realms. As the completion of the satanic plot, his return is teleological: he has pointed toward it since Book 1, and it establishes permanently redefined relations between hell's inhabitants and their assigned region. The final stage of hell's colonizing, the transfer of empire, and the triumph of the delegated governor over his subjects are included in its upending of forms.

However, this is not Satan's first staging of his own presence as God's substitute in what John Demaray calls his antitriumphs.[6] In his first public performance after withdrawing from the precincts of light, he has come forth as a sort of emperor-general:

> High in the midst exalted as a God
> Th' Apostate in his Sun-bright Chariot sat
> Idol of Majesty Divine, enclos'd
> With Flaming Cherubim, and golden Shields.
>
> 6. 99–102

He has improved upon that masquelike glitter of idols in Pandaemonium, seating himself "High on a Throne of Royal State" (2.1) not as a genius or interpreter for the moment but as the one interpreted. In these inversions of the pageantry and symbolism of empire, we sense the hidden God; but as the movement toward which God, too, has pointed in countering the satanic plot for divided rule, Satan's return to hell exposes a more substantial negative image. Expecting to speak with a godlike eloquence that will raise personal to public triumph—but helpless to resist a second incarnation in serpent form—he issues and hears only hisses. Milton could not have devised a more appropriate exhibit of rhetoric failing to rise to hymnal greeting or of pageantry failing to become triumph. All lyric crossing is stopped up in the motives of the call and the absence of the logos.

But it is also true that although Satan's homecoming fails in its attempt to reproduce God-host relations, his delegates have better luck in Eden, where they complete the movement of desire to devourable objects that Sin has anticipated and Eve enabled. Responding to a call that they take to be from him, they greet him enroute as if he warranted a venerable address:

> O Parent, these are thy magnific deeds,
> Thy Trophies, which thou view'st as not thine own,
> Thou art their Author and prime Architect.
>
> 10. 354–56

He in turn applies to them the language of priestly hierarchy, or of commanders of new empire issuing patents to colonial emissaries:

> My Substitutes I send ye, and Create
> Plenipotent on Earth, of matchless might
> Issuing from mee.
>
> 10.403–5

The terrain that once awoke spontaneous verse in Adam and Eve will henceforth feed Death. But as a final twist, we discover that

Satan is incapable of summoning anything from such distances and that the command to Sin and Death to be plenipotent would be without force if he did. Instead, it is God who arranges earth's wreckage and thereby makes death an ironic gateway to paradise, as in extreme and summary form at world's end. Lamentation thus becomes a preliminary to something like the unexpressive nuptial song that follows the weeping of shepherds.

*Paradise Lost* has still other sorts of shadowy presences behind the implication of one realm in another and the imitative performances of their inhabitants. We cannot examine all of these merely to assess Milton's topographical doubling, but some of them bear upon the nature of lyric moments as crossings of subjects to evasive objects that contain much more than themselves. In the aftermath of Satan's visit to Eden, we see innumerable infiltrations of his working as satanic doubleness creeps into the reading of signs. Like the permission he implicitly receives to rise from the floor of hell, they are the result of a partial withholding of God's rule and so are infiltrations of divine purpose also, but again ironically and indirectly. When Eve goes to work alone and Satan proceeds with the temptation, we are aware of both God and Adam as half-presences. In prediction of that shadowing, when she hears the call to come forth in her dream, she mistakenly thinks that it comes from Adam inducing her to see the beauty of the moonlit landscape and soar above it. Character is always a compound of influences, and so we find nothing surprising about that.

More broadly, narrative is itself a mixture of moments, as past and future stand behind the present, one character behind another, and one phase of character behind another phase. Eve's full course lies implicit in her early tendencies toward narcissism and ambition, in presences-as-presentiments, hints of a self lacking as yet in circumstantial development and trials of place. In Adam, too, potential remains concealed in innocence—potential for both sin and added stature. It is good narrative technique for Milton to give us such proleptic glimpses, but it is also effective moral and metaphysical shading. With Adam and Eve, it rests on a distinction between a harmless anticipation of sin and actual commitments of the will to it, the first without repercussions, since as Adam explains to Eve in interpreting her dream, evil can come and go in the mind and do no damage if it does not find lodging there. Even without reference to the Fall, traces of the future would draw Eden part way out of its passing moments, since they include the long-range plan for Adam and Eve to increase and hold enlarged dominion.

Such traces in every given moment amount to an analeptic and proleptic deepening of experience, not to the degree or with the dire effects that fallen angels torment the present with forlorn recollection and anxiety-ridden plotting but with a sense of the entire narrative process in the moment, just as a given place refers to other places and to an ultimate celestial topography. More particularly, all moments look forward to a finish foreseen by omniscience and guaranteed by omnipotence, as later Old Testament typology will import remote phases of history into present figures and events. All epochs are guided by essentially the same directions to paradise restored.

The not-present and the future are powerful solicitations, as any incomplete narrative or dramatic state is; they ask to come forth to full recognition, as full presence is hailed by lyrics. But the differences between actual and virtual presence are as significant as the one between anticipated and actual sin. Only God has unqualified standing for Milton, and even he cannot be fully present through mediation to limited intelligences. Incompleteness generates anxiety and an intensity of lyric moments in somewhat the way Eve's dream generates the morning song as a purging of confused feeling, or as wisdom, shut out at one entrance in the second invocation, generates compensatory inner light, the reverse side of which is the expectation of a triumph that gets pulled away just as one reaches for it.

Although one hesitates to set up these theologically oriented insights into lyric crossings as a model for all others, they have several advantages in that capacity. They bring lyric greetings into relation to narrative and dramatic frameworks as expressions of a sense of place and calling, as Adam and Eve in hailing Eden and its creator situate themselves in the overall design. Though their lyrics are lacking at first in reprehensible aspects of indictment and empire-making, Milton finds these too in Eve's fall. Very few aspects of language in fact do not find an origin in the combined myths of creation, fall, and redemption. This makes *Paradise Lost* useful for paradigmatic purposes. But beyond that it offers a map of historical possibilities within which Vaughan, Herbert, Marvell, and others are locatable—outside of which Spenser, Jonson, and Shakespeare stand as chief predecessors. Certainly, compared with the latter, and with Virgil and Italian heroic romances, Milton chose a singularly place-oriented epic, sparing of people until Michael's panorama of tribes and nations and distant view of the gathered saints.

Milton culminates a long process of subversion by which common Elizabethan associations of nature and social hierarchy were brought into question. Without tracing the stages by which he does so, we can see that from his viewpoint such an association would have seemed appropriate almost from the beginning of his career. Elizabethan political eulogy depended heavily on links between the delegated governance of the kingdom and natural resources. Even hampered by Richard, John of Gaunt is able to draw upon those links in pleading that "This blessed plot, this earth, this realm, this England," this "other Eden, demi-paradise" be ruled once again by kings renowned for Christian service and true chivalry. Without acknowledging Gaunt's criticism, Richard himself ratifies that alliance of prince and island blessings when he arms the native creatures of Wales against rebellion:

> Dear earth, I do salute thee with my hand,
> Though rebels wound thee with their horses' hoofs. . . .
> But let thy spiders that suck up thy venom
> And heavy-gaited toads lie in their way,
> Doing annoyance to the treacherous feet,
> Which with usurping steps do trample thee;
> Yield stinging nettles to mine enemies.
>
> *Richard II*, 3.2.6–18

Like any lyric address to place, Richard's mixes celebration and possession. His use of lurking adders for military purposes makes an unusual application of orphic powers to enemies, and it is clear elsewhere in Shakespeare as well that the alliance of civil rule and orphic address is complex and subject to misuse; but Richard's pieties are not necessarily undone by that. Even Ulysses' famous reinforcement of social degree by cosmic analogy, though no doubt partly cynical in its application, voices assumptions that very few Elizabethans would dismiss. "Degree, priority, and place,/Insisture, course, proportion, season, form, / Office, and custom, in all line of order" readily apply to both the glorious planet Sol and noble enthroned eminences. Ulysses' rhetoric rises toward the ode in the listing of such vast examples. The division of the world into parts becomes an argument for primogeniture, natural "place" among planets and stars an argument for rank and office. Any poet who makes a companionable inventory of creatures and objects—given these rhetorical commonplaces—will necessarily be political unless he first breaks that connection.[7]

Of all Shakespeare's figures of authority, Prospero makes the most effective and probably the most legitimate political use of natural and supernatural connections in turning Ariel and demi-elves loose on rebels to reseat himself as rightful duke, and it is primarily that Prospero-Ariel alliance that Milton thinks of in his own early reconsiderations of delegated rule and orphic capacity in "Arcades" and "Comus." Certainly Milton's association of the Earl of Bridgewater with Sabrina and the shepherd lad is not totally out of reach of notions that guide Richard and Ulysses. But the Genius of the Wood complicates matters by claiming orphic powers over the same region. It is he who knows the forest best, whatever titular and ceremonial command he surrenders to the radiant head of state he calls the citizenry to acknowledge—he who stakes out hallowed ground and utters "puissant words." The powers of the genius, a mask for the poet, are later based in the same spirit that enters all valid hermeneutic endeavors whether addressed to nature's book or to scripture. Like Marvell and Vaughan, Milton finds both nature's rule and civil rule thus hearkening back to the word as well as forward to a final kingdom, also quite beyond the Ulysses-Richard concept of rule.

Once the poet journeys into the forest to read its mosaic, he finds it difficult to maneuver ordinary society back into view or to take up mere laureate functions. (Herbert and Crashaw suggest that assumption of transcendental authority as well.) Though Marvell follows "Arcades" and "Comus" in granting viceregency to a local patron, he also makes a point of Lord Fairfax's retirement and becomes himself the chief reader of the woodland's "mystic book." Whether such transcendental connections undo the social bond or social disconnection comes first and throws the poet back on them, poems like "Upon Appleton House," "The Garden," *Paradise Lost,* and *Paradise Regained* abandon the nature-society-providence alliance. Milton has already turned angrily from a besotted church to hymning saints in "Lycidas" and a resumed anger is not hard to identify in Michael's vision in *Paradise Lost.* These frame the years when, as sloganeer for civil and religious reforms, he postponed further unfoldings of the orphic power he anticipated in "Arcades" and "Comus."

For the present this is perhaps sufficient to suggest that Milton's sense of a divine presence infused into times and places has a historical function in breaking the analogy between nature and the social order that Spenser, Sidney, Shakespeare, and others elaborate. I have continued to echo Heidegger's terms in describing that sense, not out of a perverse love of anachronism but because Heidegger's vocabulary reflects a masked theological bias even while translating it.[8] Heidegger's Being, which simultaneously comes forth and hides, resembles Milton's grateful vicissitude and its shading of moments and places. The difference is that where Heidegger heralds Derrida, without of course endorsing the final step into deconstruction, for Milton a creator's authoritative voice has been imposed on confusion and an even completer imparting of the divine purpose will eventually collect the scattered saints. Meanwhile, the divine presence in nature and scripture allows supplementary writing to interpret it and to make further accommodations of human limits.

PART TWO

SOCIAL PLACEMENT

*For She my Mind hath so displac'd
That I shall never find my home.*
           *Marvell, "The Mower to the Glo-Worms"*

# LOCAL HABITATION AND ITS GENIUS

CHAPTER THREE

AUTHORITY AND CONVENTION IN "LYCIDAS"

Ransom's version of relations between objects and ideas in poetry assumes that poets work with things that come relatively intact and recognizable. As a critic Ransom has minimal interest in the historical and social matters that provide most of the conditioning for those objects and ideas, nor does he consider the tension between poetic traditions and individual talent. But imagery, as opposed to objects themselves, and topoi as opposed to actual places, are the products as much of social convention and bookish discourse as of firsthand observation or individual invention. Marvell's mower, for instance, is the lineal descendant of Theocritus's Komatas and Polyphemos and Virgil's Corydon, both in his lovesick courtship of a reluctant nymph and in his naive, boastful assessment of his resources. No doubt such figures have some distant bearing on actual rustic suitors who gather up honey and flowers and go courting; but the reader knows them as conventions and perhaps as pastoral answers to epic or romance equivalents.

Though likewise not inclined to keep the literary ancestry of a genre and its interplay of tropes in full view, Kenneth Burke's suggestive essay on substance in *A Grammar of Motives* comes closer than Ransom's "image" or "texture" to at least the social circumstances of texts.[1] The word *substance* usually suggests some such circumstances, as does Burke's scene-act ratio. Both assume that poems are symbolic actions in which writers respond to their times, as Theocritus does in looking at Homeric epic through the eyes of an Alexandrian elite more interested in refined and self-conscious artistry than in a literature of "kings and battles."

Although a substance may threaten to dissolve into thin air or into the evasiveness of a body of discourse that constantly revises itself, Burke also finds that "the moment you relax your gaze a bit, it re-forms again. For things *do* have intrinsic natures" (p. 56). Neither scientists nor poets may be quite able to stipulate those natures once and for all, but they continue to make valid statements about them. Some substances are recurrent and orthodox; others carry the stamp of individual makers. Burke notes a parallel inside-outside ambiguity in the term "substance" itself: "Though used to designate something within the thing, . . . the word etymologically refers to something outside the thing" (p. 23). Thus a man of substance sits amid wealth that is part of his acquirements or his social place and is subject to circulation and common definition; yet he may also be a man of individual character, assuming that he has something to him, something substantial. Similarly in aesthetic matters, substance resides both in the interwoven meanings of texts and beyond them in the references through which they gain whatever communicative power we allow them. Literary history is largely a record of that complex inner-outer duplicity.

As I suggested last chapter, seventeenth-century poetry distanced itself from the social assumptions that had constituted a center of gravity for virtually all major texts from Wyatt through the 1590s.[2] Though the attractions of the court linger in the masque and in weakened form in the cavaliers and Spenserians, Milton abandons any idea of secular majesty after the early masques and assigns ostentatious grandeur later primarily to Satan. Marvell exiles society and its rewards at the outset of "The Garden" and in the Horatian ode transforms the offices of kingship into Cromwellian rule, albeit reluctantly. Donne considers courtly pursuits in several of the songs and sonnets but balances them against a love that outweighs them severalfold. The society Herbert invites into the temple is not civil but a special one to be sprinkled and taught by precepts and gathered into the church's "mystical repast." These are shifts not merely in individual allegiance but in the poet's orientation toward decorum, substance, and addressable objects. Parallel to them is an intensifying of the poet's personal claim for authority. Lyric personas are likely to be characters to be reckoned with and can often be mistaken for the poet himself. Donne's speakers, for instance, appear more imposing than Sidney's and at times closer to the poet we recognize from other works.

The question of authority and sincerity is a complex one, however, since any poet is prompted partly by tradition and a readership. When Astrophel says that he is anguished by love, we assume that he is expected to say that and to share with many others a heartfelt need to manufacture sonnets. The fit invention he talks about he finds mainly among predecessors. Even when he ends the first sonnet by admonishing himself to look in his heart and write, he does so as a final flourish in a rhetorically trim sonnet. The personas of the metaphysicals may not represent the poet either, but they alter the self-pretext relationship. For one thing they use fewer standard inventories of nature's graces to lay at the beloved's feet. When their tropes too turn out to be conventional, as they frequently do, their dramatic settings and attention to detail twist them away from former uses. The difference can sometimes be seen in the shift from service to a privileged calling, a shift in which the figures and devices that Puttenham and others list lose some of their appeal. The sound of "I Saw Eternity the other night," "Yonder all before us lye / Deserts of vast Eternity," "Dissolve me into ecstasies, / And bring all Heav'n before mine eyes," and "Well, I will change the service, and go seek / Some other master out" is personal enough to constitute a new lyric address, heralded by Wyatt but not really followed up until Donne. Certain risks—of eccentricity, even of solipsism in Marvell, and of egomania in Milton—accompany that personal turn and sometimes a fear of exceeding bounds, especially when the poet pretends to speak to or on behalf of God, as Milton, Vaughan, and Herbert do.

The passages of *Paradise Lost* that I cited earlier bear out this difference in voice. But the poet-nature-society-Christ relationship of "Lycidas" will serve better I think to test Milton's establishing of a persona who more or less defines his office as he goes. I want to dwell on it sufficiently to gauge Milton's departures from his predecessors and prepare for the pattern of similar departures in the metaphysicals. Hence again I have both paradigmatic and historical uses in mind for the example.

It is nonetheless not easy to decide what comes forth as something new and what Milton incorporates from the tradition, which is no doubt partly why much of the commentary on "Lycidas" beginning with Samuel Jonson has dealt with its pastoral ancestry and the problem of sincerity. Since that commentary has been rehearsed frequently, we can pass it by here. However, in one of the more interesting recent readings of the poem, Paul Alpers proposes a view of pastoral conventions that is of special interest for its minimizing both of Milton's personal imprint on the tradition and of period differences. If poets do in fact make strategic responses to their times, we should be able to determine how a pastoral monody in 1637 differs from Virgil's or Spenser's. Milton alerts us to some differences in his view of Orpheus and modern pastors, but others we must assess on our own. While conceeding that the poem challenges predecessors and fellows, Alpers narrows the "conventions" it works upon primarily to what *convenire* suggests, or the sense of community that a "coming together" creates. Taken in this sense, a convention is not the fixed procedures of genre "imposed by impersonal tradition" but the usage of a community of past singers analogous "to the community of young Cambridge poets who wrote and collected memorial verses for Edward King."[3] The persona in turn bears "witness to the community of men and nature" (pp. 476, 479). The truth he comes upon concerning that pastoral community, in Alpers's view, is not an ontological or epistemological truth to replace the convention but a social truth in keeping with it.

Such "discursive conventions" as William Empson and Kenneth Burke describe have "a solid feeling when and because they are felt to be reliable usages, authorized by the practice of some community or other" (p. 492). The goal of criticism generally and of readings of "Lycidas" in particular should thus be "to give a just account of the validity of socially derived meanings and usages—to do justice to their stability, effect, and accessibility, on the one hand, and to their historical, social, and anthropological determinations, on the other" (p. 492). And so one should stress the poet's possession of the resources of the shepherd community, which are just those conventions that have "enabled the whole poem, even where it revises and corrects them" (p. 494).

It is worth remembering, however, that Virgil's version of that community stresses its fragility, as Alpers's own very able expounding of it in *The Singer of the Eclogues* indicates. In the first eclogue, for instance, Tityrus maintains allegiances both to Rome and to his exiled friend, a victim of Rome's land policies. In an extension of Virgilian tension between factions and ways of life, Spenser's Calidore finds himself strongly attracted to the company of Melibee and Pastorella but cannot stay very long with them without forsaking his duties to the court. It is difficult for either plowland or pastureland to escape problems raised by the largest unit that claims authority over them, which in both cases lies outside the rural community. The quarrels and differences of parties within that community are also of concern to Theocritus, Virgil, and Spenser.

A relatively undifferentiated reading of "conventions" and identification of Milton with them also underplays the revisions all poets of importance make in traditions. Theocritus's bucolic epos plays self-consciously against the heroic epos of Homer, and Virgil's eclogues against the Idylls. Even simple societies do not often have the "gathering" Alpers assumes that pastoral finds in "Lycidas." Certainly Milton's society (like ours) was composed of a plurality of movements, ideologies, and overlapping but different languages. Milton turns one way of thinking against another throughout the poem, in conventions that are far from equal in validity. He turns St. Peter loose against a poisonous segment of the religious community, since churches are undermined by those who, like Bunyan's Formalist and Hypocrisy, "Creep and intrude and climb into the fold." He witnesses Orpheus's murder by the Thracian rout. The uncouth swain himself is apparently close only to Lycidas, with whom in better days he went afield "together both" (just the two of them) and heard "What time the Gray-fly winds her sultry horn." Even that fellowship—a literary exaggeration of Milton's casual acquaintance with Edward King—is past except for Lycidas's return at the end. He ultimately replaces the shepherds he has imagined at Cambridge with a society of saints who resemble angel hymnists more than shepherds. The effect of the "other groves, and other streams" in the apotheosis is to transport that society to a safer as well as a higher ground. The difference is not only between carefree college friends and revolutionaries; it is also between this world and the next, as is typical of the Miltonic realm-crossing we sampled earlier.

On the way toward that society of saints, an image of the gathered church in its final form, "Lycidas" conducts a solitary struggle with its central problems. The speaker gets along for 164 lines without addressing his fellow mourners and is alone again in twitching his "mantle Blew" and going off to fresh woods, settings for his future poems. It is not reading Christ's rejection of empire in *Paradise Regained* forward into Milton's prerevolutionary period to see a distrust of the very foundations of temporal community in the poem. Even Lycidas in returning as genius of the shore will apparently work alone to help those who "wander in that perilous flood," where the force of "wander" is to suggest not travel with a purpose but the meandering of strays.

Nor do the speaker's addresses to several parties dispel that sense of solitude until he envisions the highly selective, cultic group assembled elsewhere. Poems use addresses as required to mark rhetorical stances and shifts of ground. Triton and Aeolus are mythological conveniences, for instance, to be interrogated in place of wind and wave; Camus personifies the home ground of the lost shepherd; the Pilot of the Galilean lake serves to identify and to right a wrong. The addresses to laurels, sisters of the well, Lycidas, nymphs, Arethuse, Mincius, Alpheus, Michael, and dolphins reinforce apostrophe as a rhetorical intensifier. Milton uses it to bring fictive presences forward as though out of the musings of the speaker himself. Among these participants in the monody, the woeful shepherds that make the most convincing general company of the poem are best thought of as a kind of chorus that signals an end to mourning and mark a division of the poem. Even then the poem does not really present us with a public face. The more dominant presences, the company of pastoral elegists honored by Milton's quotations, are not only long departed but incomplete as surmises. What the society that counts exemplifies is not an easy companionship of shepherds, then, but a celebration of the redeemer and its own members, especially its newly welcomed one.

The calling to account, the interrogations, the indulgence of false surmises belong to a dramatic course that heads off any earlier assimilation of the uncouth swain completely to Milton. Perhaps the central project of Milton's poetry in fact is to assimilate one level or one realm to another with checks and balances, in a probing of each individually and of their interactions and analogies. Given that recurrent concern, it is difficult to see pastoral, particularly the flower passage, as nearly equal in recompense to paradise itself, or to read Milton's reflections upon that passage in the "false surmise" passage that follows as a recovering of its mythic attractions. But let us consider the latter passage and assess the degree to which it veers away and suggests a pastoral revisionism:

> For so to interpose a little ease,
> Let our frail thoughts dally with false surmise.
> Ay me! Whilst thee the shores and sounding Seas
> Wash far away, where'er thy bones are hurl'd,
> Whether beyond the stormy *Hebrides*,
> Where thou perhaps under the whelming tide
> Visit'st the bottom of the monstrous world;
> Or whether thou to our moist vows denied,
> Sleep'st by the fable of *Bellerus* old,
> Where the great vision of the guarded Mount
> Looks toward *Namancos* and *Bayona*'s hold.
>
> (152–62)

Conceeding that something about this passage seems realistic and that a reconsideration of the flowers does in fact take place in it, Alpers believes that the preceding passage nonetheless enables this one, with its "intricate syntax and the delicate solicitude of a word like 'perhaps.'" That "these lines prove what the flower passage seemed to disprove—the adequacy of poetic imagination" (pp. 486–87)—seems to me dubious. An imagination that is adequate to the monstrous element may not be adequate to what comes from the next level of myth. Although sleeping by the fable of Bellerus qualifies an otherwise harsh realism, as "visit'st" also does, not pastoral representation in itself but the appearance of "the dear might of him that walk'd the waves" brings forth awe and mysteriousness, precedents for which are scarce in either the classical tradition or English pastorals based on it. Spenser's choral group on Mount Acidale, for instance, rises above the shepherd games of the plain but is of another kind from Milton's and obviously lacks the Reformation overtones of Milton's saints, following as they do upon the Thracian rout and false pastors. Certainly the temperament of radicalism is powerful in the poem, no less in the replacement of flowers and soft lays with saints than in the denunciation of corrupt clergy.

Even so, it is possible to overdo the severing of "weep no more" from its preparations, and Alpers and others have ably pointed to some of the reasons. Lesser pastoral idealizations even when upset by winter storms and corrupt clergy have an imaginative power of their own to be sure, which is no doubt why Milton proceeds by a combination of lyric involvement in, and dramatic sufferings of them. Similarly, the edenic delights of Adam and Eve are never discredited by the Fall or rendered obsolete by the new paradise that Christ promises for them in Book 3 and Michael again in Book 12. Milton typically seeks not an exalted communion of saints in itself but a balance between the visionary level it represents and an easier sociability of the kind that husband and wife find in meet conversation. Adam wanted that conversation to begin with precisely because lengthy colloquy with God promised to be a great strain for him. In "Lycidas" the trademark of vertical differences in style is changeability passage by passage and a breaking up of conventions in a structure of advances and retreats. The connection between shepherd sociability and higher communion is primarily contrastive, as even the bond between husband and wife becomes for Adam the minute Eve forces him to choose. Quarrels and debates are one side of such discrepancies in community in *Paradise*

*Lost,* and Pandaemonium is the extreme they come to when the satanic gathering replaces the holy one. "Lycidas" has some elements of that larger myth (without the fallen angels), and we recognize its final vision from other poems as well, in "Ad Patrem," the hymnal sections of the Nativity Ode, "At a Solemn Music," "On Time," the end of "Il Penseroso," and parts of *Paradise Regained.*

The distinguishing of the saints from Virgilian pastors is only one sign of Milton's imposing of a personal, visionary signature on pastoral conventions. We are aware from the start that the poem is struggling with a task set by the sort of gathering that elegy summons, by the rendering of funeral tribute by fellow shepherds and specifically a speaker aware of his obligations. One of the things that earlier passages indicate is that the poem's making is crucial to Milton personally. Even what collects early in images and echoes of pastoral—in its considerable sedimentation—Milton overpowers by rough handling. The opening of the poem imposes a complex, developing voice at a point at which a first reading has as yet no help from reversals and no anticipatory sense of the final vision. It thus makes a fair test of the imprint of the speaker's authority and what separates Milton from predecessors and prepares for his redefinition of calling. The occasion of the poem (the assembling of an anthology of verse) encroaches upon his self-moved initiative and gives him an opening set of questions about his readiness.

We recognize the special Miltonic nature of that concern, posed in its usual gravity—recognize it, I think, much as we do Beethoven's imprint on symphonic form. It is not really much like anything Virgilian or anything in Spenser or Sidney:

> Yet once more, O ye Laurels, and once more
> Ye Myrtles brown, with Ivy never sere,
> I come to pluck your Berries harsh and crude,
> And with forc'd fingers rude,
> Shatter your leaves before the mellowing year.
> Bitter constraint, and sad occasion dear,
> Compels me to disturb your season due:
> For *Lycidas* is dead, dead ere his prime,
> Young Lycidas, and hath not left his peer:
> Who would not sing for *Lycidas?* he knew
> Himself to sing, and build the lofty rhyme.
> He must not float upon his wat'ry bier
> Unwept, and welter to the parching wind,
> Without the meed of some melodious tear.
>     Begin then, Sisters of the sacred well,
> That from beneath the seat of *Jove* doth spring,
> Begin, and somewhat loudly sweep the string.

The differentiating features of style here are a matter of movement as well as image or theme, as someone's gait is as much a personal mark as facial features. One can understand why Isabel MacCaffrey would think that "we hear the unmediated exclamation of a speaker who is not yet identified as an uncouth swain,"[4] that is, hear Milton himself and not merely a dramatic persona as his stand-in. I would prefer "mediated" and find an acknowledgment of echoes necessary from the outset as part of the assertion of difference; but the speaker's concern for his unripeness might seem gratuitous if we come to it only from the tradition and not also from Milton's recent past, or since we have that privilege, from his entire canon, including the prose treatises. One of the Miltonic signatures is an obsession not just with starting a vocational phase but with beginnings in general and the poet's capacity to find links between them and the providential scheme of things. Milton seldom enters into an enterprise lightly or lets others do so. For the poet setting forth, at a crisis in his career with each major project, questions about how to begin prove impossible to answer beforehand—what forces are to gather, what connection can be made between his talent and the divine will, what the relation of the new undertaking is to past ones and to guiding traditions. The questions are embedded in the working out of the task in hand, as again in the Nativity Ode and "How Soon Hath Time." In *Paradise Lost* the retreats to fundamental origins in the first sin of angels and men and in the creation; in the Nativity Ode the birth of Christ; in "L'Allegro" and "Il Penseroso" the genealogies of joy and melancholy—these all develop connections between primal origins and new moments. The invocations of *Paradise Lost* lend additional retrospective credence to the personal imprint here, where even at the end of the poem both Lycidas and the uncouth swain are still embarking on new careers.

It is nonetheless difficult to determine just how, technically, Milton makes the opening of "Lycidas" personal. Despite its elaborate periphrasis and its assembled traditions, its rhetorical figures are fewer than those with which Colin Clout delights E. K. Already in "O ye Laurels," which halts the progression of the first line, we have a prediction of "But O the heavy change, now thou art gone," "Ay me, I fondly dream!" "Alas! What boots it," and "For so to interpose a little ease . . . Ay me!" The speaker intermittently acknowledges his and tradition's incapacity to proceed with equanimity. He comes upon some assurance of a future in the shepherd's trade early in the poem—a future independent of any equivalents to a courtly career or a temporal sociality—but that future still depends primarily upon discovery of a realm that will support not just the fame of poets but the substance of their social and topographical hope. Such a vision will eventually be filled out imagistically; it will even out the rhythms of the poem and offer a forward movement of some gravity.

For all its haste and violence, the initial complaint manages a foretaste of that gravity and an implicit assurance that is entirely characteristic of Miltonic calm. We find it also in *Of Reformation, Areopagitica,* and other tracts; in the flurry of uncertainty and impatience in "When I Consider" that comes to closure in "They also serve"; and in the maturing youth of "How Soon Hath Time," reconciled to the pace of his great task-master, however undefined the means and the specific accomplishments. Not mastery alone, however, but disturbed mastery characterizes the voice. Troubled paragraph development brings the persona's mask very near the self behind it in the complex syntax, the latinity, and even the verbal eccentricity that to T. S. Eliot marked an unfortunate divergence from Virgil. The special quality of the evergreen endurance of "Ivy never sere," the half-hesitant manner of "compells me," the way of posing questions about due regard and rewards, the unusual diction of "build," "welter," and "melodious tear" are all recognizable Miltonic flourishes.

This generating of a language is inseparable from the growth of a self; Milton stages both in the poem as a subset of the "beginnings" theme. In *Paradise Lost* where growth centers in Adam and Eve, Adam's recognition of his special existence—his difference— leads quickly to what God teasingly calls a very precise and subtle concept of happiness. Milton grants a great deal of freedom to other creatures as well—freedom to dwell differently in their settings from anything else, if not always to develop. Members of the species come forth determined to wreathe a lithe proboscis or burst with kindly rupture. At the other end of his career, the individual kiss that greets arrivals into "Long Eternity" in "On Time" seals approval of a personal achievement, just as the husband in "Methought I Saw My Late Espoused Saint" expects to see his wife with "Full sight... without restraint," resuming personal relations at the point at which individual being passes into a fixed state. As Eve demonstrates, a rebellious individualism can lead to egoistic extremes in this quest for a higher, final place, but within the limits of kinds and rules Milton finds room for self-expansion. Where

Sidney plays at that individual development, then, and Spenser in Colin's shepherd costume is almost apologetic about claiming it, Milton makes it necessary for the poet's coming forth to his tasks.

It is partly as a son of Adam, then, and as future advocate of self-invoked callings that the uncouth swain begins "Yet once more": before Virgil, before Theocritus, in Milton's scheme of things, humankind began addressing its myrtles and its ivy in the tradition of the first parents. It is Eve who voices what we might regard as the first pastoral elegy:

> O flow'rs,
> That never will in other Climate grow,
> My early visitation, and my last
> At Ev'n, which I bred up with tender hand
> From the first op'ning bud, and gave ye Names,
> Who now shall rear ye to the Sun, or rank
> Your Tribes, and water from th' ambrosial Fount?
> 
> *PL*, 11: 273–79

How many times in how many places humankind has had its relationship with home places disturbed (always surprisingly, always before due season) Milton knows to be countless even in "Lycidas." He is not dependent upon Virgil to tell him so, merely to suggest an important variant of the lyric voice that can be used as a comparatively recent and very high standard.

It is not necessary to extend this commentary on "Lycidas" further merely to observe Miltonic authority emerging from predecessors whom it corrects or to locate in outline the historical difference between Milton's view of the poetic vocation in shepherd mask, in the landscape he proposes for it, and others before him. What I earlier called the poet's cultic tendency might better be conceived of as simply a commitment to reformed institutions and a self guided by them, and a review of literary traditions accordingly. "Cultic" is not apt of course if it is taken to suggest small groups that meet secretly, since Milton's future associates declared themselves openly and set about altering church, state, and family with some programmatic determination. A "calling" for them, as for Milton, was a point of departure instigated by providence or assumed under its corrective guidance. The historical point is that the society with which Milton identified, whose language he used to test received literary traditions from sonnets to epics, was sufficiently of the same mind, and active enough, to form almost a period of its own. As a subculture it fed ideas and institutions into an already multicolored society in a stream that reached some distance before it blended in. Like all strong movements, it was revolutionary at first, no less in literary than in doctrinal matters and politics, as "Lycidas" indicates, and hence no less in landscapes than in other matters. Milton was its most extraordinary literary proponent, but the earlier century produced a number of lesser revisions of the traditions Milton subverts.

These too I want to read partly as reactions to the courtly modes of predecessors, but whatever they respond to, they tend to be staged as the reactions of personas seeking either private or marginal places to be and therefore needing to redefine their relations to an audience that cannot be taken for granted. That rethinking of rhetorical address brings in its wake a metapoetic concern for the nature of lyric. The claim for personal authority, to return to it, gets inserted somewhat problematically into it. It continues to draw upon the authority of tradition, as "Lycidas" does in echoing Virgil and Theocritus, but it tends to do so with something of the same egocentrism that "Lycidas" displays. In the background are larger questions of class allegiance and for Milton, revolution and its active ways of bringing about the gathering of saints not merely in poetic myth but for a time in actual social reform. It is difficult to judge such intrusions of politics into fictions, but they constitute part of the extrinsic substance of others besides Milton—of Marvell, for instance.

## HOBBES'S GENERIC REGIONS AND THEIR INHABITANTS

The sorting out of either individual or period differences is not assisted much by renaissance criticism, which in England concentrates on generic differences rather than on influences and cultural allegiances. But that task is unquestionably important to any understanding of lyric localities. As James Turner and Raymond Williams have indicated, landscapes are not necessarily socially or politically neutral even when they seem remote. The most painterly of poems may be concerned not merely with sylvan, river, or mountain scenes but with ways of life and may assume an audience of a certain kind as well. Thus in Turner's view, when a poet like Aldred Revett presents a lad in russet coat melting his soul "through the vocal oate" and finds nature all gentility and ease, he indirectly supports the status quo and accepts a recorder function for the pastoralist. Certainly he urges no one to take up Miltonic questions about authority, possession, or social order. Shadows, colors, heights and depths, placement and relation of objects, textures, and the disposition of nature are relatively untroubled in such ideologies of dissociation, whose "Inliv'ning by transcription" puts a screen of art between us and actual rural life.[5]

A notable exception to the silence of apologists on poetry's more specific social allegiances is Hobbes, spokesman for a conservatism equal to that of the landscape poets. Together with Denham's "Coopers Hill," his "Answer to Davenant's Preface to *Gondibert*" is the most serious midcentury challenge to the sort of literary and civil disruption Milton represents. Basically, he assigns places and genres to social-geographic spheres according to the reigning renaissance ideas of decorum. Poets from time in memoriam have "lodg'd themselves in the three Regions of mankind" for heroes, urban dwellers, and rural dwellers.[6] What falls to each district respectively is the heroic, the scommatique, and the pastoral, toned down and particularized variants of the philosopher's celestial, aerial, and terrestrial regions. Crossing these with narrative and dramatic deliveries produces six specific genres in all, epic, tragedy, satire, comedy, narrative bucolic, and pastoral comedy (p. 55). In Hobbes's rudimentary taxonomy, these unfortunately are the sum total. The princely mode has the closest alliances with god-given governing powers and thereby warrants an epic style.

Hobbes's brief list is obviously challengeable from a number of directions, although its correspondences between provinces and poetic modes are not necessarily unsound in principle. Herbert's temple, for instance, gathers figures and themes from an Anglican institution that Hobbes could have included had he wanted to expand his scheme. Presumably he might also have taken notice of fairyland and other regions in the general area of romance. He could not have foreseen of course the topographical spread and complexity of a poem like *Paradise Lost*, which would have challenged the symmetry of any overly neat classification. Of all his omissions, however, the most puzzling is that of lyric, and we can only speculate as to why he found no place for it. He may have decided that whereas satire, comedy, and tragedy depict a society directly and are either generated within it or staged before it, lyrics are usually monologic addresses to an object or dialogues of some intimacy. But privacy should not have made them seem independent of social implications, even in descriptive settings and painterly topographies such as those of "Coopers Hill," "L'Allegro" and "Il Penseroso." Festive lyrics, for instance, share with comedy a celebration of communal well-being and rituals, as in Herrick's Mayday and country house poems. A trace of that communal element clings to public commemorations and epithalamia as well and may be inferred from elegiac losses. The community of saints in "Lycidas" eventually contributes to Lycidas's reception and replaces other forms of lyric, coming in fact very close to Hobbes's celestial heroic mode, beyond the bucolic landscapes of lads in russet coats. Lyric's public nature even in apparently private sanctuaries is further indicated by the fact that crossing to prized or lost objects can be checked by disapproval real or anticipated, as in "The Sunne Rising" and "The Canonization," where Donne wards off censure, or as in "The Garden," with its awareness of social constraints to be set aside. In a good deal of seventeenth-century landscape poetry, society is made out to be counter-lyrical. Rather than assuming something like a tourist-reader and enthusiast for orderly variety and painterly excursions, the poet requires the reader to become an initiate and to separate himself from others to join the poet in solitude and share his reading of nature's book.

Hobbes's exclusion of lyric from his generic scheme suggests that he may have turned the relations of text to social spheres the wrong way around. Assuming that "the subject of a Poem is the manners of men, not natural causes" (p. 56), he makes physical settings incidental to, rather than extensions of, the sociality of poems. Those who would call in sonnets, epigrams, "and the like peeces" do not summon true genres in Hobbes's view, merely parts of an "entire poem," which sounds like notes toward a supreme fiction in the celestial-heroic mode. Any individual egocentrism or subjective interest thereby becomes difficult to acknowledge. Nor does he question that princes, as men of conspicuous luster and influence among men, display the best of manners. The rest are either inconstant and troublesome, or plain and dull, one in accord with impure city air and the other with earth. Hobbes is clearly not joking in that reduction (which would perforce classify Milton in the mobile blustery sort), and he shows no inclination to retreat from the "three sorts of Poesy" themselves. But one must remember his provocations in the civil war setting and the reinforcement his scheme receives from his theory of faculties, in which experience, memory, judgment, and philosophical precepts are expected to keep tight reign over fancy, the faculty of imagistic innovation. Sound wits are tethered to ancient thought and sound government; innovation that smacks of enthusiasm threatens a tradition whose most conspicuous continuity lies in royalty and what attends it. As the preface to Homer's *Odyssey* also remarks, the virtues of heroic poems can be comprehended in one word, "discretion," which hangs upon profitable design buttressed by prudence, justice, fortitude, and "the example of such Great and Noble Persons." Though praiseworthy as that in which the sublimity of poets consists, fancy is restricted mainly to harvesting ornaments from unusual places, which are not to become permanent harbors of self.

Lyric's emphasis on the speaker and points of view in distinct places have given trouble to other theories of literature-society relations besides Hobbes's, but Hobbes's time was not one in which those relations could be easily set aside—the "I" not only of lyric but of sectarian tracts and heroic modes gets such prominent staging. What seems distinct in such landscape excursions as Milton's, Marvell's, and Vaughan's is a commitment to a persona's usually troubled movement toward possession and celebration in some attempt at transcendental crossing. In the triangulations of speaker-object, speaker-audience, and poet-tradition, the second is left more or less implicit and the last becomes highly revisionary. What the final speaker of "Lycidas" must decide before his career can go on is how far the pastoral voices of the past, the destructive power of nature, and the corruption of the church will be allowed to extend their influence over him. Not until he hits upon the mythic power of him who walked the waves, a new Orpheus, can he redefine nature, the shepherd-pastor-poet, and his own future.

Tudor panegyric, in contrast, depends not on that seizing of individual privilege but on public values and moral persuasion within a collective sense of decorum. Settings may be far removed in places like Sidney's Arcadia or Spenser's fairyland, but even these borderlands maintain strong associations with the court, not less so in the visionary experience of Redcross seeing New Jerusalem and of Calidore on Mt. Acidale than in their active pursuits of virtues to assemble into the perfect knight. The story of that courtly centrism is already familiar from Russell Fraser's *War Against Poetry,* Richard Helgerson's *The Elizabethan Prodigals,* Daniel Javitch's *Poetry and Courtliness,* and several biographies of major figures.[7] It need not be recalled here except for the contribution that emphasis on service makes to the guilt of the prodigal writer in Gascoigne, Lyly, Greene, Lodge, and Sidney. As Helgerson demonstrates, those who turned to writing in the later sixteenth century—often after failing to secure positions at court—found it difficult to reconcile the careers they were expected to assume with what their peers considered to be literature's uselessness. Lyric and romance were especially vulnerable, given their preoccupation with amorous matters and self-concern. Stephen Gosson's *School of Abuse* in that light was less an anomaly in its attack on poetry than Sidney's *Defense of Poesie* in looking for poetry's socially redeeming value.[8]

This is not to say that courtly poets always speak in some way for unified culture. They appear to be attracted to solitude and tempted by the same remote settings as Colin Clout and Musidorus. Arcadia is traditionally a retreat from empire or is presented in such a way as to contrast with it, and it or an equivalent is so handled by Spenser, Sidney, and Shakespeare. No one probes the tensions between courtly service and poetic vocation with greater subtlety and sensitivity than Spenser, especially in the masks and disguises that pastoral provides. It is often from the periphery of the court that he examines the poet's access to it and duties toward it, beginning with *Shepheardes Calender* and proceeding to the Colin Clout episode of *The Faerie Queen*, Book 6. In "Colin Clouts Come Home Againe," the shepherd-poet returns from his expedition to London reconciled to the fact that both the glory of Elizabeth's court and its corruption are better left where they are by those who have learned to survive in the spare, rocky land under Mole. However, the poem's concern remains the *relations* between that center and the poet's outpost. As Spenser and Sidney realize, by leaning toward educative modes and panegyric and pursuing the literary vocation *as* service, the poet can try to have it both ways. He can do so provided only that he either returns from remote places, as Sidney's princes and Spenser's Calidore are obliged to do, or comments on the capital from his borderland perspective.

From the viewpoint of either their Tudor predecessors or Hobbes's conservative classifications, the metaphysicals and Milton are displaced: they make their excursions into landscapes, temples, and private chambers with no intent to reenter public service as Sidney or Spenser understood it. Although royalist apologetic finds renewal in the cavaliers and Drayton and more seriously in Dryden, survivals of what Hobbes would call the celestial-heroic mode tend to look belated after Donne. Overall, the range of new seventeenth-century settings is as impressive as the speakers who explore them. Precisely as relocations, they question what place signifies and how one is to respond to it. Modes do not stay as they were except in lesser poets. As we have seen, for instance, pastoral in Milton becomes unsettling and unbucolic in a different way, as an instrument of career-making in "Lycidas" and as a segment of epic in *Paradise Lost,* in which both pastoral and epic elements are reassigned to Adam and Eve as the domestic rulers of Eden before empire-making becomes a satanic habit. Despite his repeated search for a position at court after his marriage, Donne insists in the *Songs and Sonnets* that he has no regrets in abandoning one career for another. Herbert is certain that the temple is the real center of the world, not a substitute for something else. Although Marvell is more restive, "The Garden" expresses confidence in nature's capacity to provide all one needs. Indeed, one can be a poet only there: it is in and to trees that the soul sings, gaining proleptic glimpses of paradise in the most appropriate place.

These examples will need to be looked into further in due course. Before that, however, I want to consider Jonson's in-between sociality and reconstruction of classical standards in genres that by Hobbes's classifications would be mixed. Jonson reinvents Horace's country house as an appealing supplement to courtly kinds and finds in cultivated rural settings new advantages for the poet. The Sidney estate of "To Penshurst," for instance, combines providential abundance with concern for manners and social place. It is both heroic and rural. It does not carry the poet so far abroad as Eden or the Bermudas but keeps to a relatively small provincial dominion—small by comparison to the realmic scope of Sidney, Spenser, Shakespeare, or Drayton's *Poly-Olbion*.[9] At the same time, it gives the poet an extensive classical tradition of praise. The country household in general provides a sanctuary from public life for the Sidneys, Pembertons, Saxhams, and Wroths, until Lord Fairfax retreats more decisively from national responsibilities to the Appleton estate. It allows lyric, discursive, and descriptive modes to coexist in a comparatively low-keyed middle style that does not encourage outright rapture or apostrophe or attempts at celestial-heroic panegyric. It does not need a commanding genius loci to orchestrate the blessings of place, and so the poet figure is more secretary or guest than authoritative seer, at least until "Upon Appleton House."[10]

Jonson's other alternatives to a courtly orientation are even more far-reaching, and together with Donne's, set up models for later placements and an attitude of independence relatively free of the rhetoric of patronage. They also assemble their own educated audiences who are not taken as given but constituted for the occasion. The poet's authority is thus exercised less over objects that he interprets or appropriates on his own than over situations in which he turns nature's resources into social resources. His goal is the reestablishing of a classics-oriented set of standards and a moral subsociety that he can count on to read him in the right context, more or less as directed from within the poem itself. A hint of Milton's reformative zeal is suggested by that rudimentary programming of a special group and by Jonson's putting before it both exemplary models and satiric examples.

*First give me faith, who know
Myself a little. I will take you so,
As you have writ yourself. Now stand, and then,
Sir, you are sealed of the tribe of Ben.*
   "An Epistle Answering to One that Asked to be Sealed of
   the Tribe of Ben"

*How summed a circle didst thou leave mankind
Of deepest lore, could we the centre find!*
   "To the Immortal Memory and Friendship of That Noble
   Pair, Sir Lucius Cary and Sir H. Morison"

# JONSON AND THE POET'S CIRCLE

CHAPTER FOUR

ISSUING INVITATIONS

Jonson's circle was a curious phenomenon in literary history. It met on occasion, and it provided the substance for a figure of some sophistication in the poetry itself. The actual circle and the trope are too entertwined to be completely distinguished, but insofar as the latter can be sorted out I want to consider it by itself. In both phases the circle points up the poet's situation outside the court. It is urbane but not necessarily of the city. In his relative independence, the poet defines his own gathering and imagines settings for it such as the households of the Sidneys and Wroths, the chambers of the poet-inviting-friends-to-supper, and the Apollo Room of the Old Devil Tavern. As a presumed audience, the circle becomes a coterie conditioned by the poet's manner of address and articles of association. Neither the select group nor the broader one is the same as the audience of office-holders and courtiers created by the social structure and taken more or less as conditions dictate by the courtly poet.

Jonson's poet-centered group also differs from other audiences. By comparison Donne assumed a more dispersed set and used primarily verse epistles and commissioned poems to address them and sometimes gain their support. Henry Goodyere was not highly placed; others such as Countess Lucy of Bedford, Lady Huntingdon, and the Drurys were capable of offering substantial patronage but did not constitute a circle.[1] Although Donne held out hope for preferment at the court itself until late in his career, he found neither a secure position there nor a substitute for one among scattered friends. Nor did his best verse address a definable group. The *Satyres,* most of the *Songs and Sonnets,* and the religious verse—most of the poetry we still read—are largely independent of the connections that the verse epistles cultivate, although Donne no doubt thought of his correspondents as apt readers for anything he wrote. Jonson's following is more directly implicated in his major verse. Whether he addresses them directly or not, he is aware of the criteria his associates must meet and of his own status among them. The poet is not greatly concerned with services of the sort that were expected of a Raleigh or a Sidney and assumes the circle's innocence of public dealings. No one seems inclined to raise philosophical or metaphysical questions, and even the moral ones that come up can be readily posed and understood. Instead, the poet identifies what is upstart or false and instills a commitment to decorum and a loyalty to common standards. The circle avoids not only malice, then, but complication and moral confusion.

Because the circle assembles at the poet's bidding, he calls upon his choice words to define it and coax people into it. He forms it by exclusion, as any imposer of standards does, yet his is not really a strict order. It does not observe rituals, set up idols, forsake society, or push rhetoric to serious beseeching. Unlike Donne in his chambers, Jonson does not seek to include a world by epitome or command symbols that devalue the outside by comparison, as compasses, beaten gold, and hermitage do. The atmosphere is more of clubroom than of vested institution. The poet's invitations to supper make no long-range claims, merely seal off a moment into which no haggard fates intrude. The requirements for admission do not allow much lyric effusion, and apostrophe usually moves toward epistolary address, which again is quite different from Donne's. Actually, Jonson's best verse often reveals a tension between lyric grace and the heft of reasonable theses struck as though in conversation. That tension can be seen as an outgrowth not merely of his own taste but of a group that mixes poetry with commentary and makes reason and judgment inseparable from praise.

Jonson's restraint has a direct bearing on the nature of the circle-as-trope in that an exact apportioning of praise to worth requires a careful estimation of candidates who appear for initiation or commemoration. The circle cannot be safeguarded and cannot foster well-being among its members unless they are open to each other and aware of the dangers of posturing. Certain Jonsonian lyrics have the look of toasts or formal scrolls read at festive occasions; others suggest an intimacy based on mutual values, when "not to sing, were enemie to reason." The poet whom we see in the *Epigrams* is at home in a place selectively urban but not open to the streets except when it ranges into satire (as in "On Something that Walks Somewhere," "On English Monsieur," and "The New Cry"). Nothing drops in from alien or transcendent spheres and nothing rises unexpectedly from a demonic underworld. Jonson's lyric personas are not susceptible to the appeals of remote places, to alchemy, the general flimflam of the times, or the broader appeals of London and other cities populated by Volpones and Sir Epicure Mammons. Despite Jonson's avowed patriotism and occasional soldierly temperament, it does not extend to national issues, empire, or even Petrarchan loves.

If in country house poems the bounty of rural life assists the hospitality and manners with which the estate manages its provincial community, the London circle has comparable bonds and some distractions. In "An Epistle Answering to One that Asked to be Sealed of the Tribe of Ben," Jonson is especially leery of gossip, faddishness, and the brittle lifelessness that he tags nicely the "animated porcelain of the court."[2] He is also skeptical about military service and honor, although he does not belittle them:

> But if, for honour, we must draw the sword,
>   And force back that which will not be restored,
> I have a body yet that spirit draws
>   To live, or fall a carcass in the cause.
>
>                                         P. 209

He is as troubled by the "earthen jars" of court and the coarsening of values as he is by animated porcelain. Continuing that metaphoric distinction, he is determined to be his "own frail pitcher," which requires that he remain aloof from the crowd that jostles and cracks individual vessels. He seeks to "Live to that point I will, for which I am man, / And dwell as in my centre as I can" (59–60). It follows from that brief manifesto that anyone who wishes to join the circle—as a third alternative to becoming clay or porcelain—must be "well-tagged, and permanent" in friendship, "Not built with canvas, paper, and false lights / As are the glorious scenes at the great sights":

> So short you read my character, and theirs
>   I would call mine, to which not many stairs
> Are asked to climb.
>
>                                         P. 210

The bond is that of reason and taste rather than an elaborate code or sense of status, and it suggests a lyric dominated by sententiousness. It discourages fanatical commitment and momentary enthusiasm. The short climb contrasts to the more elaborate initiations of knighthood; Jonson's statement of his few initiatory stations are purposely blunt and unceremonial. The candor of "carcass in the cause" brushes aside the intricacies of honor: sword play is not ballet; one does not pose or model class standing in heroic duels. Lyric possession in the second quotation comes to a minor outbreak in "mine" as a preliminary to lyric commemoration, which amounts to the welcoming of friends, and both are based on character above average. Good sense demands that one be readable and plain: the surprises of complex character and unmaskings are reserved for the Volpones and their tricky servants. Jonson's circle thus avoids the elaborated manners that a Calidore sorts out in arduous quest and all the intricate relations among courtesy, love, and friendship that a Cleopolis converts into sets of expectations. It meets at appointed times for special purposes, although its values are presumably not to be forgotten when it disperses.

No single poem reveals that standard of hospitality, the ritual use of an occasion and its objects, and the resisted temptation to push to the edge of Mammonlike rapture better than "Inviting a Friend to Supper," which proposes a tentative program in its call to the occasion. It has a sense of place, but convivial doings are more important to its tempered lyric grace. I agree with Ian Donaldson that this sort of poem, rather than moralizing poems like "An Epistle to a Friend to Persude Him to the Wars," best represents Jonson.[3] His self-proclaimed devotion to morality, reasonableness, and consistency are evident in it, but we also glimpse another Jonson—the gourmet, the man-among-men arranger, the epicure aroused to song, the classical scholar who knows what degree of spirituality and intellectual achievement is proper to such gatherings. As a host he is concerned with objects at hand and presumably with furnishings as well as with conduct and manners. His initial mock deference is not a sign of stiffness but is an open pretending, staged for the occasion, which allows for performances and social fictions:

> Tonight, grave sir, both my poor house and I
>   Do equally desire your company;
> Not that we think us worthy such a guest,
>   But that your worth will dignify our feast

> With those that come; whose grace may make that seem
> Something, which else could hope for no esteem.
>
> P. 55

Rhyme heightens that self-conscious artifice, which the speaker (as honest charlatan) exposes by exaggerated formality.

That the speaker should describe the menu in such detail may seem a surprising descent from higher concerns. But as providential supply sustains the cheer of "To Penshurst," abundance reinforces this urban well-being. Some of the delicacies, however, he holds out and then retracts in order to confess that the friend's presence is worth lying for:

> Yet shall you have, to rectify your palate,
>   An olive, capers, or some better salad
> Ushering the mutton; with a short-legged hen,
>   If we can get her, full of eggs, and then
> Lemons, and wine for sauce; to these a coney
>   Is not to be despaired of, for our money;
> And though fowl now be scarce, yet there are clerks,
>   The sky not falling, think we may have larks.
> I'll tell you of more, and lie, so you will come:
>   Of partridge, pheasant, woodcock.
>
> P. 55

Although he ritualizes his items, he obviously does not invest them with the talismanic dimensions that Sir Epicure would give them. He restricts enthusiasm even as he suggests legitimate reasons for it. Economy and taste govern the selections, and he knows how far he can go before he begins to suggest the trickster.

Such a circle is not summoned to roister and is not to break down its cohesiveness with gossip. Its opposite in this respect is the audience of the town crier offering news of the day to urban masses. Those whose activities the crier broadcasts are very busy and make up a society of sorts, but their intelligence in "The New Cry" is all of conspiracies and men in the know:

> The counsels, projects, practices they know,
>   And what each prince doth for intelligence owe,
> And unto whom; they are the almanacs
>   For twelve years yet to come, what each state lacks.
> They carry in their pockets Tacitus,
>   And the *Gazetti*, or *Gallo-Belgicus*;
> And talk reserved, locked up, and full of fear,
>   Nay, ask you how the day goes, in your ear.
>
> P. 48

Jonson's table will be mirthful but not part of a costume Arcadia. Nor are his guests, at the other extreme, pilgrims of truth seeking the ends of Socratic dialogue while they banquet—merely men in sound company who know their Virgil, Tacitus, and Livy.

With the issuing of such invitations, which I have dwelt upon to suggest the conversational tone, the equippage, and the atmosphere, Jonson assembles the group, defines an informal code, and offers a middle range of language for its model closer to epistle than to song. He does not pretend to achieve tight organization or to offer the Bacchanalian gifts that poets promise from time to time. (He would have been embarrassed I expect by Herrick's faery feast and swooning devotion to sack.) He aims for a loose association that will find its festivity in the specific occasion rather than in such calendar holidays as Herrick's Mayday, which are open to a wider community and refer to a greater expanse of times, places, and peoples.

If James Howell's account of one such occasion is to be trusted, Jonson's actual gatherings were very similar to the one "Inviting a Friend" proposes. Howell speaks of good company, excellent cheer, choice wine, jovial welcome. However, he also sounds a note of danger that stems from the self-centered nature of the poet's call, his demand for personal loyalty, and his dislike of criticism. "An Epistle Answering" is right to see gossip and clannishness as serious dangers to such a coterie. Having no functions other than sociable ones, such a group is paradoxically more vulnerable to antagonisms than a court where enmities are expected and do not necessarily undermine the authority of the system or its titular head. The stakes are high enough around an Elizabeth or a James to attract would-be initiates in great numbers whatever the difficulties they face; standards can survive the failure of individuals to measure up. When such an evening as Jonson plans descends to carping and defensiveness, however, it is poisoned at the root—in the trust the coterie must have in the taste and judgment of the poet-host. At the particular gathering that Howell remembers, Jonson villified certain others "to magnify his own Muse"—an "ill-favour'd solecism in good manners" in Howell's opinion. Normally willing to abide by the tone of the privileged group and normally adulatory toward Jonson himself, even Carew disapproved of that tendency. After Jonson's intemperate response to criticism of *The New Inne*, which must have been voiced to friends as well, Carew asked rather pointedly:

> Why should the follies then of this dull age
> Draw from thy Pen such an immodest rage
> As seemes to blast thy (else-immortall) Bayes,
> When thine owne tongue proclaimes thy ytch of praise.[4]

However, these criticisms apply more to the actual than to the figural group, in which the personality of the host can be idealized. Whatever Jonson's temptations to self-inflation and excess in chastizing literary foes, an important part of a fictive chartering of a group is its assignment of just reputations by a speaker who undergoes preparation for the role in the poems he presents. The best safeguards against carping and envy are the good judgment he assumes—obviously easier to achieve hypothetically than in action. One of the poet's functions as critic and moralist is precisely to sort out legitimate from illegitimate enthusiasm and justified dislike from personal spite. The forward march of classics into modern settings depends upon him, and as a persona he seldom disappoints. Lyric, satire, and encomium get mixed and somewhat redesigned from their sources when they come within his influence. For one thing they cannot be dressed in the style they have in poets seeking patronage, which may partly explain Jonson's superiority over Donne in verse epistles and his preference for reasonable praise. His epistles lie on the fringes of lyric, seldom finding legitimate opportunities for apostrophe. Nor do they play with Platonist ideals of love or social grace or take round-about ways through golden ages or Mount Acidales, where the poet might find a place momentarily apart from associates. Locating the circle in the midst of society, the poet runs different risks than he might in these other places.

Although the circle is not strictly speaking besieged, when we consider the comedies as well as the lyrics we discover quite different host figures and purposes for the gatherings they arrange. Where country estate poems examine the standards of private households and their generosity, and where the invited supper group collects to confirm and enact standards in a convivial format, the comedies concentrate on assets exuberantly catalogued and pursued as spoils, and of course upon upended ideals. Indeed, it is in the plays that Jonson scrutinizes in-groups most closely and anatomizes the gilded expectations that lead men by their appetites—lead them to inflated ideas of their own worth and correspondingly to inflated inset lyrics addressed mainly to personal possessions.

FLEECING THE GUESTS

The overestimation of goods that brings sheep to their shearers is probably Jonson's most frequent satiric target. Intriguers extend to their victims promises of clothes, plate, and jewels and the talismanic object gold. Although a universal transformer of the ordinary into the grand and a catalyst of quick agreements and contracts, gold creates at best a loose circle that must break up at the unmasking, as temporary allies scatter in the face of judicial order. Jonson's strength lies both in depicting those fixations on spoils and in giving an assortment of con men a striking language with which to entice a following. Those men are reverse images of Jonson's better hosts and thus of the motives that pull people into complicities.

Their language is often lyric, albeit ironically so, and it indicates the strict limits of permissible enthusiasm in the epistles and epigrams. But the relationship between the positive circle and its negative images is more complicated than mere inversion might suggest. As Arthur Marotti has pointed out, Jonson's Horatian pose of sanity and moderation has little to do at times with his true strength.[5] When we consider the outbreaks of lyricism in the plays and masques, we are struck by the variety of items that enlist enthusiasm and the styles in which they are celebrated. Freed from the constraints of his own voice and preference for a moral constituency, Jonson can let a Sir Epicure Mammon rise to ecstasy over potential holdings and humanitarian projects. On the one hand, Jonson in his own voice praises plain language, as in *Discoveries,* and wishes to be known as a poet of morality and reason: "Many Writers perplexe their Readers, and Hearers with meere *Non-sense,* . . . Pure and neat Language I love, yet plaine and customary."[6] He connects that spareness and lucidity with both the nature of things and character: "The conceits of the mind are Pictures of things, and the tongue is the Interpreter of those Pictures. The order of Gods creatures in themselves, is not only admirable, and glorious, but eloquent; Then he who could apprehend the consequence of things in their truth, and utter his apprehensions as truly, were the best Writer, or Speaker" (p. 628). On the other hand, the excess that certain characters gather in the plays generates a linguistic richness that is also reflected, but more under control, in "Inviting a Friend." It cannot be automatically discredited, although from Volpone, for instance, money extracts a clearly over-blown apostrophe:

> Good morning to the day; and, next, my gold:
> Open the shrine, that I may see my *saint.*
> Haile the worlds soule, and mine. More glad then is
> The teeming earth, to see the long'd-for sunne
> Peepe through the hornes of the celestiall *ram,*
> Am I, to view thy splendor, darkening his:

> That, lying here, amongst my other hoords,
> Shew'st like a flame, by night; or like the day
> Strooke out of *chaos*, when all darkness fled
> Unto the center. O, thou sonne of Sol,
> (But brighter then thy father) let me kisse,
> With adoration, thee, and every relique
> Of sacred treasure, in this blessed roome.[7]
>
> 1.1.1–13

Volpone perhaps remembers the functions of the logos in shooting light into darkness and in organizing chaos, but he looks past all such instructive parallels that he might have found between gold and the sun. What he sees is a rival center or god figure seated in a domestic shrine. He not only disregards what might have been there but cancels the creation's relationships of places and objects. The little corner filled with gold becomes the world, not as analogy or epitome but as obsession. Actually to possess what one worships is to be doubly blessed. Such a shrine clearly does not stand in the gathering place for reasonable friends but compresses paradise into transportable property, hidden in a niche. As Mosca observes money can even be medicinal: "This is true physick, this your sacred medicine, / No talk of *opiates*, to this great *elixir* (1.4.71–72).

Despite this depravity Volpone masters a diction and an imagery that would do credit to a religious adept. To celebrate substances of such status, words must rise toward the logos that originally assigned all things their worth. In this respect Jonson's alchemists, illusion-makers, and deceivers are cousins to the visionary poet. After Volpone has demoted the sun in the presence of his treasure, he drives away the rival joys of dream, love, and beauty with the same "dumb god" that gives speech to others but has none itself:

> Thou are vertue, fame,
> Honour, and all things else! Who can get thee,
> He shall be noble, valiant, honest, wise.
>
> 1.1.25–27

His victims have similar views: they hope to invest a little to get a lot in plate, money, cortines. Thought of doing so turns them into songbirds.

In *The Alchemist* Jonson gives Sir Epicure Mammon a similar appraisal of gold's transformative power, as close to hymn as conversation is likely to get:

> He that has once the *flower of the sunne*,
> The perfect *ruby*, which we call *elixir*,
> Not onely can doe that, but by it's vertue,
> Can confer honour, love, respect, long life.
>
> 2.1.47–50

Sir Epicure is exuberantly detailed in both the goods he hopes to accumulate and the social works he plans to accomplish with them:

> We will be brave, *Puffe*, now we ha' the *med'cine*.
> My meat, shall all come in, in *Indian* shells,
> Dishes of agate, set in gold, and studded,
> With emeralds, saphyres, hiacynths, and rubies.
> The tongues of carpes, dormise, and camels heeles,
> Boil'd i' the spirit of Sol, and dissolv'd pearle. . .
> And I will eate these broaths, with spoones of amber,
> Headed with diamant, and carbuncle.
> My foot-boy shall eate phesants, calverd salmons,
> Knots, godwits, lamprey's.
>
> 2.2.71–81

This amounts to a fool's golden age or at least a redemptive program to achieve it. That he is not totally preposterous, merely ninety percent so, is suggested by the hopes that even so sober a man as Edward Dyer entertained for alchemy.[8] He is as much taken with gourmet delights as Subtle is with those properties that magic converts into gold, beginning with *material liquida* or "unctuous water" and going on to dirt:

> a certaine crasse, and viscous
> Portion of earth; both which, concorporate,
> Doe make the elementarie matter of gold:
> Which is not, yet, *propria materia*
> But commune to all mettalls, and all stones.
>
> 2.3.144–49

As any child could have told him, of course, viscous portions of earth and water make mudpies, not gold bars.

Both Subtle and Mammon range to the far ends of earth for imagery to sustain their hopes. Although Subtle's language is more apparently scientific and exact than Mammon's, he ransacks the Egyptians, scripture, and the fables of poets; he disentangles perplexing allegories and interprets mystic symbols looking for what lies within substances that might commune with kindred. After all, devotional emblems and apostrophes to divine beings also expect marvelous transformations of earthly things into celestial ones. The language of symbols that seers use is a mixture of hope and lunacy, not calculation or ordinary intimacies. Both Subtle and Mammon are devotees of recipes and remedies: they assume that substances have a life of their own and can be personified, addressed, coaxed forth, reformed, or combined to startling ends if only one applies the right verbal formulas. Words become charms, gestures, magic; and bystanders are entranced by them.

Objects are not only addressable but capable of improving those who believe in them: they will return youth to the aged and health to the sick. Thus Volpone's "Oglio del Scoto" is as powerful a household remedy as gold itself. As in Subtle's chemistry, the secret lies in the mix of elements, which may be individually undesirable but in their common ties release rare properties that a literalist of the imagination would not dream they had. Like Surley, Corvino is happy to provide a parody of that magical recipe:

> All his ingredients
> Are a sheepes gall, a rosted bitches marrow,
> Some few sod earewigs, pounded caterpillers,
> A little capons grease, and fasting spittle:
> I know 'hem, to a dram.
>
> Volpone, 2.6.17–21

Such unpromising ingredients reportedly will reseat one's teeth "did they dance like virginall jacks" (p. 57) and make them white again; they will restore hearing and cure one's ailing liver.

Knowing his own power in the invention of verbal dodges and selling of formulas, Mosca likewise rejoices in the powers of gold and the illusions it encourages. As trickster, he has in common with his masters and with the poet the spell of words and the realization of secret kinships:

> I feare, I shall begin to grow in love
> With my deare selfe, and my most prosp'rous parts,
> They doe so spring, and burgeon; I can feele
> A whimsey i' my bloud: (I know not how)
> Successe hath made me wanton. I could skip
> Out of my skin, now, like a subtill snake,
> I am so limber. O! Your Parasite
> Is a most precious thing, dropt from above,
> Not bred 'mong'st clods, and clot-poules, here on earth.
> I muse, the mysterie was not made a science,
> It is so liberally profest! almost
> All the wise world is little else, in nature,
> But Parasites, or Sub-parasites.
>
> Volpone, 3.1.1–13

For any such spell to succeed, of course, the illusionist must make his listeners into believing participants, but the key is fixation on the object. A practiced conjurer can convert a bat's wing or a fly's leg into a marvel, using one item that appears no different from the rest to bind them and make them work.

Thus issuing extraordinary powers all around, the comedies give free reign to Jonson's imagination—until the moralist steps in to condemn those who have gathered for the spoils.

CHARMING THE LISTENERS

Whereas the goal of tricksters is to give a nudge to hopeful illusions and a tug at pocketbooks, the poet is admonished to use his fictions for educational and moral purposes. In this respect, as

Marotti suggests, Jonson has it both ways, especially in the comedies: the imagination gets its outing among objects rescued from ordinariness, but final authority belongs to reason, Then, too, lyrics can be legitimately enthusiastic when the objects of praise so argue. Addressing the power of moonlight in *Cynthia's Revels,* for instance, Hesperus counters the extremities of the chase and the disturbance of night with a shining image of stately dignity. Where Volpone races beyond the limits of reason in his apostrophe to gold, Hesperus finds a relatively spare language for the silvery order of Cynthia:

> Queen and huntress, chaste and fair,
> Now the sun is laid to sleep,
> Seated in thy silver chair,
> State in wonted manner keep:
>   Hesperus entreats thy light,
>   Goddess excellently bright.
>
> Earth, let not thy envious shade
> Dare itself to interpose;
> Cynthia's shining orb was made
> Heaven to clear, when day did close:
>   Bless us then with wished sight,
>   Goddess excellently bright.
>
> Lay thy bow of pearl apart,
> And thy crystal-shining quiver;
> Give unto the flying hart
> Space to breathe, how short soever:
>   Thou that mak'st a day of night,
>   Goddess excellently bright.
>
> P. 348

The trochaic measure here suggests an energy that charges and yet is contained by the intricate balancing of lines and stanzas. The meter extracts and holds every syllable (as in "excellently," for instance), and raises to a singable level certain words that are normally more evaluative than enthusiastic. The song itself not only enacts but calls for ceremony. It seeks to preserve a wonted state of light and order whose reigning brilliance will sustain station where night prefers blindness and changeability. The poet's reiterated plea and the glitter of his appointments for Cynthia suggest the joy of spectacle and anticipated blessings. Cynthia herself is usually assigned other occupations, including the chase and the kill, and other significance, especially mutability. But Hesperus here would make her bow and quiver ornamental and adorn her order in a stately propriety. The refrain returns ceremonially to an identity the goddess need only claim.

Jonson assigns flights of imagination not only to dramatic characters but to himself or a close imposter, as in the aging lover of "A Celebration of Charis." Such poems tell us a good deal about his combinations of satire and lyric and special means of countering the poet's impulse to scale heights.[9] Proceeding first through self-deprecation and various reasons for an old man's plunge into love's excesses, Jonson finds his best lyric pretexts in Charis's beauty and truth, though even these issue an ambiguous call to an unchivalrous lover. He frames them initially in the sober utterance of a sage almost immune to ardor:

> And it is not always face,
> Clothes, or fortune gives the grace,
> Or the feature, or the youth;
> But the language, and the truth,
> With the ardour and the passion,
> Gives the lover weight and fashion.
> "His Excuse for Loving," p. 129

The word "fashion" is curious after "truth" and "grace," but then to love is ordinarily to be fashionable and thereby to join the pursuits of youth. Jonson is again indirectly concerned with the appropriate circle and its rites, as love's publicist seeks to explain his infatuation to an implicitly skeptical audience. His beloved is not divine but human, and her triumphs are of dubious value when she forces men to abandon their habits. If Donne in *Songs and Sonnets* is preoccupied with the passage back and forth between the world and the lover's private affair, Jonson's speaker can neither wait to have his discovery of Charis acknowledged nor bear to hear the mockery of onlookers. His candor admonishes us to beware of the posing and stylization of other poets, who idle reason's motor in passion's fast current. Self-concern keeps before us the issue of proprietary interest in the beloved, but its irony says clearly that mismatches result in great foolishness; failure to recognize that would be disastrous to one's moral and psychological health. Obviously, a good deal of brush has to be cleared away before true monuments to love can be erected.

In "What He Suffered," the poet prepares to abandon self-satire for a "dexterous," straightforward song, and in "Her Triumph," he offers an authentic lyric on behalf of Charis. The latter poem ends with the pretty amplitude and rhetorical grace of a musical encomium:

> Have you seen but a bright lily grow,
>   Before rude hands have touched it?
> Have you marked but the fall o' the snow,

> Before the soil hath smutched it?
> Have you felt the wool o' the beaver?
> Or swan's down ever?
> Or have smelled o' the bud o' the briar?
> Or the nard i' the fire?
> Or have tasted the bag o' the bee?
> O so white! O so soft! O so sweet is she!
>
> P. 133

The anapest-iambic combinations and the rhetorical accumulation of the stanza suggest that what matters is less things that gain tangibility (by being compared with lillies and swans) than what can be made of them. Verbal gamesmanship transforms the ordinary into the marvelous despite the near-banter of rhyming "touched it" with "smutched it." In so balanced and so careful a measure, statement becomes ritual just as the triple "O's" and exclamations of the last line mark a formalized counting off and a pretended passion rather than a reaction to compelling love.

Such poems have a less finely tuned sensitivity to nature than Shakespeare's songs and less of the haunting local mythology that gives voice and animation to nature in Milton. The Spenserian resources of contemporary poets such as Drayton are also missing from them. Or to put it in terms of more distant precedents, even here, as the cultivation of a rationalized style urges, Jonson is more Horatian than Ovidian. But Jonsonian songs also exploit the melodic foundations of Elizabethan lyric and its stake in performance, especially in the masque. Actually, nearly all Jonson's poems read as though staged, usually before a cordial, small audience, and it is partly the expertise of the performance that holds our attention. The range of his entertainments from epigrams to masques allows for a varied craftsmanship. Neither musical grace nor the devices of the performer are necessarily opposed to the interests of the moralizer, but the latter tends to disappear when the voicing of "O so white" or "Goddess excellently bright" is granted center staging.

Another element missing from Jonson's lyric performances is the questing persona or first-person intelligence whose own reading of situations and reactions to them is of some moment. Jonson does not throw the circle into perplexity by setting forth on voyages of discovery. His persona is usually possessed of what he requires from the outset, though the course of reason and intricacies of syntax may not be easy to decipher. By comparison to Herbert's or Donne's dramatic presences or to the apparent sincerity of Vaughan, Jonson is more ventriloquistic than we ordinarily expect a lyricist to be. His masks and antimasks are not antipathetic, like those of Blake or Yeats, but are those of an extemporaneous performer whose feelings find only limited scope for development. Nothing takes a quick way to crescendos or conclusions. Jonson does not accept subjects of ready-made acclaim that would allow the persona to become a public spokesman or showman. He is not a circus master, despite his love of theatricality and despite the cordiality of his circle. Nor is he broadly public, which is partly what I meant earlier in saying that he is only selectively cosmopolitan. He is more likely to condemn outright showmanship. When he encounters a piece of court walking by he finds it without praiseworthy features, though it tries desperately to be at the heart of things:

> At court I met it, in clothes brave enough
> To be a courtier, and looks grave enough
> To seem a statesman. As I near it came,
> It made me a great face; I asked the name;
> A lord, it cried, buried in flesh and blood,
> And such from whom let no man hope least good,
> For I will do none; and as little ill,
> For I will dare none. Good Lord, walk dead still.
> "On Something that Walks Somewhere," p. 11

Such a great personage has lost its human qualities in becoming a walking showcase. Similar complaints fly like arrows into the stuffed shirts of diplomats in "The New Cry." By such portraits Jonson makes clearer the restrictive membership of the circle.

The word *grave*, used ironically in the second line above, appears again in the portrait of William Camden, where it bolsters legitimate praise and indicates a compromise between judgment and lyricism of the sort that Jonson brings to his most judicious moments and his best candidates for membership. His praise is typically not of influential but of sound men whose inborn worth is reinforced by good deportment and extensive learning:

> Camden, most reverent head, to whom I owe
> All that I am in arts, all that I know,
> (How nothing's that?) to whom my country owes
> The great renown and name wherewith she goes;
> Than thee the age sees not that thing more grave,
> More high, more holy, that she more would crave.
> What name, what skill, what faith hast thou in things!
> What sight in searching the most antique springs!
> What weight, and what authority in thy speech!
> Man scarce can make that doubt, but thou canst teach.
> Pardon free truth, and let thy modesty,
> Which conquers all, be once overcome by thee.
> Many of thine this better could than I;
> But for their powers accept my piety.
> P. 13

Except for the reiteration of "what," Jonson permits very few stylistic flourishes or elaboration. Since Camden possesses mainly old-fashioned virtues, the poem does not try to be clever, despite its one outlandish claim that the country owes its renown to an antiquary and a teacher. The sequence *grave, high,* and *holy* rises by degrees above the mean, as do *name, skill,* and *faith* in coming to an exclamation against the general hindrance of plainness. The "things" in which Camden has faith are not exalted, or at least the word Jonson chooses is not, but they suggest both confidence in the world's rightness and the resources of Camden's scholarship. The renown and the sweep backward to the classics imply a circle almost as wide as a nation in this case but without the pomp of greatness.

Perhaps the most noteworthy—certainly the best known—example of Jonson's epigrammatic constraint is "On My First Son." Back of the poem lies an implicit household crisis and perhaps again a readership of a limited kind. In the foreground is a personal relationship seen in an elegiac phase framed by an implicit narrative. Constructed out of three four-line units, the poem limits grief partly by formality and movement from the past, when the father's sin was to hope too fondly, to the present wish to lose all father and thereby master grief:

> Farewell, thou child of my right hand, and joy;
>   My sin was too much hope of thee, loved boy.
> Seven years thou wert lent to me, and I thee pay,
>   Exacted by the fate, on the just day.
> Oh, could I lose all father now! For why
>   Will man lament the state he should envy?
> To have so soon 'scaped world's and flesh's rage,
>   And, if no other misery, yet age?
> Rest in soft peace, and, asked, say here doth lie
>   Ben Jonson his best piece of poetry;
> For whose sake, henceforth, all his vows be such,
>   As what he loves may never like too much.
>
> Pp. 26–27

The economy of the first unit limits the complaint and acknowledges the providential source of all gifts, the collection of all debts on schedule. The definite allotment of seven years is both intentional and just. Wisdom and discipline, however, do not prevent the poet from struggling against his own rationalizations. One should cease to be a father, but if possessiveness refuses to depart? And can one commemorate without some trace of possession? The questions of the second section indicate an anguish not easily quieted and an inability to settle immediately for epitaph, a form of dismissive closure that says in effect, "Here find the dead summed up." But in the poem's overall development, even the relatively expansive complaint at the center yields quickly to constrictions in feeling and in style. The concluding four lines rewrite the opening four with greater control, setting aside the exclamation and the questions of the second part. As Jonson modestly subordinates the speaking of praise in "To William Camden" to its object, he concedes here that a poem does not make up for the loss of his best product. The only addition the poem makes to concluding epitaph formulas is the adjective "soft," and even that has parallels in such conventional phrases as tread softly, go quietly, pass gently.

However, in the juxtaposition of "soft peace" and "best piece" and in the fictional quotation from the son, Jonson does complicate the tone. As the son lies quietly, the father, making a poem in and of his remembrance, stresses the making itself: peace to one is a piece to the other, and even if not his best piece, at least a peaceful product of his right hand. Such wordplay might seem in questionable taste, but it is in keeping with the close distinction between love and like, which also calls attention to the verbal pieces out of which an exacting poem is made. Without adding to W. D. Kay's and L. A. Beaurline's speculations on that distinction,[10] I am struck by the fact that making it to begin with requires a precise gauge of feelings. Discernment is imposed on feelings now and must be in the future, as the poem ends with a controlling resolution against temptations to stray ever again into self-gratifying excess.

The parallels between the lost son and the poem are curiously undeveloped, however, despite Jonson's momentary attention to them. The poem is fully the poet's and cannot be taken away as the son has been. It helps him curb excessive feeling and yet retains a memorializing hold upon the dead. But these advantages do not interest Jonson as much as self-assessment and control of the legitimate grounds of complaint do. The distinction between loving and liking is obviously important and is akin to the one between possession and praise. I take it that what one loves may be celebrated; what one likes must be owned as well. In any case Jonson prepares for the dismissal of the poem by making it not only second to the son but a further demonstration of refused possession.

In both "On My First Son" and "To William Camden," Jonson avoids ornament and odic intensity, which is a kind of self-denial or poetic deference. To say that he also avoids irregularities and contains perturbations is not to say that he allows judiciousness to squeeze feeling completely dry, however. The course one takes to self-denial may not itself be thoroughly disciplined. The impulse to attach great hopes to what one loves will always need watching. Jonson's tendency is to reveal passion rising, against counterchecks, from a justifiable attraction to what is worthy before locating superior reasons for disciplining it. Where deference rings true, it usually suggests that those who merit praise are in the image of classical and English predecessors of the kind that William Camden studies as a Latin scholar and historian. Back of men and women of standards and good taste are the writers Jonson brings forward by citation and indirect allusion.

Imitation, in fact, is the chief form that deference takes. The refusal to claim personal possession is related to it, but not in any simple way, since imitation is more than mere copying. As Richard S. Peterson remarks, Jonson's use of classical materials results in a metaphorical and mythical complexity; allusions are meant to be recognized as "signs in the finished work that its originality, organization, and continuing life depend on suggestive links to the great writers of antiquity."[11] John Hollander's version of that allusive structure, which is not always distinguishable from plagiarism, holds that "between the intimately private and the didactically public, there are many modes, and Jonson played in them all." The public dimension comes not merely from a hoarding of lines, as Edmund Wilson remarks, but from an ambition to aim "at the one great statement that will render obsolete other sayings, which is part of the search for an ideal community guided by literary precedents."[12] Wilson's way of putting it suggests more pride in personal authority than is justified, but as the circle expands to include former writers and their types and figures, the poet can claim to be reviving the best parts of a civilization and making them part of the current performance. The circle absorbs the classics as its second nature. Most of the proper names cited in the epigrams belong to acquaintances who reconstitute just such an ancient standard.

It may seem by all this that the locus of lyric for Jonson sacrifices real places for traditional topoi and is more bookish and social than natural or topographical. If so, there would be nothing unusual about that, and certainly Jonson deals frequently with an already-processed nature. But itemized resources are also important to him, especially in "To Penshurst," "To Sir Robert Wroth," and the raptures of Sir Epicure. What is the relation between that provisioning of the circle and what inspires lyric apostrophe? I mentioned earlier the coincidence of decorum and possession in lyric, or *appropriateness* and *appropriation* (also the tendency in some kinds of lyric to challenge these by disorder.) For Jonson that is a key confusion or running together, because all genres take experience piece by piece and assign its parts names and places according to schematic tropes. The poet is chiefly the arranger, or in refashioning genres, sometimes rearranger; it is he who knows best the categories and storage places out of which the host fetches the choice pieces of his entertainments. The provisions of "To Penshurst," for instance, are first stationed in the terrain for estate picture-taking around the modest, well-modeled house. Some of them are then brought in for the fire or the table in support of the country economy centered in the baronial power of "the great lord."

The natural resources of the estate are obviously not publicly available in the sense that anyone can select a tree or a deer for his own; but a given item once entered in the steward's ledger can be administered to guests. The poet-beneficiary of such generosity becomes perforce a minor laureate figure, not an orphic bird. He has no commission to disentangle mysteries or issue fables for riddle-solving intellects; if he celebrates nature's marvels, it is *as* provisions, not as a hieroglyphics to which he, rather than the estate owner, holds the keys. Indeed, he first of all controls enigmas and ambiguities, because these have a way of challenging mastery, not only withdrawing certainty from words and images but generating awe and generating as successors not Cotton or Carew but Vaughan and Crashaw. (It takes a true equilibrist and juggler of meanings like Marvell to salvage both Jonson's domestic rule and the topographical mysteries it normally discards, which is what makes "Upon Appleton House" so singular a poem, the key to its main difference from Jonson being its prolonged plunge into the woods.)

Giving a domestic twist to celebration and possession, Jonson acknowledges simultaneously the Sidneys' mastery of nature and his own status as a kind of poet-in-residence or songbird in the family tree, taking possession of the well-prepared provisions allocated to him after their improving journey through the pantry and kitchen:

>     And I not fain to sit, as some this day
>       At great men's tables, and yet dine away.
>     Here no man tells my cups, nor, standing by,
>       A waiter, doth my gluttony envy,
>     But gives me what I call, and lets me eat;
>       He knows below he shall find plenty of meat,
>     Thy tables hoard not up for the next day.

65–71

This may seem to place the poem on some byway of courtly encomium, with stress on patronage; but I look upon it as less that than a tentative breaking loose signaled by the poem's contrast between Lord Lisle's place and extravagant "piles" elsewhere. The image of patronage is prominent to be sure in the host-guest relation as well as in the possession that fat aged carp agree to as they rush to get themselves hooked, listed, and tabled. But the estate is also simple: in every detail it declares its dislike of ostentation and its self-sufficiency. If Milton too claims a share in the local rule of nature in "Arcades," and Marvell finds it possible to move off to the *silva* where a poet can read the enigmatic lessons of creatures and trees, the way for that independence has been prepared, in Jonson's strange menu-minded way, by the bold declaration that "the same beer and bread and self-same wine / That is his lordship's shall be also mine" ("To Penshurst," 63–64).

CLOSING THE CIRCLE AND TYING THE KNOT

The relationship between poetic commemoration and the circle is elaborately charted in "To the Immortal Memory and Friendship of That Noble Pair, Sir Lucius Cary and Sir H. Morison." Its way of putting the poet's relationship to a selected group has been acknowledged often enough to require little amplification here,[13] but it is pertinent that Morison is himself the primary circle. The poet redefines his own role accordingly. Morison's "fair example" gets abroad for others to heed without a great deal of help from the poet. Through the turns and counterturns of the ode the substance of brave minds and "simple love of greatness, and of good" (105) impose their force, and lyric rises naturally from them. Jonson thus claims to invent nothing except perhaps ways to showcase that reality. The circle makes of the poet not a myth-maker who spellbinds or hoodwinks but someone who identifies truths for his listeners and advises loyalty to them. Whether he joins others or they join him is a matter of indifference, so long as all parties recognize the same examples. Jonson ends with the same deference, subordinating the written record to deeds in which friendship is written "with the heart, not pen."

The image of the circle serves him as well here to limit the poet's powers as it does elsewhere to assign them. It again suggests containment and the intimacy of a discerning group. Such functions of the circle trope are not surprising, and all told, in its several occurrences, it strikes a balance between consistency and variety. However, Jonson requires other figures to fill out the concept of the audience he would address and furnish with a state of mind. He does, after all, stage plays and masques for a broader society as well, less of his own selection, more interested in myth and more accustomed to pageantry. The style of the masques and of the lyrics that go with them is accordingly more elevated than that of the epigrams, and the objects they assemble are more conventionally emblematic. Since my purpose is to explore the privacy of a poet escaping courtly dominance, I will not assess in detail the implications of that broader audience. However, Jonson is sometimes no less zealous on behalf of the poet's formative influence over it than he is with the coterie itself, which partly explains his hectoring of audiences and bitter disappointments in them at times. He wants a national sphere of influence only if it can be managed without weakening the poet's rightful authority.

One of the figures Jonson chooses for the relations of this larger ensemble is the curious knot, which in Daedalus's song in *Pleasure Reconciled to Virtue* builds a bridge from the rationalized lyric to pageantry and puts its appeal in theatrical terms. The dance figure stands roughly for intricacies of an entertainment that can combine pleasure and instruction. It suggests the forming of a group more given to demonstrative and symbolic play than a small circle is— but equally devoted to morality:

> Come on, come on, and where you go
>   So interweave the curious knot
> As even th' observer scarce may know
>   Which lines are pleasure's, and which not.
> First, figure out the doubtful way
>   At which a while all youth should stay,
> Where she and virtue did contend
>   Which should have Hercules to friend.
> Then, as all actions of mankind
>   Are but a labyrinth or maze,
> So let your dances be entwined,
>   Yet not perplex men unto gaze;
> But measured, and so numerous, too,
>   As men may read each act you do.
> And when they see the graces meet,
>   Admire the wisdom of your feet.
> For dancing is an exercise
>   Not only shows the mover's wit
> But maketh the beholder wise,
>   As he hath power to rise to it.
>
> Pp. 362–63

In other invitation poems, Jonson is less openly concerned than he is here with the expressive mode itself. If in inviting the friend to supper, he holds out the attractions of food, poetry, wine, and friendship, and in the Cary-Morison ode instructs Lucius Cary to reaffirm the bond that friends establish over "love of greatness, and of good," here he assumes that art will synchronize its audience even as it gives it interpretive problems.

A difficulty lies in the perplexities of humankind, however, and in a confusion of values that undermines the common bond when the circle expands. Where a William Camden or a Henry Morison sets a pattern that reasonable men follow, the actions of greater humankind here are "but a labyrinth or maze." Any dance that displays them will weave a curious knot, composed first of pleasure's doubtful lines and then meeting virtues. If pleasure *is* to be reconciled to virtue, opposing things must interact without confusion, perhaps as in the circles of Spenser's dancing graces. Measure and number are useful to any such coordinated end: an orderly dance is both pleasurable and good and therefore meant to be witnessed (as Spenser's dance apparently is not, if Calidore is an indication). When movement is patterned in the right way, the audience sees the aesthetic design; form becomes answerable to mind, or as Jonson says, "wit." Such a discernment of pattern is musical or lyric in that it follows a course of rising realizations through rhythm and melody. In the two key words "power" and "rise," Jonson brings meaning and form together in a single impression and proposes that a community fall into place precisely as the audience of an expressive act. He binds its members to the same insights and times their recognitions by his cadence. Where such graces meet, following wit—seizing the design—reconciles pleasure's motions to virtue's discipline.

I confess to finding the interpretable acts of that knotty dance vague even in the context of the masque, but presumably Jonson has in mind something like the stimulus to virtue that poetry's concrete universals have for Sidney in the *Apology*. Enacted patterns of virtue—as opposed to those that philosophy presents abstractly—gain commitment by the charms of music and lyric. Theoretically, no barrier exists to the showing of such art to a broad audience, though again Jonson wishes the poet to assemble and command it. Even here it need not necessarily be courtly, though most audiences of masques and triumphs were.

It is difficult to define precisely the extent of the authority Jonson would assign the poet in this performative function or the degree of difference between the poet's circle thus broadened and the courtly circle that commissions masques. But it seems reasonable to say that Jonson is like Donne in seeking a contract with whatever portion of a society he can entice within range if not into committed membership. He takes a more significant step toward the marginality of the major lyricists of the seventeenth century than such followers as Carew, Suckling, and Herrick might suggest. His originality in conceiving the poet's authority and readership is still too seldom recognized.[14] That originality is no doubt due in part to the fact that the times have forced him out of the courtly mold, which he looks upon uneasily and sometimes slips into. Among poets whom one might expect to find writing verse like his, such as Wyatt, Gascoigne, Raleigh, and Sidney, we discover very little of precisely his kind. He differs from them both in song and in plain style epigram. But more importantly, he does not repeat a great many of the rhetorical exercises and attitudes that appeal to the writers of romance, sonnets, and the anthologized pieces of *Englands Helicon*. Nor is he satisfied with the musicality of a Campion or the Spenserian graces of a Drayton. To speak in a lower-keyed voice, he changes the sound of praise and puts aside its most popular formulas. Partly because of his turning to classical predecessors, it is easy to overlook the house-cleaning he performed before he sat down to plan his entertainments and to write.

He is too seldom credited also with the variety of occasions and styles he expects his listeners and readers to absorb. In some ways he follows a more difficult course than Donne, whose showy breaks with predecessors in *Songs and Sonnets* yield a harvest of triumphs over antagonists real and imagined. Jonson is more conservative, though no less combative. The continuities between modern poetry and its classical precedents call for the sort of social lyric that scholars like Camden drill into new generations of schoolboys under the influence of humanist educational theory. He avoids eccentricity as Donne does not. He does not seek out private chambers or woodland retreats in order to circumvent society, but corrects it to its face even while beckoning selected and qualified members of it to become complicitous in the occasion.

*Cities are Sepulchers; they who dwell there*
*Are carcases, as if no such there were.*
*And Courts are Theaters, where some men play*
*Princes, some slaves, all to one end, and of one clay.*
*The Country is a desert, where no good,*
*Gain'd (as habits, not borne,) is understood.*
*There men become beasts, and prone to more evils;*
*In cities blockes, and in a lewd court, devills.*
                    *Donne, "To Sir Henry Wotton"*

# DONNE'S SILHOUETTES AND ABSENCES

CHAPTER FIVE

THE *SATYRES:* FIVE VIEWS OF COUNTERFEITS
AND THE SOCIAL CONTRACT

No renaissance poet except Jonson points up so effectively as Donne the reinforcements that lyric and satire may gain from each other, and none is so absolute in what he expects of true dialogue. These two propositions are related and bear upon the topography of Donne's imaginative world: lyric for him is often either a witty probing of relations-of-two or an enactment of communion in an enclosed place; satire reacts to the failure of personal relations and looks abroad to the court and the city. Lyric and satire are the systole and diastole of his secular poetry. Their portrayal especially of vicissitude prepares for his view of the world's betrayal of the soul in the devotions and sermons and his rescaling there of the soul's difficult ascent. The secular Donne prefers the closeted intimacy of dialogue and often finds other situations suspect. Besides having sins peculiar to them, as he tells Sir Henry Wotton by epistle, the greater settings of town, court, and country combine each others' vices "as in the first Chaos confusedly." And "So pride, lust, covetize, being severall" are also each in all, "And mingled thus, their issue incestuous."

In contrast private triumphs of the "The Good-morrow's" kind are founded upon trusted union and avoidance of potential short-circuits, at which Donne glances in ironic asides. In the satiric songs and sonnets and in the *Satyres* themselves, he measures the fickleness of "fondling motley humorists" and others by the standard of personal loyalty and constancy. As he remarks in the first satire, "For better or worse take mee, or leave mee: / To take, and leave mee is adultery" ("Satyre 1," 25–26).[1] The speaker's displeasure with the court and the city (he usually ignores the country) rises out of what he regards as the treachery and the counterfeiting that reign abroad. Where the speakers of *Songs and Sonnets* base true dialogue on the openness of one party to another, the satirist finds himself among those whose first inclination is to impress and to use others. He may be further isolated, as some readers think, by his own moral aloofness and holier-than-thou view of human error.[2] Whether or not he is, he gathers nothing resembling Jonson's associates within his chambers, nor is his rough-hewn language calculated to set a standard of reasonableness for like-minded people.

One of Donne's more impressive statements on erosions of trust comes in the "Fourth Satyre." Pope's translation gives us a valuable slant on it, because unlike Donne's original it assumes that the satirist addresses a compatible group. The difference shows clearest at the climax, where Pope capitalizes on Donne's fury to make somewhat different points. He had this to work with:

> And, My Mistresse Truth, betray thee
> To th'huffing braggart, puft Nobility?
> No, no, Thou which since yesterday hast beene
> Almost about the whole world, hast thou seene,
> O Sunne, in all thy journey, Vanitie,
> Such as swells the bladder of our court? I
> Thinke he which made your waxen garden, and
> Transported it from Italy to stand
> With us, at London, flouts our Presence, for
> Just such gay painted things, which no sappe, nor
> Tast have in them, ours are; and naturall
> Some of the stocks are, their fruits, bastard all.
>
> 163–75

Donne's puppets, Italian wax-works, and counterfeit nobles compose a confused theatrical world that makes the real and the fake almost indistinguishable. The splendid clothes of nobles end up in plays, and the theater's wardrobe is in turn rented out to poverty-stricken courtiers. Truth is worth an idealist's enthusiasm, but no one knows where to locate it. Nor is the speaker's own style impeccable in its rush to assail what offends him, as Donne uses enjambment and a hurried style to reinforce his impatience. Whereas Jonson never strays very far from apothegms for an implicit group that can profit by them, Donne's speaker calls out from his isolation like a Jeremiac prophet never far from diatribe.[3]

Pope's view of the wax works is naturally very similar, but his persona is less over-wrought at having to turn away from his fair mistress:

> O my fair Mistress, *Truth!* Shall I quit thee,
> For huffing, braggart, puft *Nobility?*
> Thou, who since Yesterday, hast roll'd o'er all
> The busy, idle Blockheads of the Ball,
> Hast thou, O *Sun!* beheld an emptier sort,
> Than such as swell this Bladder of a Court?
> Now pox on those who shew a *Court in Wax!*
> It ought to bring all Courtiers on their backs.
> Such painted Puppets, such a varnish'd Race
> Of hollow Gewgaws, only Dress and Face,
> Such waxen Noses, stately, staring things,
> No wonder some Folks bow, and think them *Kings*.[4]
>
> 200–211

More of the beau monde shows in Pope's idle blockheads, and the sin of his courtiers is a deficiency in taste, dress, decorum. Donne is more concerned with a general lifelessness and betrayals of trust that create bastards, or in a word, truth, not taste. Neither version has any great difficulty identifying waxen evils, and the chief counterfeiter in both is a bore who corners the speaker and fills his ear with public scandal.

Also, both are concerned with credibility, or as Pope concludes:

> Scar'd at the grizly Forms, I sweat, I fly,
> And shake all o'er, like a discover'd Spy.
> *Courts* are too much for Wits so weak as mine;
> Charge them with Heav'n's Artill'ry, bold *Divine!*
> From such alone the Great Rebukes endure,
> Whose *Satyr's sacred,* and whose Rage *Secure.*
> 'Tis mine to wash a few slight Stains; but theirs
> To deluge Sin, and drown a Court in Tears.
> Howe'er, what's now *Apocrypha,* my Wit,
> In time to come, may pass for *Holy Writ.*
>
> 278–87

Donne had written with somewhat less aplomb:

> I shooke like a spyed Spie. Preachers which are
> Seas of Wit and Arts, you can, then dare,
> Drowne the sinnes of this place, for, for mee
> Which am but a scarce brooke, it enough shall bee
> To wash the staines away; Though I yet
> With *Macchabees* modestie, the knowne merit
>   Of my worke lessen: yet some wise man shall,
>   I hope, esteeme my writs Canonicall.
>
> 237–44

The differences are partly tonal and stylistic, but in writing of the court Pope also implies common views of propriety that Donne does not. Donne's isolated speaker in the wilderness finds a discrepancy between the truth that claims his personal allegiance and "gay painted things," and he speaks his mind regardless of who may be listening. In the conclusion, too, where Pope's concern is a general acknowledgment of wit, Donne's speaker hopes at best for a single wise man who might some day take him to heart. The weakness of his own wit drives him from court and makes him a less effective instrument for its correction than heaven's artillery. The satirist finds himself prying into things better left unseen except by the final judge—compared with whom no secular moralist has much cleansing power. For Donne's speaker, then, it is all society, not merely the strength of his own witty attack, that is in jeopardy.

One senses a would-be lyric speaker behind this, defeated for the time being by a lack of worthy communicants and a place to stand but prepared to welcome both. He prefers another sort of community altogether from the one available to him, built upon openness and secure in its intimacies. As it turns out, the intimacies that appeal to him will be mainly those of lovers, as in the *Songs and Sonnets,* or of writers and receivers of epistles, or later, of confessor and God; they will never be broadly social or even selectively sociable. Donne will invariably refuse to let them be compromised, which in the case of the itinerant soul in the Anniversaries means abandoning the world altogether. The intensity of the union that Donne pursues washes out or reduces to shadow all peripheral substances and all lesser contracts and mediating institutions. The listener is the other party, or on occasion an onlooker. In the verse epistles, too, Donne addresses a friend or a patron, sometimes through someone else simply to add a third party.

But that is to look ahead. It is the *Satyres* that initially set forth the nature of trust and its violation, and they warrant close scrutiny both for the preparation they offer in reading the lyrics and for their own sakes. In dramatizing the contrast between the integrity of the private place and the role-playing of the street, "Satyre I" follows a short-story line from the arrival of an acquaintance at the speaker's chamber to their encounters with several satiric types outside and eventually to the friend's abandonment of the speaker and return. Language is slippery; books are not shared; no rituals of food and entertainment serve to draw a circle together. Movement is toward dispersal and centerless street wandering rather than centripetal and contractual. Manners are subject to revision according to one's sidewalk opportunities. Parting is less resonant with morality and disintegration here than the parting of lovers but is nearly as disturbing to the speaker. The place into which his visitor comes, virtually a closet, suggests both the privileges of Donne's private harbors and their constrictions. Since the ladies of the *Songs and Sonnets* have not yet put in an appearance, the speaker's companions are divines, philosophers, statesmen, historians, and poets, both miscellaneous and print-bound, all of them difficult to apply to street life except in contrast. In that respect the integrity of the book and the power of writing already throw out predictions of "A Valediction of the Booke" and "The Canonization," the first concerned with lasting bonds and the second with contrasts between the ostentatious power of the chronicled great and the integrity of lovers residing in their small sonnet rooms. But for the moment the studious speaker's statesmen are "jolly" figures who teach us "how to tie / The sinewes of a cities mistique bodie," and his poets are "Giddie fantastique" fellows—better companions certainly than the one who comes to drag him forth, and perhaps supportive of membership in Jonson's circle if the speaker were more inclined to talk about them. If they do tie a mystic body together, it can only be hypothetically, not by exercising real influence through him.

Where books offer an intangible and inapplicable society, sidewalk traffic is readily visible but in costumed disguise. The speaker's "wild uncertaine" friend calculates the worth of each passerby according to the cut of his cloth, though for the speaker himself virtue alone gives satisfaction:

> At birth, and death, our bodies naked are;
> And till our Soules be unapparrelled
> Of bodies, they from blisse are banished.
> 42–44

Despite this outbreak of sermonizing, the speaker portrays with some wit and economy the flightiness of his companion:

> Now we are in the street; He first of all
> Improvidently proud, creepes to the wall,
> And so imprison'd, and hem'd in by mee
> Sells for a little state his libertie;
> Yet though he cannot skip forth now to greet
> Every fine silken painted foole we meet,
> He them to him with amorous smiles allures,
> And grins, smacks, shrugs, and such an itch endures,
> As prentises, or schoole-boyes which doe know
> Of some gay sport abroad, yet dare not goe.
> 67–76

What he identifies is similar to what Oliver Wendell Holmes's autocrat of the breakfast table calls simply publicity-seeking by those who expect to leap into the limelight at a single bound: whereas true fame comes when one is not looking, the ladder of notoriety is easily climbed but it "leads to the pillory which is crowded with fools who could not hold their tongues, and rogues who could not hide their tricks."[5] What subjects the court and the city to fluctuating confusion is a lack of common standards and just such quests for prominence. Where all that shows in "lace, pinke, panes, print, cut" (1.97) is transitory, surfaces prove to be either impenetrable or merely whimsical.

In exploring the failings of poetry and the law, "Satyre II" turns up two other phases of betrayed trust. Although critics have sometimes found the two interests of the poem less related than they might like, the speaker considers both poets and lawyers in the context of language and unites them in Coscus, once a poet and now a lawyer. The poem's concern with language is another side of society's failure to commit itself to open, recognizable truths. The judgment that Donne implies is similar to that of Jonson's *Discoveries:* "Wheresoever, manners, and fashions are corrupted, Language is. It imitates the publicke riot. The excesse of Feasts, and apparell, are the notes of a sick State; and the wantonnesse of language, of a sick mind" (*Discoveries,* pp. 592–93). Or again, in Jonson's words, "*Language* most shewes a man: speake that I may see thee. It springs out of the most retired, and inmost parts of us, and is the Image of the Parent of it, the mind. No glasse renders a mans forme, or likenesse, so true as his speech" (p. 625). Performance for pay undermines that rendering in both lawyers and poets. A good poet should be an asset to a community that seeks models of behavior; but the sorts of poets who are Donne's target here pirate the wit of others and assist counterfeiters and waxworks in obscuring truth.

Coscus's plague of legal terms corrupts specifically the language of courtship. It trivializes what should be the strongest bond of a society by making its intimate addresses jargonish with "continual claims," "injunctions," "rival suits" and "proceedings." Stringing such things together, one can actually assemble whole sentences, as in "If I returne next size in Lent, / I should be in remitter of your grace"; or, "in th' interim my letters should take place / Of affidavits" (54–57). The speaker is not amused:

> words, words, which would teare
> The tender labyrinth of a soft maids eare,
> More, more then ten Sclavonians scolding, more
> Then when winds in our ruin'd Abbeyes rore.

57–60

It is difficult to gauge the decibels of ten tongue-lashing Slavs, but the effect is that of Babel.

The affectations of a Coscus are different from those of "Satyre I," but they have similar repercussions. In effect in a noisy world people seek the most noticeable way to sally forth and the most imposing speech. Meanwhile, the good works for which lawyers should be trained go undone, and connections between the private soul and public works are broken. The results Donne finds equivalent to misreadings of biblical texts:

> when he sells or changes land, he'impaires
> His writings, and (unwatch'd) leaves out, *ses heires,*
> As slily'as any Commenter goes by
> Hard words, or sense; or in Divinity
> As controverters, in vouch'd Texts, leave out
> Shrewd words, which might against them cleare the doubt.
>
> 97–102

Clear sense and correct explication are the foundations of received truth and therefore of community:

> But (Oh) we'allow
> Good workes as good, but out of fashion now,
> Like old rich wardrops; but my words none drawes
> Within the vast reach of th'huge statute lawes.
>
> 109–12

Mere words even of a more open and rational sort are helpless to guarantee a social contract in these confusions of the city and the court. Perhaps for that reason the third satire turns to religion and frames a quest for a church, both to reinforce truth and to give it institutional stability. We know the gravity for Donne personally of that search, which occupied him through most of his mature years. At the sequential center of the five satires and at their spiritual and conceptual center as well, he tries to locate just what truth should be in its doctrinal form. In doing so he passes momentarily close to the boundaries of lyric but in a mode closer to that of the *Holy Sonnets* than *Songs and Sonnets*. The soul's first pursuit must be just such a truth, by which Donne means not the sort of truth that attaches to incidents and occasions, to axioms, or even to the postulates of science and credos, but truth absolute, centered, universal:

> On a huge hill,
> Cragged, and steep, Truth stands, and hee that will
> Reach her, about must, and about must goe;
> And what th'hills suddennes resists, winne so;
> Yet strive so, that before age, deaths twilight,
> Thy Soule rest, for none can worke in that night.
>
> 3. 79–84

The image of this free-standing, exalted truth Donne stations in a privileged position in a passage that has been rightly recognized as crucial to him. He delays the phrase "Truth stands" syntactically and plants it unqualified and sturdy in the center of the line, where it is readily visible from all regions. Ostensibly, he means such a truth to be theological and doctrinal, but it can just as well be personal and serve the functions of the poet's centering myth. Though he persisted in his efforts to find employment at court and continued to praise kingship lavishly in the sermons, none of Donne's statements about majesty or those who serve it leads us to believe that he subsequently saw any possibility of a secular or public equivalent to such truth or even strong reinforcement of it. His hope here is to find a religious institution to enshrine, propagate, and defend it

The attributes of the hill do not transfer to truth itself, however, which is momentarily beyond concretion; they apply rather to the pathway one takes, or to the circumstances of pilgrimage. What Donne sketches is "the way" that occupies so much Reformation questing and gives Bunyan the central metaphor for *Pilgrim's Progress,* which as we will see later is partly a metaphor for discourse. Indeed, as the focus shifts from truth to him who climbs toward it, Donne slips away from the goal, much as Bunyan's Christian frequently falls back and starts up again. The passage trails off on the topic of an old age that seeks rest—that comes not to light but to twilight. Where truth stands aloof as the living substance the intellect should grasp, night marks the onset of obscurity and the borderlands of elegy.

The quest for truth embodied in a church runs into other difficulties as well. The higher truth stands, the more it blinds the beholder:

> hard knowledge too
> The mindes indeavours reach, and mysteries
> Are like the Sunne, dazling, yet plaine to'all eyes.
>
> 86–88

Seemingly, no one can find a way to domesticate it or attract a membership to it. It seems literally to have no place. Pursuit finds its most formidable barriers not on the steep hill, however, where one might be inspired to win most where the way is hardest, but in its human byways where kings, vicars, and men of law set the rules. Souls that will be tried by truth's high standard at judgment find themselves exhorted to live, in the interim, by the charters of magistrates:

> So perish Soules, which more chuse mens unjust
> Power from God claym'd, then God himselfe to trust.
>
> 109–10

In the larger structure of "Satyre III" as well as in the passage on truth itself, the gleaming vision that could unite men gives way to shabby substitutions—primarily of a social sort that the other satires identify.

If "Satyre III" sets a standard for the soul's pursuit—putting abstract truth in place of communal norm—"Satyre IV" establishes a psychological or affective locus for one who seems increasingly vulnerable to isolation. The speaker's assailant in this case is not the harmless flutterer of the first satire or the comparatively harmless poets and lawyers of the second but an informer who spreads malice simultaneously through the social body and the speaker's mind. No preparatory exposure to corrupt language can immunize one against him:

> Pedants motley tongue, souldiers bumbast,
> Montebankes drugtongue, nor the termes of law
> Are strong enough preparatives, to draw
> Me to beare this: yet I must be content
> With his tongue, in his tongue, call'd complement:
> In which he can win widdowes, and pay scores,
> Make men speake treason, cosen subtlest whores,
> Out-flatter favorites.
>
> 4. 40–47

His language is subtler and more insidious than Coscus's and his art of lying surpasses even that of chroniclers. Like Jonson's town criers and spies in "The New Cry"—the gossipy sort expressly not invited to supper—he libels great men, names the princes they have paid for their offices, describes their sexual habits, and gives the inside dope on foreign affairs. Like Jonson's ripe statesmen, they talk in whispers and spread anxiety. Jonson's court spies, of course, also deal in the coded language of insiders; they

> talk reserved, locked up, and full of fear,
> Nay, ask you how the day goes, in your ear;
> Keep a Star-Chamber sentence close, twelve days,
> And whisper what a proclamation says. . . .
> They all get Porta, for the sundry ways
> To write in cipher, and the several keys
> To ope the character. They've found the sleight
> With juice of lemons, onions, piss, to write,
> To break up seals, and close 'em.
>
> "The New Cry," 17–29

Donne is less concerned with the ciphers and the secrecy and more with the poisonous reception of intelligence, which in the spectrum of kinds of information and truth comes at the opposite end of that hard-won variety that stands on the eminence:

> I more amas'd then Circes prisoners, when
> They felt themselves turne beasts, felt my selfe then
> Becomming Traytor, and mee thought I saw
> One of our Giant Statutes ope his jaw
> To sucke me in; for hearing him, I found
> That as burnt venom'd Leachers doe grow sound
> By giving others their soares, I might growe
> Guilty, and he free.
>                                           129–36

Donne imagines a metamorphosis of men into beasts and makes the speaker himself momentarily not merely one such but a lesser one about to be devoured. Rather than taking refuge in a safe chamber that reduces the world to manageable proportions, the victim of courtly conspiracy finds himself entering a great orifice, the location of false words and a place to be eaten. When the "makeron's" barrage of words ends in a request for a loan, he is able to buy some peace; but the aftereffects of the visit are as disturbing as the visit itself, as though a circle has after all been established—of the devil's kind. In the inmost self, even in his dreams, the speaker feels contaminated:

> At home in wholesome solitarinesse
> My precious soule began, the wretchednesse
> Of suiters at court to mourne, and a trance
> Like his, who dreamt he saw hell, did advance
> It selfe on me.
>                                           155–59

To the image of corruption and vanity that "Satyre IV" presents, Donne adds one further portrait in "Satyre V," which concerns a narrower but related matter—the failure of the court and its officers to render justice to suiters. We do not need to consider it in detail, but it adds to the portrayal of social disruption the notion that without a last resort—an honest authority—anyone no matter how sound can be beggared. Suitors are like streams swallowed by "a vast ravishing sea." Consumed alive before worms can get them, they are vulnerable to such as the Pursivant, who breaks and enters, declares them heretics, and delivers final judgment. Although less concerned with language and manners than the other satires, "Satyre V" is equally bitter about this corruption of the courtly system and the part of the social contract that should guarantee privacy and property but does not—sufficient reason, if Donne were Jonson, to form one's group and begin looking for private shelter.

I have not wanted to abbreviate too much in this initial stage, because the *Satyres* have not been as well connected with what follows as they might be. From here on I will select the fewest possible instances to cover the ground and follow up the inside-outside contrast in Donne's gathering of the greater into the lesser in his own kind of synecdochial minimum. The court that he glimpses off and on in the *Satyres* and *Songs and Sonnets* operates under a disregard for codes similar to the disregard Wyatt found objectionable in Henry VIII's court and Spenser discovered in journeying from Kilcolman to London. Donne was clearly prepared to explore different settings for the poet even before the ostracism that came of his marriage and led to his search for refuge at Pyford, Mitcham, and Drury Lane. The stage is also set for the cultivation of epistolary addresses to Lucy Harrington, Henry Wotton, Henry Goodyere, Mary Magdalen Herbert, and the Countess of Huntingdon. More important to the styles he developed in establishing the margins of private bowers, he learns to counter spies, false women, costumed peacocks, and opportunists by playing irony against Petrarchan formulas and the values of streetwalkers and court worldlings. The satire embedded in *Songs and Sonnets* belongs not to a Jonsonian man-among-men but to a critical observer who holds to a privileged truth that thrives only when two people give their undivided attention to each other and use their wits to inform their feelings.

TWO IN ONE: THE SUBSTANCE OF LOVE
AND SETTINGS OF COURTSHIP

The satires describe and criticize a social vacuum that renders most urban and courtly contacts of little value to Donne in the figure of the poet. Love cannot be socialized or individual strengths brought into general use without standards that begin in fidelity. Where the loves of Spenser's illustrative knights and ladies are useful in the poet's tying together the parts of a chivalric whole, Donne's lovers begin by removing m ''ations between them and their personal truth. The fulfillment of self is guided by intellect and framed by dialogue without the Spenserian propensity for landscapes and adventures. Behind the rugged (and sometimes ragged) attack of the *Satyres* on vices is a vulnerability to isolation that suggests no further quests or initiations, merely further threats of abandonment. In the offing is Elizabeth Drury's forsaking of the world as its principle of order and spiritual life, but that is an enlargement of the desertion theme. More immediately and personally, several songs and sonnets explore the breaking up of love's fragile arrangements, as in the desertion of the beloved, for instance, that leaves the speaker spiritless in "A Nocturnall upon S. Lucies Day," spiritless and deprived not merely of social contact but of metaphysical essence and the substance of truth.

The implications of Donne's encompassing negativity hang upon love's uncompromising demands. When he writes in "The Sunne Rising," "She is all States, and all Princes, I, / Nothing else is," he gives a new twist to an old macrocosm-microcosm figure. Unlike his predecessors the poet feels no need to lament being so devoted to love, although he is sometimes defensive. As "The Canonization" indicates, the lovers themselves may even become objects of worship or models of truth for those on pilgrimage from the country, court, and city. As the language of the songs establishes its own habitation, seekers may approach its expressed pattern and share the substantiating power of hymns that have their living emblems in love's hermitage. Not only the united bodies and souls of two, then, but a certain population can be present to love, which needs only tangible signs and dialogue to be set in view and sustained more broadly. But that expression requires the reform of loves' onlookers also, and so love replaces other indoctrinations with the self-created and *proclaimed* truth of the poet and his love in their showcase. I'll return in a moment to that need for publicity and the difficulties that attend it in the bookmaking occupation it entails.

If Donne makes such large claims jokingly at times, he appears to do so not to undermine conviction but to disarm skepticism. Both the brashness of "The Sunne Rising" and the reverence of the last two stanzas of "The Canonization" are complicated by playfulness and read better with the *Satyres* and the satiric wit of other *Songs and Sonnets* in mind. Even so, "nothing else is" and "by these hymns, all shall approve / Us Canoniz'd for Love" stand as bold assertions of a secular faith and a social possession seen entirely in their terms. So surprising are the claims of some poems that readers have been tempted to assume an undercutting of the speaker, in the way Robertsonian readings of medieval courtly love literature find in it a clerical championing of *caritas* over audacious passion. I do not detect that particular kind of irony in *Songs and Sonnets*, which use their double-edged language typically to protect lyricism or prepare for it. The beloved is herself said to be not merely like something, as a partial substitute for it, but to be the thing itself—or so "The Sunne Rising" asserts. No prince as such needs more than his state; and as it fully occupies him, so the lovers' room is total planet to the sun: "Shine here to us, and thou art every where; / This bed thy center is, these walls, thy sphaere." This must be said in awareness that the sun shines indifferently on a vast globe of things and creatures, but it serves to underscore the speaker's indifference to that globe. Within reach simultaneously are both center and periphery, essence and embodiment, the thing and its expression. No rupture divides any phase of one's possession from another phase, and time itself becomes irrelevant.

If something about that uncompromising grasp of love's substance seems familiar, it is perhaps the language of sacramental union that it resembles. Donne borrows from devotional thought frequently, much as Petrarchans do but without using love as an upward avenue or as in Herbert's love for another object in "Let me not love thee, if I love thee not": it concludes in itself. Despite his echoes of such thoughts, however, it is difficult to locate anything just like love's sacred sites even among later poets who have his example before them. When the cavaliers exaggerate the appeals of love, they do so by way of gallantry; no one takes them seriously. Ordinarily, the concept of sacred places and privileged moments attaches to something like Marvell's garden or Vaughan's enigmatic topography. The compression of everywhere into one place is common enough, of course. Herbert's follower Ralph Knevet is typical in finding the body itself to be a compressed world, though a problematic one:

> Man is no Microcosme, and they detract
>   From his dimensions, who apply
> This narrow terme to his immensitye:
>   Heaven, Earth, and Hell, in him are pack't:
>
> Hee's a miscellanye of goods, and evills,
> A temper mixte with Angells, Beasts, and Devills.
>
> Yea the immortall Deitye doth daigne,
>   T'inhabite in a carnall cell:
> So pretious gemmes in the darke center dwell,
>   So gloomy mines fine gold retaine
> But by vicissitudes, these Essences
> The various heart of Man wont to possesse.[6]

A frequenter of commonplaces, Knevet repeats that sentiment in "The Mansion" in which the Lord, to show the miracle of his humble love, establishes godhead in a stable and in the low province of "despis'd Galile," brought down from "his bright Throne above." Thinking of Herbert he also finds his own volume, *A Gallery to the Temple*, a body of "letters" available to special entries of the spirit, until body, world, and book all become God's vessels. Thus in "The

Imprese," he imagines ingraving some fine motto to display "High Dignityes, / And honours gay" (p. 133) in the ruby God has given him; but only the "blessed Name" of Christ and the image of his "death of shame" makes a true motto, since residence lies in the privileged name itself—not in metaphor or analogy.

Such poets as Herbert, Vaughan, and Knevet each in his way fills sacred places with a plenary truth of emblematic things and holds that locating the soul among them helps it. I will explore some tactical advantages of such places later; the pertinent matter here is Donne's daring in sanctifying his own chambers by the presence of the lady or co-presence of the two-in-one. Their possession of each other seals off the lyric site and permeates them with the undying substance of revealed souls. They may thus set aside other programs for self-improvement—careers, religious conversions. But in reverse any place once favored can also be betrayed, and for this Donne again suggests a pattern for later poets. In "The World" for instance, Knevet asks "What magicke spell / Confines mee to this Circle Wide?" and wonders if the special power of letters has not gone (literally) to the devil:

> What characters devis'd by arts of Hell,
> Have my affections to this prison ty'd?
> This place of exile, where my life,
> No better is then lingring death.
>
> "The World", p. 138

Far better to be buried alive in a cell, which "habitation is / Better then Hell" (p. 146). More tellingly, when love is removed in "A Nocturnall upon S. Lucies Day," Donne makes the void that results equivalent to the mystic's dark night. Even a love that merely wanes in "A Lecture upon the Shadow" drops instantly into dark.

The latter poem is especially instructive in its interplay of shadows and full substances and its construction of a standard of truth that the mind can seize upon to make love permanent. It also finds a middle style between outright lyric and irony in its quasi-lecture mode. The speaker is not blindly devotional but inclined to translate feeling into principles, as handles for love's intangibility. Having done so, he makes one of Donne's more resolute claims for self-fulfillment in the context of internal threats to fidelity. In their recognition of each other's true selves, these lovers, too, arrange a world about them and make possessing, being, knowing, and celebration all virtually identical. Where "The Good-morrow" recognizes that possession depends upon candor, "A Lecture" is preoccupied with the repercussions of deceit, which comes, the lecturer says, in two phases, before love's zenith and after, *if* it declines:

> Stand still, and I will read to thee
>     A Lecture, Love, in loves philosophy.
> These three houres that we have spent,
> Walking here, two shadowes went
> Along with us, which we our selves produc'd;
> But, now the Sunne is just above our head,
>     We doe those shadowes tread;
> And to brave clearenesse all things are reduc'd.
>     So whilst our infant loves did grow,
>     Disguises did, and shadowes, flow
> From us, and our care; but, now 'tis not so.
>
> That love hath not attain'd the high'st degree,
> Which is still diligent lest others see.
>
> Except our loves at this noone stay,
> We shall new shadowes make the other way,
>     As the first were made to blinde
>     Others; these which come behinde
> Will worke upon our selves, and blind our eyes.
> If our loves faint, and westwardly decline;
>     To me thou, falsly, thine,
> And I to thee mine actions shall disguise.
>     The morning shadowes weare away,
>     But these grow longer all the day,
> But oh, loves day is short, if love decay.
>
> Love is a growing, or full constant light;
> And his first minute, after noone, is night.

The lecture comes appropriately at a moment when love's truth and therefore the implications of potential decline are clear. Love's language at this stage is not that of courtship or adulation and is just barely that of lyric. In the line "And to brave clearness all things are reduc'd," the first stanza opens out modestly—in a combination of declaration and commemoration. This expansion climaxes the narrative order before a concluding axiom and an analytical phase have fully explained the parallels between love's growth and the sun-shadow movement. The thrust of the lecture as a whole is in fact toward usable axiom—usable because the situation is dramatic and admonition is crucial to it. Although in its growing stages love may be fearful of exposure, in the full sun it has the courage to be exhibited, to be showy, and reduce all else to itself. A love still diligent is not capable of scaling that height because its concealments force a breach between the lovers and society. Since they cannot openly practice the graces that love is supposed to foster, the reactions to the world that "The Canonization" dramatizes are not possible.

More difficult to account for is Donne's extremity in denying half-way measures in love's decline. It may be that having discovered the essence of love and become defined by it, one does not settle for less, any more than Bunyan's Christian once located in the celestial city could live outside its gates. In the terms of "The Good-morrow," deception between lovers who have once understood each other exposes a fatal defect in their union; that which was not mixed equally dies. The "Oh" of the second stanza recalls the pitch of "brave cleareness" and moving beyond lecture signals both the realization of love's substance and its potential loss. However, the outbreak does not remove the cautionary "except" or the two "ifs." Admonition prevails, not love's decline, since love need not follow the sun's course. If all one requires to break the parallel is continuation in the truth, any elegiac feeling for fragile love is premature. For the time being, love is qualified only by wise council and foresight, as in the final couplet's balancing of the potential plunge against defiance. Behind that defiance must lie a mustering of the resources of the psyche, a gearing up of the intense soul to choose its own immortality through love's covenant.

As "A Lecture" suggests, one trademark of Donne's recurrent view of love is the way in which it controls onlookers. All readers need a text, however, and love's body is a better book for some than invisibly united souls. The question of texts and their readability and thus of symbols and their efficacy becomes foremost. "The Exstasie" and the final stanza of "The Canonization" are concerned with love's interpreters, what sort they are, what they have to interpret. Moreover, Donne is frequently torn between privacy, as "The Good-morrow," "The Sunne Rising," "Valediction: forbidding Mourning," and other poems stage it, and the need to exhibit, one of the besetting sins of the *Satyres*. The *Songs and Sonnets* are full of tokens, hieroglyphs, and love's special figurative instruments. The writing of sonnets or making of pretty rooms obviously helps evangelize, since in that form all may see, approve, hymn. But Donne can never quite make up his mind whether lovers should actually refashion the world through special revelations that only they can make or leave it to its own devices. The sonnet as pretty room compromises: it is intimate and private, but the right sort of visitors may approach it. Either way, the union of two-in-one depends first upon the lovers' own waking souls: they must meet in affections and faculties and in dialogue to gain strength from their union and only then offer something to bystanders and begin to repair the damaged personal trust the *Satyres* anatomize.

How much the lovers know about their love is also open to question and is not a matter to be brushed aside lightly. Mysteries trouble their union in "The Relique," "The Exstasie," "Valediction: forbidding Mourning," and "Lovers Infiniteness"—in which possession outruns recognition and analytic powers. Any failure in either possession or understanding is likely to raise the speaker's wrath:

> Some that have deeper digg'd loves Myne then I,
>   Say, where his centrique happinesse doth lie:
>     I have lov'd, and got, and told,
>   But should I love, get, tell, till I were old,
>   I should not finde that hidden mysterie;
>     Oh, 'tis imposture all.
>
> "Loves Alchymie"

This both assumes the hidden mystery and in exasperation finally denies it, but clearly what others say love is the speaker doesn't see. Where love is more open, the need to know what elements it is less pressing; where street experience prevails, it is difficult to say exactly where the center is unless cynics and sensualists are allowed their reductive answer.

One usefulness of the world-as-audience is that it requires explanations. In offering misreadings it forces the lovers to articulate love's principles and discover what they truly possess. It opens a window in the lover's chambers, or gives them something like a balcony on which to come forth. Presumably cerebral understanding cannot hurt their union and may shore it up against invasion and dispossession. Thus in "The Relique," thought of future inquiries and of the messages one might leave behind prompts the speaker to translate love into symbols and interpretive statements. To correct an idolatrous age, one might, for instance, leave a message behind simply to say that "we lov'd well and faithfully." Beyond that basic certainty, however, lie miracles about which neither "this paper" (the current poem) nor a relic will be able to speak directly:

> These miracles wee did; but now alas,
> All measure, and all language, I should passe,
> Should I tell what a miracle shee was.

It is not clear just how much all this will mean to an idolatrous age anyway, or to its curious grave-digger, who will speculate somewhat bemusedly upon the device he uncovers. Certainly the lovers have no real need to explain themselves, although if the past tense, "Shee was," is what the future uses and not the poet's,—thinking of an already departed lover,—the speaker may even now be sorting things out with her. In either case he is paying tribute as well as explaining. Taken as a pledge and keepsake, the bracelet of bright hair, like the poem, will betoken fidelity and unbreakable union to any apt interpreter. Indeed, all interpreters of love's mysteries resemble religious adepts. They must turn away from a broader social discourse to understand love's special language. What one might wish to say beyond that—about the essence of love—surpasses reason, measure, language.

Symbols and tokens provide at best problematic ways for lovers to convey love's totality to interpreters, still less for them to understand themselves. Explaining incomplete or failed love is no easier. The psyche in Donne's close quarters often dwells in vacillation. By supreme acts of overreaching, it climbs to highs of satisfaction and seems to see all the way to eternity's gateway, as in "The Anniversary" and "The Good-morrow." But it needs signs for its scaling equipment. Articulation and definition are but the tools of its faith; or to vary the language slightly, souls cannot go far without mind, which requires a good deal of learning in Donne and some honing by argument. Well-worked metaphors and conceits are more important than formal logic in that honing. Conceits like the bracelet are valuable partly because they can be held up to prolonged scrutiny before one discovers their limits and the borderlands of reason itself.

An image similar to "The Relique's" bracelet is changed in "The Funerall" to "That subtile wreathe of haire, which crowns mine arme." Less brilliant and less starkly contrastive to the grave, the token in this case does not hypostatize love but calls into question a relationship the speaker himself claims not to understand, although he puzzles through it. Love and its betrayal are both beyond reason but not as miracles. The poem finally must make obscurity its instrument of revenge: burying the lady or a piece of her carries her into an oblivion that "this paper," unlike the paper of "The Relique," refuses to explicate. The wreath itself will not hold or retrieve the absent spirit, of course; both remain riddles. The word "bravery" brings into the conclusion some of the confidence of "A Lecture upon the Shadow," but in a vengeful mood:

> As 'twas humility
> To'afford to it all that a Soule can doe,
>   So, 'tis some bravery,
> That since you would save none of mee, I bury some of you.

This has ringing finality in a context that otherwise stresses speculation and posturing. But despite its determination, the answer to the lady is not altogether satisfying, and no amount of assertion can fill the vacancy she has left; "some" is a lesser piece of her than the total of the speaker she has attracted and then rejected. A certain lyric force resides in the speaker's anger, but the apostrophe it generates stops up the expansion of self that comes with other celebrations of love's staying power. In effect, the poem announces a failure in the lyric crossing to the other.

It is partly that staying power that validates love's publicity and preempts other subjects of panegyric for Donne in the *Songs and Sonnets*. The glory that counts to the idealistic speaker of those lyrics is the lovers' own and sometimes its reflection of the divine state that they anticipate. "The Anniversarie" anticipates it with less antagonism toward detracters and less trauma than Donne's lyrics ordinarily exhibit. It is perhaps Donne's most forthright poem. For once he supplies no tokens or emblems to carry love's image, only comparatively lesser things to gauge its height:

> All Kings, and all their favorites,
>   All glory'of honors, beauties, wits,
> The Sun it selfe, which makes times, as they passe,
> Is elder by a yeare, now, then it was
> When thou and I first one another saw:
> All other things, to their destruction draw,
>   Only our love hath no decay;
> This, no tomorrow hath, nor yesterday,
> Running it never runs from us away,
> But truly keepes his first, last, everlasting day.

The speaker is content to be unironic and without his lecture materials for a moment, but even so we recognize his simplicity here as that of a complex poet who comes to such moments of repose the hard way. The narrative of love's growth incorporates some of the richness of "The Good-morrow's" celebration of the first day's discovery and "Loves Growth's" management of love's seasonal expansions. The magnificence of the several "alls" and the context of worldly glory, in the rising crescendo of abstraction that takes into its sweep all tomorrows and all yesterdays, are justified by love's endurance. In the longer concluding line, Donne approaches a liturgical language that veers from chronicle and toward books of prayer. Declaration gains its lyric force from that simplicity, as also in "Only our love hath no decay."

The final line of the first stanza of "The Anniversary" capitalizes on an accumulated sense of the "abler soul" of two-in-one, pits it against a decaying world of deceptive splendor, and projects an eternity for love's lyric possession. The second stanza, however, is more somber:

> Two graves must hide thine and my coarse,
> If one might, death were no divorce.
> Alas, as well as other Princes, wee,
> (Who Prince enough in one another bee,)
> Must leave at last in death, these eyes, and eares,
> Oft fed with true oathes, and with sweet salt teares.

Once Donne has established the possibility of a private glory equivalent to that of princes, the short journeys of corpses to graves is less dampening than it would otherwise be. That the present love, or an increased version of it, will return to them when "soules from their graves remove" gives basis enough for love's dialogue. However, the "Alas" and emphatic "wee" give timely point to the parting that must come. One's final chamber is not the little room that is an everywhere but the grave where none embrace.

Making love known and durable is a worthy project for the poet as love's publicist, then, but it has its dangers, and all love's expressive modes have their limits. Donne pays some attention to the potential erosion of meaning in love's bodies and its emblems in poems like "The Exstasie" and "A Valediction: of the Booke." In the latter posterity as well as present onlookers must learn to know the lovers, primarily through annals compiled from letters. There love is "sublimed" by fire, and "Rule and example" may be found, which suggests no disastrous falling away from reality in transcription. Indeed, divines, lawyers, and statesmen may throw away other studies and find all they seek in this one volume:

> This Booke, as long-liv'd as the elements,
>   Or as the worlds forme, this all-graved tome
>   In cypher write, or new made Idiome;
> Wee for loves clergie only'are instruments,
>     When this booke is made thus,
>     Should againe the ravenous
>   Vandals and Goths inundate us,
>   Learning were safe; in this our Universe
> Schooles might learne Sciences, Spheares Musick, Angels Verse.

Such books are love's true records, "To make, to keep, to use." They have at least one advantage for most onlookers: where spiritual people look to a disembodied heaven, an embodied beauty can be studied in its very forms: "where love doth sit, / Beauty'a convenient type may be to figure it." Such is the power of apt words that even a lover's name scratched on his beloved's window represents him to her in "A Valediction: of my Name in the Window." Thus if they are not housed mutually in a room, his soul, he says, can still be emparadised in her. At the worst, letters on the window may be his "ragged bony name" or "ruinous Anatomie":

> The rafters of my body, bone
> Being still with you, the Muscle, Sinew, 'and Veine,
> Which tile this house, will come againe.

At best, by such odd ciphers and dialogue, lovers may be made known to each other and thereby held steadfast. Let others pay heed to that; their own courses may depend on their hermeneutic skill.

No sooner do both these valedictions propose a mode of writing that will make the absent lover present, however, than they take it back. "The Window" concludes after progressive retractions from its initial confidence:

> But glasse, and lines must bee,
> No meanes our firme substantiall love to keepe;
> Neere death inflicts this lethargie,
> And this I murmure in my sleepe;
> Impute this idle talke, to that I goe,
> For dying men talke often so.

Though this retraction could be construed a number of ways, the simplest psychological explanation would seem to be that the speaker sets up all sorts of overt acts including subscribing and inscribing love, but only fidelity really works. Words and souls must correspond before lovers can "letter" each other. The dying is merely cavalier hyperbole for "without you, dear, I perish." A substantial love is an erotic, immediate presence that no phallic pen can replace; a less carnal substance must coexist in them if their words are not to lie. No substitute for either can really sustain them.

The valediction of the book ends even more "cryptically":

> Thus vent thy thoughts; abroad I'll studie thee,
> As he removes farre off, that great heights takes;
> How great love is, presence best tryall makes,
> But absence tryes how long this love will bee;
> To take a latitude
> Sun, or starres, are fitliest view'd
> At their brightest, but to conclude
> Of longitudes, what other way have wee,
> But to marke when, and where the dark eclipses bee?

Again Donne plays with a critical absence-presence, this time without removing the book as intermediary. The distinction between great and enduring love is a nice one in both senses of the word. Heated or great love, as passion, requires physical presence; the second love, enduring and therefore spiritual before being brought to book—if it in fact exists—is tested by the unfilfillment of passion. The lover must choose the best expressive mode and hermeneutic principle for the case in hand: any navigator-interpreter can take a latitude from obvious bright stars, but to chase down an eclipse traveling at a fast rate across Europe, and thus to see the something in nothing that love-in-absence has, requires great learning and skill. To "mark" is to write, and to write of such an absence is to scout out the eclipsed borderland, where light has just now disappeared and its very absence tells us what it was and why we craved it. The dynamics both of "A Lecture upon the Shadow" and "A Nocturnal" show here in the paradoxes of writing, not to undo writing altogether but to discover the true substance the book should reveal precisely in and through a lover's absence.

Again, then, at its best love's engraved and printed language may allow love to transfer its substance momentarily into a representation. But a single soul that tries to stand alone finds that it cannot do so, and one who has grown used to love and been deprived of it goes precipitously to ruin. In love's *permanent* absence, unless pretty sonnets give it a place to dwell, the force of its presence is doubly proved, but a void nonetheless opens just beneath the sacred place. In neither realized nor abandoned love does Donne find a sustaining public order or feel the need to adopt acknowledged codes of courtship. In effect, he seeks to build the logical, redeeming power of the logos into love's lyrics and to find incarnation granting love its best and most visible forms; lacking that living form of love, he turns to writing.

### RETURNING TO THE FIRST NOTHING

Donne is obviously not convinced that natural settings contribute much to one who seeks meet dialogue and interprets its tokens, which is perhaps another reason that his poetry is removed not only from society but from the birds, trees, gardens, and animals of the medieval encyclopedia and renaissance *topographia*. ("The Exstasie" and "Twicknam Garden" are exceptions in their use of descriptive topoi, but neither seems concretely outdoors; they turn a spare number of decorations into virtual stage props.) Emblems in his book of love are defined by renaissance geometry, chemistry, and other learned disciplines. He concentrates on essences, quintessences, patterns, epitomes, and individual items that can be elaborated into conceits, such as the window pane, compasses, spider love, and mandrake roots. Although he is sometimes an urban poet, he does not dwell on the colors of urban street life either, which he reduces to general elements, actions, and silhouettes. Not even music, arts, foods, rites, folk customs, trades and professions, or character types can be said to give body to his verse, which brings into view instead the realms of reading, intellect, and personal relations. As John Carey points out in his speculative search for Donne's shaping imagination, when Donne is concerned with bodies, it is mostly with their insides. He is a vivisectionist and physician, and even that mostly in the prose: "His language responds richly to the task, fabricating abhorrent and coagulated textures for the world's decaying materials."[7] That is well put, and it points up one of the peculiarities of love's symbols as well—their obsession with the mechanisms of movement, inscription, and recovery by readers. The mechanics of writing on windows and the conditions of interpreting count almost as much as the messages themselves. When Donne elaborates on the grave digger's situation in "The Relique," for instance—what he will do, what others will say, the condition of the token and its marvelous survival in the grave—he entrusts love's truth to a strange mechanics of clues and their interpretation. A window pane, too, is a very difficult medium for writing and reading and not very expressive without the addition of colors and pictures. Better are sonnets that serve as pretty rooms but even there such rooms must be carefully defended and the audience prepared. Donne offers no furnishings or even acts and phases of love for helpful particulars.

The sites and surfaces of love are not textural or filled out with qualities, then, though they have operations. It is by a miraculous leverage that the private places of "The Sunne Rising" and "The Good-morrow" lift worlds into view. In both we are made aware of the scurrying activity of explorers, the king's men, and the sun itself, and of the reductive trading of all these for love, as though a large world were compressed inside a water-filled paperweight in one's hand. This mechanistic sense of how to bring a world into view is peculiar to Donne until Marvell augments it, and it is related I think to the private powers of self-completion he wished for the psyche. By rigorous acts of exclusion and denial, as the reverse motion of its plunge into truth, the psyche earns its own way, or finds (mainly in the *Holy Sonnets*) how short it falls and thus when and how to petition for help. One also needs to add to Carey's view of the vivisectionist at work the poet's translation of objects into the ideas they illustrate and the acts they perform. Bodies are not always decaying debris even in the Anniversaries and the sermons; they can be expressive symbols in those illustrated lectures that make specific points more persuasive in order to ensnare an audience. Where surfaces count, then, it is not their most tangible properties and not always their mechanics that interest Donne but often their likeness or unlikeness to other things.

Donne's exhibition of ruin in "A Nocturnall," however, includes two words, *chaos* and *absences,* that look more directly toward the world of objects and the sermons' obsession with disintegrating bodies. They are used partly in the way of alchemy, since matter behaves according to formulas, and the secrets of its chain reactions may be extracted by forced experiment. Where fulfilled love argues for the redeeming, incarnate expression of united souls in eyes, hands, and gestures, bodies deserted by love are deprived of all value and all self-mastery. The mechanics take over. Love's now permanent absence carries the speaker back to a primal state of nothingness, before correspondences among things had come forth at the command of the logos. Even the composition that chemists deal with is not very textured or descriptive, nor does Donne dwell on the larger arrangement of discrete bodies that makes up the total order, which begins with the infusion of spirit. The absence of these and of reason as well leaves matter a dead husk or inert mechanism, as absence has left the lovers mere "carcasses." This negating of arrangement and form releases elements back to their original disjunction, as death and the lightless void of Saint Lucies' day destroy the integrity of wintry things. Chemistry and cosmology, the small and the large, are interdependent, and both are deprived of significance and expressive power by the death of the beloved, the world's center.

Donne's extraordinarily undoing of a world in "A Nocturnall" is no more than one might expect from his elementing a total world from love to begin with. He has assigned virtually the power of creation to lovers or at least made them second Adams and Eves without need of an outdoor Eden. Cosmos and chaos are inseparable concepts, as in other seventeenth-century poets as well. As we have seen in Milton, for instance, creation is composed of highly individualized things and creatures raised from the conglomeration of chaos; its negation is a hubbub of uncontrolled particles. In the "state" of chaos, nothing coheres:

> Before thir eyes in sudden view appear
> The secrets of the hoary deep, a dark
> Illimitable Ocean without bound,
> Without dimension, where length, breadth, and highth,
> And time and place are lost; where eldest *Night*
> And *Chaos,* Ancestors of Nature, hold

> Eternal Anarchy, amidst the noise
> Of endless wars, and by confusion stand.
> For hot, cold, moist, and dry, four Champions fierce
> Strive here for Maistry, and to Battle bring
> Their embryon Atoms.
>
> *PL* 2. 890–900

In contrast in the created cosmos each atom joins others in intelligible relation, and their interactions under the "Arch-chemic Sun" produces the best mixtures of heat, "Terrestrial Humor," air, and fertile soil. The chemistry of the four elements is no more impressive than its cosmology. No one feels that fortunate participation of elements in the universal order more than Adam, who is the opposite of Donne's speaker in "A Nocturnall," the latter taking one step past Eden and its embowered love all the way to the world's "first nothing." While Donne's speaker is unmoved by the sun, Adam celebrates its derivative light, as all things reveal their principles to him in its light and warmth. Adam's naming of the separate bodies of the creation presupposes both their discreteness and their availability to sense and reason, until nothing of the universal blank or the godless void remains to be filled. The defect of loneliness that he recognizes and overcomes with the creation of Eve affects Donne's speaker in unexpected and extreme ways, since love's dialogue has not only completed the creation for him but given it value and held it together.

The mode of "A Nocturnall" carries beyond both satire and elegiac lyric to a kind of negative anatomy that repeats and savors the extinction of love's sites—the grave, the book, the window pane, the household or pretty room, the bed. Even so, Donne suggests that all this erasure, which is the drift of elegy and of satire both, is simultaneously a cleansing or preparation for a phase to follow. I take that phase to be in some vague way paradisal and thus suggestive of love's higher location, but the poem is not specific. The present is devoted to a definition of the emptied state and to a vigil that will presumably carry beyond the bitter isolation of "Love's Alchemy," "The Funerall," "Twicknam Garden," and the *Satyres*. The beloved is even now in that unstipulated place toward which one prepares with gestures of spirit and the purging exercises of word power. The emptying of the enumerated world may after all be the beginning of a communion beyond specific objects and occasions, in a place that need not be imagined so long as the union of lovers is not forbidden there. In that respect "A Nocturnall" is an early version not of the sermons but *Devotions upon Emergent Occasions,* which begins with the individual sinner in his room, confined to bed and stricken with mortality, ready for translation elsewhere and therefore willing to assume that the world is already hopelessly ruined. In Donne's rewriting of the epitome in prose versions, the new center is often such a ruin, beginning with the self having discovered early limits to its powers.

Hence it seems appropriate to conclude this mapping of Donnean topography with two passages that remove sustaining substances and go on to devotional preparation for the next world, in which Donne imagines a new self bolstered by grace and freed of all awkward mechanisms. That "elsewhere" in the *Devotions* appeals to him more and more as time passes. Having appeared in the *Holy Sonnets* and the Anniversaries earlier, it counterbalances the suffering of the *Devotions* with a glimpse of the "weight" of glory:

> This is natures nest of boxes; the heavens contain the earth, the earth, cities, cities, men. And all these are concentrique; the common center to them all, is decay, ruine; only that is eccentrique, which was never made; only that place, or garment rather, which we can imagine, but not demonstrate, that light, which is the very emanation of the light of God, in which the saints shall dwell, with which the saints shall be appareld, only that bends not to this center, to ruin; that which was not made of Nothing, is not threatned with this annihilation.[8]

Light's emanation in this setting reworks the satire-lyric interplay of negative and positive forces, here held in equilibrium by the special movement of Donne's syntax. The extremes demand each other and force each other more clearly into view.

More impressively, in the Second Prebend Sermon, Donne enters "that *pondus gloriae,* that exceeding weight of an eternall glory" as merely one small clause in an extensively structured list of sufferings and future expectations of the same, in which, without that glory, "we are waighed downe, we are swallowed up." In love's place he establishes a glory that is unpossessable and unknowable except by faith or by repute but that nonetheless merits celebration. In place of love's betrayals and struggles with the mechanism of bodies and tokens, he lists clause after clause of physical and psychological tortures until almost miraculously he engineers the upward turn and its sense of repossession. This resurgence comes in full view of onlookers, whom Donne the preacher implicitly invites into the communicative act, not merely as onlookers seeking a pattern from above but as participants. In that broadening of the communicative circle, the preacher perhaps finds at last an answer to the isolated satiric speaker and the abandoned lover.[9] In apostrophes to God, he forges a lyric crossing to replace other dialogues. A substantial world, still cited largely to be discarded, forms the topographical setting for that crossing and a gauge, in its destruction, of a huge recompense that must remain without body or name.

PART THREE

NATURAL AND SUPERNATURAL PROVINCES

> *Thy power and love, my love and trust*
> *Make one place ev'ry where.*
> "The Temper I'"

> *O fix thy chair of grace, that all my powers*
> *May also fix their reverence:*
> *For when thou dost depart from hence,*
> *They grow unruly, and sit in thy bowers.*
>
> *Scatter, or binde them all to bend to thee:*
> *Though elements change, and heaven move,*
> *Let not thy higher Court remove,*
> *But keep a standing Majestie in me.*
> "The Temper II"

# HERBERT'S INTERIM AND FINAL PLACES

CHAPTER SIX

The pairing of Jonson and Donne reveals differences both in temperament and in seclusion topoi as well as styles. It is not altogether convenience that has divided their successors roughly into cavaliers and metaphysicals, and my next pairing, of Herbert and Herrick, will take advantage of the logic of that division. But succession is complicated by a significant mixing, Herbert, for instance, being as Jonsonian in plain style as he is metaphysical in fermenting wit. The traditional classification breaks down almost totally with Vaughan, Marvell, and Milton. And so again we do a little better, I think, both with them and with Herbert, if we keep to topical charts. These give us not only stylistic but formal, metaphoric, and thematic ways to read the dynamics of literary response.

   On those charts Herbert veers sharply from his three most important predecessors, Sidney, Jonson, and Donne. He does not presuppose a courtly circle as Sidney does, nor even the necessity to constitute his own substitute for it. But he does have to guide readers toward altered expectations, assuming that they come from Jonson's classicism or the love tradition with its elaborate rhetoric, its habitual periphrasis, and its procedures for approaching (yet never possessing) the beloved. Negotiations with God are a quite different matter, not necessarily more direct but more dangerous to play with, and the church of course provides a unique setting. It virtually awards its own readership. But if Herbert were not broader than that readership suggests, it would be difficult to distinguish his lyrics from the anonymous medievalism Rosemond Tuve discovers in back of them. The secular literary tradition has intervened, Donne's part of it especially, and Herbert's difference to a large extent is the product of an unusual combining, as again and again he crosses the secular and the sacred. Whereas he addresses his readers in general terms in "The Church-Porch" as primarily a collection of sinners needing to be sprinkled and taught with precepts, the lyric poet who presides over *The Temple* lets them in mainly as implicit witnesses of the speaker's approach to the divine presence, in so many ways like courtship of an Eliza or a mistress. Jonson's careful cultivation of a social context and Donne's secular lover's seclusion are obviously of little use to that new courtship and the high stakes it causes the reader to wager over the outcome. For these Herbert substitutes a paradigmatic spiritual drama in which God not only becomes the beloved but is a quite special case in his anticipation of anything the poet might say.

This special critic, the reader who counts most, raises foremost the question of authority. The poems go back and forth from the poet's desire to author that presence to an acknowledgment of his helpless passivity. This too is an important substitution for the kinds of forlorn address the secular lyric makes, and Herbert clearly feels the added difficulties it poses, the chief one being simply the strain of locating God in words and places. The poet craves enclosure, for instance, but having to place God within an object or poem breaks open the container. Receiving him requires the reform of the sinner beginning with the "Church-Porch's" moral handbook, since only prepared receptacles can hope for occupancy. But knowing what to do is easier than doing it. Humanly built memories are "quarries of pil'd vanities," and hearts are stockpiles of sin that leave their owners pleading, "Oh fill the place, / And keep possession with thy grace" ("Good Friday"). Preachers themselves are not much better as God's conduits, being as "Church Windows" says but "brittle crazie glasse" that require virtually a miracle for the divine story to be annealed in them. "I am both foul and brittle," the speaker of "The Priesthood" confesses, "much unfit / To deal in holy Writ."

God is thus stationed at two removes unless the poet can induce a change, which amounts to a kind of double sacred periphrasis, the first, the incarnation's reduction; the second, flawed verbal, artistic, and church-sponsored relivings of the son's episodic progress, the source of all rites and rituals. Actual biblical places and the topoi made of them so interfere with God's true, inexpressible nature that the extra barrier of the sinner's obstinancy and resisting heart can altogether block off its presence. Hence much of *The Temple* is devoted to examining—and denying—paraphrase equivalencies, not only for God but for the soul, for certain doctrines, and even for the simplest of truths. In "The Quidditie" Herbert lists a number of erring paraphrases for verse itself, which is *not* a crown, hawk, lute, sword, or most of the things the secular traditions assume. As the Jordan poems add, neither is it quaint words, trim inventions, or winding stairs. These aspects of the inheritance have to be discarded at the outset. In "Deniall" similar errors of paraphrase apply to the soul and heart, which, being poured into broken vessels and disorderly verse, find no sense of accord between what the rhyming tongue says and the self feels:

> Therefore my soul lay out of sight,
> Untun'd, unstrung:
> My feeble spirit, unable to look right
> Like a nipt blossome, hung
> Discontented.

If one's own heart and soul cannot find proper form, how much more is God put out by the crazed glass and limp words of human devising.

To be sure, in certain seasons—particularly Easter and Christmas, seasons of hope—metaphors come streaming to both priests and poets: the word is a pasture, the soul a shepherd; the flock it feeds are thoughts, words, deeds; and we all "sing one common Lord" ("Christmas"). Doctrines, too, collect a quantity of truth, as the trinity and incarnation are stately cabinets full of the Lord, whose sweets "are packt up" in them ("Ungratefulnesse"). But this only leads to vacillation between emptying out and filling up vessels. That vacillation is by now a familiar story to Herbert's critics, as are his expectations for simple style. If the poet could not promise some usable metaphors—if scripture, for instance, did not give him the apostle's "grain" to convert into "bread"—there would be no gathering of a reader-flock for the mystical repast, no conveyance of true substance, no recounting of Christ's life story as the basis of all images, doctrines, and sacraments. At the same time, there seems to be little the poet himself can do to initiate a divine indwelling to which he can summon the flock. "The Holdfast" concludes that no one can claim authority in such matters; one can merely observe that, paradoxically, all things human that have served the divine nature are "more ours by being his," not by having been his, but by being currently and always his if he chooses.

The difficulty for lyric address in that otherwise consoling thought is similar to the drawback of a plain style that produces only "My God, my king": the outgoing impulses are stopped up except as correctable leaps into authorship, and except for pleas and complaints. The divine substance flows only one way. Thus the poet's contribution in "A True Hymne" is a longing "O, could I love!" and God's conclusion a simple, abrupt (if total) "Loved." Similar endings come up fast and close down with preemptive mystery in "Prayer I," "Redemption," and even "Love III" as the final writing of "loved." They do without the indirections of trope and traditions of periphrastic location. God's residences are unpredictable and indifferent, finally, because they are obliterated by his descent into them, all sacred paraphrases being much more radically unlike the truth than, say, the moon is unlike Diana or the sun unlike Phoebus.

One of Herbert's legacies to Vaughan and the several others who followed his lead is nonetheless a practiced attempt to balance self-abasement and high ambition. As we have seen in "Lycidas," Milton seeks his own version of that balance, and Marvell experiments with it momentarily in "The Coronet," "On a Drop of Dew," and "A Dialogue, between the Resolved Soul, and Created Pleasure." But Milton goes much further than Herbert would dream of going in claiming the gifts of the seer, and Marvell is too skeptical to believe that he or anyone can actually set forth the divine nature. The Neoplatonist alternative to its embodiment that Marvell proposes in the latter two poems undermines not only nature's forms but the poet's own artfulness. Unwilling to go that far on other occasions, he pulls back to a different kind of self-reduction in "The Garden" and "Upon Appleton House," where a wise passiveness keeps him at arm's length from both Miltonic genius of place and Herbert's struggle to negotiate further for a place. (He is somewhat overwhelmed by the vast design of *Paradise Lost,* though he acknowledges its success.) Both Milton and Marvell, then, inherit the risky venture of founding the poet's authority without courtly functions, but neither suggests quite the readership or the seesaw drama so pervasive in Herbert's best lyrics.

As a poet for all realms, Herrick takes an easier way, and I glance at him here primarily as a contrast to the those who pursue transcendental placings of lyric address. It is revealing that when he finds himself detained in a place without attraction, he does not analyze a subtle dissociation of mind from what it surveys or initiate proceedings to escape to another plane; he merely crosses it off his list with a reverse charm or curse, which implicitly sets up reception of a well-mannered nature:

> *Dean-Bourn,* farewell; I never look to see
> Deane, or thy warty incivility,
> Thy rockie bottome, that doth teare thy streams,
> And makes them frantick, ev'n to all extreames;
> To my content, I never sho'd behold,
> Were thy streames silver, or thy rocks all gold.
> Rockie thou art; and rockie we discover
> Thy men; and rockie are thy wayes all over.
> O men, O manners; Now, and ever knowne
> To be *A Rockie Generation!*
> A people currish; churlish as the seas;
> And rude (almost) as rudest Salvages
> With whom I did, and may re-sojourne when
> Rockes turn to Rivers, Rivers to Men.[1]

This dislike of the rude countryside may seem to argue for courtly preferences, but Herrick has actually little explicit interest in establishing a consistent decorum by which to judge an outlying province. He only knows what he does and does not like and sets aside "The Country Life" and "The Hock-cart, or Harvest home" to distinguish further. The point here, however, is simply that Herrick is open to the varied charms of country harvests, petticoats, veiled beauties, fairyland, bed chambers, and countless other places available for pictorial vignettes. Milton and the metaphysicals are less catholic and more driven to locate central and ultimate places.

Herbert of course makes the one realm, the temple, subsume all others. Few poets have studied a single locality as closely for intimations of end things. At the same time and in the same place he gauges the powers of word and image to express the divine presence—often in images as emblems and in words as abstractions beyond icons or tortured and broken into elements, as in the word-game poems "Jesu," "Anagram," "Love-Joy," "Paradise," and "Heaven." Neither abstraction nor emblematic concretion can offer more than an approximation of what the poet seeks—which is to be as close to God as he dare try to move. Terms such as "bliss," "peace," "love," and "trust" provide some preliminary access to that position, especially when they are coupled with God's presence everywhere, locally and universally, temporally and eternally. Unlike a normal human addressee, such a party can be evoked only by some use of theological terms, but he makes himself sufficiently available to allow overlapping between divine petition and the more ordinary situations of address. He dwells in the heart, in frames, in arks, cabinets and cupboards, houses, and windows, for instance, as well as in scripture and sacrament.[2] To situate him there, Herbert comes recurrently to the lowly preposition "in" among other words that signify an in-dwelling presence as opposed to a transcendent law giver. He thinks in terms of interpenetration, filled places, and mutual habitations of body and spirit. The temple is the chief place of presence, but it opens onto external realms and transplants the plenary world into its own enclosed space, where the poet can establish relations between man and creator. Rites, charms, rituals, word games, and festivities assist its sacramental manipulation of presence.

Even so, all means of bringing God into localities are imperfect, and for the poet no placement less than paradise can be fully satisfactory. As "The Flower" indicates, any request for permanent union with God is prideful. It cannot be granted and should not even be made—although that does not prevent the poet from lamenting, "O that I once past changing were / Fast in thy Paradise." Even the soul, God's "subtile room," like all things connected with the transient state, is subject to corruption and displacement. Sin can occupy it, and other competitive lodgers wish to dwell there and in the heart. Hence the poet must practice certain tactics of expulsion to make room, alternating appeals for divine presence with complaints and confessional purgations.

Herbert's quest for a fixed accord and a defined career is inseparable from such matters of placement. In "The Temper II," he calls for what he terms a fixed chair of grace to discipline his own unruly powers and to extract from himself songs of praise and reverence. Among his various offices, the poet prefers to render true hymns in an elevated style, but it is usually in ordinary things made special by grace that the divine presence registers. Under the right circumstances, virtually all images and their topics are expandable into vehicles of revelation, but they are also expendable and no sooner offer a glimpse of the divine presence than they betray their shortcomings. Their unreliability precipitates several crises in Herbert's affliction and unemployment poems, in which God seems to be no place, certainly not in a fixed chair of grace. The poet may make some progress limping along in his vocation, as "Affliction I" indicates, but his better moments tend to be strung out and anecdotal and his gains reversible.

In "Affliction I" he has been mistaken to think in the early days of his service that God's blessings were being openly and generously extended. Up to the reflective present of the poem, each new turn of service reveals new errors of perception and ever-perplexing entanglements that leave him without a sense of mission or place to serve:

> Yet lest perchance I should too happie be
>     In my unhappinesse,
> Turning my purge to food, thou throwest me
>     Into more sicknesses.
> Thus doth thy power crosse-bias me, not making
> Thine own gift good, yet me from my wayes taking.[3]

In the first of the alternating long and short line units here, Herbert turns the paradox of the feast on nothing into a searing irony saved from irreverence only by its humor. The same thought spills over into the second unit and prevents any comfortable adjustment of event to narration. The stanza works toward a typical closure beginning with a "thus" and an encompassing counter movement that leaves him momentarily stalled, but even as the unit closes formally, it keeps open and even raw the relationship itself.

When neither service nor the study of service succeeds, the poet turns about in a series of reversals and comes to a riddling conclusion, which breaks free of place, service, and all forms of rootedness:

> Now I am here, what thou wilt do with me
>     None of my books will show:
> I reade, and sigh, and wish I were a tree;
>     For sure then I should grow
> To fruit or shade: at least some bird would trust
> Her houshold to me, and I should be just.
>
> Yet, though thou troublest me, I must be meek;
>     In weaknesse must be stout.
> Well, I will change the service, and go seek
>     Some other master out.
> Ah my dear God! though I am clean forgot,
> Let me not love thee, if I love thee not.

Perhaps no ending in Herbert is more up in the air about the poet's possibilities for a household or a church to serve in. Yet it is also definitive in dramatizing an in-between state and in capitulating at the last moment. Coming at the end of an extremely busy movement of changing tonalities, it tightens up certain realizations of status and the rewards of service. In contest with himself, the poet alternates between weakness and assertion, which is roughly equivalent to alternating between a human logic that tries to define the servant's place and a passive faith in inscrutable divine purposes. The attractions of treeness are several. Trees are dumb and feel no pain, which would be an improvement over human tribulations.

Primarily, they simply grow and are useful, especially to birds. But Herbert gives the trope an added turn in "*I should be just*"; God, who should be his tree, has not been. Certainly at a minimum, masters should be to servants as trees to birds: not that trees do anything explicitly for birds, but they are there to be nested and sung in. However, as the subjunctive mood indicates, the speaker's desire for either vegetable painlessness or safe perch is desperate; no permanent comforts are to be expected.

A more satisfying way to handle affliction would be to resign oneself to it. But that idea, too, Herbert abandons in coming to a conclusion that reveals the dialectical skill of the rubrician, who shuffles three implicit matters, service, love, and reward, in such a way as to reveal their close relationship. The services of poets to masters and to Petrarchan ladies in predecessor complaint lyrics are reducible to a single formula in this revised master-servant relationship. As the "Ah" suggests, Herbert comes to that realization with conviction. The outbreak signals a new self-awareness as the argument struggles to higher ground. Service is to be rendered simply by love, which is its own reward. Although they abandon most of the aggression of the complaint, the final lines do not come to an unconditional surrender, as "clean forgot" indicates.[4] What is new about the concluding formula is an emphasis equally on love and on "thee," which reminds us that love is theological or Pauline as well as personal: "If I love *thee* not" (as opposed to thy rewards), "let me not *love* thee." Such a balancing of love's proper object and the willed action of the servant would take away the reward where the service is not appropriate. By reversing the emphases—"If I *love* thee not, let me not love *thee*," or perhaps "*not* love thee"—the speaker could also suggest a paradoxical removal of the service whenever the attitude goes awry. Either way, whatever previous relationships may have clouded the poet's sense of place, God has not contracted his service in any way that obligates him to pay for them in comforts nor of course in any way recognizable to those who seek careers through patronage or acknowledgments from mistresses. Both the complaint lyric and the love lyric shift their ground as the speaker cancels the secular analogies that have fed his own grievances. The good servant may not deviate into other courses that translate God into a providential well-wisher or compress him into the doings of prosperity. All expendables have been discarded, all analogies questioned.

The structure of the last two stanzas is more intricate, however, than any such summary can indicate. Herbert has by this point played with a great many variations of the basic narrative stanza in a seemingly over-extended numbering of grief's phases. Here he progressively shortens the emotional lines and winds into a counter movement that challenges the leisure of the stanza, turning one section against another. The psychological tension is all inside the speaker, the charges being entirely one-sided and without reply; but that makes all the more devastating the rejoinder he applies in the final couplet and the check he gives in advance to any future impulse to get up bills of grievance. The first long-short unit, "Now I am here, what thou wilt do with me / None of my books will show," opens the hands in a gesture that says in effect, "here I effectively and entirely am: honesty and recollection can bring forth nothing further to bear on the case." The speaker does not pout over the futility of books, which we can assume to include all divine ones and perhaps all he himself has written as a clue to what he might still do, certainly all that a student with painstaking research might discover in the libraries that record the tasks and contracts by which God rules ecclesiae, poets, and ordinary men.

The ground has been surveyed, then, and no act of intelligence remains to be exercised, no human help brought up; and so the case being indeed quite helpless, he can only move from narrative to current trials and put that helplessness on display: "I read, and sigh, and wish I were a tree." Herbert exploits the stanza's second unit not to open a new topic or to augment by illustration and example but to pry the lid off that great reservoir of futility. After a stop and a regrouping of thought, the follow-up can then be released: "For sure then I should grow / To fruit or shade. . . ." That afterthought comes from a harbored imaginative world of quite another kind, and we begin to see that a stanzaic turn in Herbert's close unfolding is a self turning, a ransacking of every corner of consciousness and pious feeling and its harbored rebellion for enticements to change the terms of service. That so much stanza remains with which he can elaborate this hypothetical unthinking state of bliss remembers in smaller form the many elaborations of grievances and narrative ins and outs of this very flexible and surprisingly ample verse unit throughout. In its capaciousness here, the stanza is allowed to spread until God might have room to enter should he see fit, as on other occasions the poet hopes he will through cracks in the poem's surface. But it is also rigorously disciplined in conducting the drama, which for the moment holds the public outside until the doors can be flung open and the drama published.

It is not entirely clear at this point how much that publication may be anticipated by the act of speaking, which after all sets a pattern from which others may profit; but if any closure proves to be possible, it will have to proceed not from instructions offered in some definitive way to readers but from the tentative approach of poet to God, just as the mystical repast that outsiders are expressly invited to share is first of all the product of a similar speaker's reluctant progress toward love. The stanza here allows only a brief turnout in place to let us think of its larger context. Actually, *The Temple* permits similar well-managed but often longer glances in its excursions into the outer or historical world, from which it looks back at the temple-sanctuary and its special discipline. The manipulation of overall and limited points of view is part of that placement of units within a whole and is a suspension as well as a pacing, as points of view we have already recognized are held in abeyance while others are inserted. I note in passing that this art of insinuation is akin to the technique of third-person narrative in which point of view is sufficiently inside a character to render his perceptions, but also sufficiently flexible to allow concurrent or intermittent authorial judgment. The control of small inner spaces and reflections of larger ones—like the leverage of subordinate thoughts uttered in asides that lift edifices into view—no one has ever managed as Herbert does. (Getting so much into the short compass both of stanzas and colloquial lines is one of his singular triumphs; another is constant circulation through events and types from the greater story, as "Easter-wings," for instance, identifies the present request for inspiration with the sinking and soaring of all mankind from Adam.)

It is only in retrospect from "Love III" that we are allowed to see how much a given turnout depends upon the security of the whole and the sense of place at table the servant anticipates as the enactment of a final, ceremonial contract. In "Affliction I" the stanza allows just such small satisfactions as will mislead the speaker and us awhile into thinking that self-assertion offers something independently, as again in "*I* should be just," or even more loudly and incriminatingly "I should be *just.*" But even in that false pride (as though a mere human could solve the world's injustice), the speaker does not yet allow a hint of petulance. It is simply that one must be permitted a satisfying self-estimate now and then if other rewards are scarce. The rhyming of "tree" with "me" suggests one sort of answer to the opening question of what to do with me, and the rhyming of "grow" with "show" virtually finishes that answer.

"I would make me a tree to thrive and show; I would let me at least produce, as poet or simply as man." The rhyming of "trust" and "just" escalates a notch toward grand yet tight abstractions for the contractual bonds and of master-servant relations. All such bonds, of course, would depend upon trust and justice—would if men controlled their destinies, were just, or could be trees.

Taking off from that self-satisfying fantasy with its lingering indulgence of the complaint, the last stanza proceeds first to some timely bracing. Herbert expends just the first unit on that task, the time being short. The moment is obviously right for a gathering of some sort, but the problem still remains, what actually does one do? What substantial progress can one show from the complaint, upon which to base a change? That first unit substitutes a convenient axiom and an attitude for a real answer, and its show of strength proves to be hollow. The speaker knows that the thorn is still in his foot; he simply vows not to limp anymore. Herbert gives that forbearance a semblance of possibility by the interrupting acknowledgement "though thou troublest me" before settling into a deeply rooted Christian stoicism which, unsatisfying as it is here, has in fact ended many a similar debate over God's unfathomable ways. But the first new searing pain usually drives out such resolve in the truly tender; and the second unit here, so well deployed now as an antithesis in this quickening pace, allows petulence to emerge from hiding at long last. It has issued enough disguises, rationalizations, and wayward plans to throw the unwary off the scent; but now that it has stood up in "Well, I will change the service," it will be satisfied with nothing less than a complete apology, or a reversal of policy. The "some other" master betrays its lack of will, however, and makes it appear an idle threat, uttered to indicate simply that the last straw has fallen with all the back-breaking weight it is reputed to have.

It is just when one can't go on that one discovers that one can go on, and why. In a final movement unpredicted by earlier stanza closures despite their variety, Herbert riddles to a high plane we had no right to expect from the speaker without divine intervention but know to be exactly right as soon as the view from there unfolds. Such formal skill, in which every syllable comes down with the right weight at the right moment, can come only out of psychological adeptness and great wisdom. None of those who learned from Herbert discovered quite how to do precisely that with a stanza, each of whose lines is right, each of whose repetitions builds a poetic whole that in turn finds a place in a singular volume—self-contained, complete, yet locating its place in a greater universe outside.

What contract between master and servant does the final couplet propose? Actually none that is binding both ways, and so the closing even here remains open in important respects. By floating several possible readings of the lines in their hovering stresses, Herbert accepts unconditionally the cross-biasing he has complained about earlier. He stops all conceivable escapes from the one course that will work, which is to serve by love and forget the rest. The proper scene for that role is the temple, where rites and sacraments are seated in their doctrinal context. In effect the speaker proposes an agreement against his own temptations to profane the place where love for its own sake prevails. Whether or not God also loves does not really figure in his calculation, which is strictly preventative. However, even if such paraphrases (among others that are conceivable) managed to disentangle the main elements of the riddle, the final line would still not be definitive or sacramental in itself. No answer comes from God, who is not imagined to have descended either into symbols or into ritual acts. Nor does "Affliction I" suggest that he should. This is only one among a good many spiritual exercises and small dramas on the way to the definitive enactment of service and love in "Love III." What Herbert requests for the moment is a safeguard against the inclination to bargain too much. As rhythm and emphasis hesitate among possibilities, the ending is glimpsed and postponed; it tends to become pausal, as though in an alternation of earned repose and renewed struggle. The implicit household topic assures us that all quarrels are in the family. The placement that the poet requires, to return to it, is not a well-substantiated position or a permanent chair of grace but a spiritual condition that will survive cycles of hardship and prosperity and begin to rise toward the everywhereness of divine love and trust. The speaker thereby extricates the soul a little from its circumstances and its autobiography. Ultimately it will require no furniture or objects except those of communion and love's substance served therein.

"Affliction I" is not the only Herbert poem to cast a longing eye on the advantages of rootedness and the still more attractive prospect of rising into God's place directly. As two other employment poems, "Temper I" and "The Flower" indicate, Herbert had difficulty reconciling his ambitious desire to be a poet of transcendence with his awareness of the fixed state to which he is consigned along with all other mortals. In "Employment II" the speaker defines the soul as motion—certainly as stirred by emotion:

> Man is no starre, but a quick coal
>     Of mortall fire:
> Who blows it not, nor doth controll
>     A faint desire,
> Lets his own ashes choke his soul. . . .
>
> Life is a businesse, not good cheer:
>     Ever in warres.
> The sunne still shineth there or here,
>     Whereas the starres
> Watch an advantage to appeare.
>
> Oh that I were an Orenge-tree,
>     That busie plant!
> Then should I ever laden be,
>     And never want
> Some fruit for him that dressed me.

However, even busy trees sooner or later come to an end. As "Vertue" reminds the rose, "Thy root is ever in its grave, / And thou must die." In "Employment II" the speaker is even less hopeful:

> But we are still too young or old;
>     The Man is gone,
> Before we do our wares unfold:
>     So we freeze on,
> Untill the grave increase our cold.

Thus manhood disappears before the poet gets his fortune made or his volume out, and the well-manured soil claims the plant it grew. The soul is more definitively smothered by the general conditions of bodies than it is by the ashes of its own past activity. In "The Flower" Herbert would break loose altogether from the botanical cycles of productivity and freezing and be transcendent, transplanted past changing. But to gain that ultimate garden requires a disciplined recognition of mortal rootedness and patience to endure it.

Herbert comes to a similar realization of the poet's wayward inclinations in "The Temper I," which at first laments the torments of spatial extension and the vast discrepancies between earth, heaven, and hell.[5] Stretched to extremes and trying desparately to adjust to them, the speaker comes to prefer any secure place however small to the vast universe. But again a seasoned spirit accepts all places, even displacements, and the inclination to roost near God gives way to a willingness to run risks in order to encompass a greater arena:

> Yet take thy way; for sure thy way is best:
>     Stretch or contract me, thy poore debter:
> This is but tuning of my breast,
>     To make the musick better.

The service here is not merely love but music of a tempered kind and hence a form of employment. It finds its best balance in the final stanza, which I take to be one of Herbert's crucial statements about placement. It is an answer of sorts to the discrepancy between mortal rootedness, or cohabitation with God in limited frames and cabinets, and transcendent soaring. Its style has some of each level:

> Whether I flie with angels, fall with dust,
> Thy hands made both, and I am there:
> Thy power and love, my love and trust
> Make one place ev'ry where.

The paradox here is more definitive than that of "Affliction I" but equally riddling. A satisfactory notion of placement both for the professional maker of praise songs and the typical sinner comes with the realization of God's omnipresence and his agreement to be represented to men by love. If one place *is* everywhere, as the chastened would-be hymnist decides, then one time must be all times, and any moment God choses to enter takes on the quality of eternity. It may also follow that activity is really disguised repose. One can be rooted in place as a mortal but busy and encompassing as a mind and spirit. The definitions are again theological, but the experience is no less personal for that.

Knowing this with some certainty, the poet reaches into a reserve of power by means of abstractions that are often his best "topics" or placements. They are terms of inaction inasmuch as they do not require a busy copiousness to encompass God's blessings, as "Providence" does—except as "make" requires an exercise of love, trust, and power to bring one to rest. The solution is much more impressive than the bland coziness of "Even-song," which concludes:

> My God, thou art all love.
> Not one poore minute scapes thy breast,
> But brings a favour from above;
> And in this love, more then in bed, I rest.

Granted that an evening song properly ends in bedtime prayer, the style is that of one who muses to himself and comes to a sense of blessedness without struggle or a sense of outside distances, with all their possibilities for alienation. "The Temper I" does not define any further uses of poetry to help one arrive at an awareness of God's everywhereness, but it does suggest that the better music of the preceding stanza both moderates the extremes of complaint and high praise and paradoxically extends moderation toward wonder and mystery. When "everywhere" is thus filled with divine presence, one can go nowhere in the cosmic vastness without encountering it. Godlessness has been expelled in the most inclusive of all Herbert's cleansing operations.

That momentary confidence does not prevent the poet's lapsing into a sense of uselessness in the sequence that follows, which includes "Employment I" and its realization once again of the perils of rootedness:

> If as a flowre doth spread and die,
> Thou wouldst extend me to some good,
> Before I were by frosts extremitie
> Nipt in the bud;
> The sweetnesse and the praise were thine;
> But the extension and the room,
> which in thy garland I should fill, were mine
> At thy great doom.
>
> For as thou dost impart thy grace,
> The greater shall our glorie be.
> The measure or our joyes is in this place,
> The stuffe with thee.

The poet would have God materialize a place in which to be served, not only now but after judgment. His use of "extension" and "room" is curious, however. Sweetness and praise fly up in words like spiritual essences and become God's "stuff" (the poet's substance and matter lodged in the perfect reader), while the tangible residue (that which has dimension and placement in metaphor?) remains with the poet. Presumably it is the shell of the poem or its mechanics of saying, the "measure," that belong to him and thus all the labor, while grace can be imparted with ease should God choose. Certainly being will dilate only when moment and place are filled with such a gift. But at the moment, though he has measures aplenty, he languishes uninspired, without produce or sweet smell, not as an orange tree but a tuneless reed:

> I am no link of thy great chain,
> But all my companie is a weed.
> Lord place me in thy consort; give one strain
> To my poore reed.

Even the parallels with natural processes, limiting enough in themselves in "The Flower," break down when the poet falls into such unproductive periods, and then no place will serve as meeting ground. The quandary of the unemployed is here compounded; where the sixteenth-century poet often felt injured by denials of the service he had been trained for, Herbert's poet is deprived of much more: his membership in the natural species; the great chain joins low to high without him, giving placement to all degrees but nipping his potential poetic flowers in the bud.

Apart from the failings of language in such unsupported moments, Herbert does not usually celebrate nature for its own sake. Nature must either receive special visitations or shrivel and in neither case manages to stay healthy for long. Nor can the poet exploit its potential worth for elegiac feeling as the reverse of celebration. In "Vertue," for instance, the daily cycles and the seasons serve primarily to set off the soul's passage beyond them, as we have seen. Spring contains things that are sweet and perishable and therefore tempting, but the poet assesses them cooly and in the final stanza converts all intimations of elegiac feeling into a sense of the soul's marvelous escape. He gains considerable leverage from the fact that the soul is superior to those sweet days, roses, and springs that we ordinarily prize. The final fire clears them away almost as rubbish.

The poet's impulse to move within the precincts of God's protection has the outstanding drawback that he cannot stay there and still live a temporal life. An incarnate word presents an alternative, however, and also a transferable word power that escapes the disadvantages of abstraction and the perils of rootedness in place and time. Herbert finds its descent into the frame of bodies and poems even as he discovers it in cabinets, the heart's lodgings, and houses. Word-shapes such as "The Altar" and "Easter-wings" suggest a hieroglyphic capacity for the divine being to be inscribed in materials, just as "Sepulchre," "Good-Friday," and "Obedience" look for engravings on surfaces. The poet too would engrave rhymes in steel and locate immortal love, "author of this great frame," within the compass of poetic forms. But it is the incarnation of deity that makes such things possible, or as "Anagram" remarks concerning the letters of Mary's name:

> How well her name an *Army* doth present,
> In whom the *Lord of Hosts* did pitch his tent!

Juggling the arrangement of letters renders different paraphrases of the same word, each version of which is an implicit comparison to the original word. Not only is Mary improbable as God's housing, no ordinary tent will hold the entire celestial host. Yet this one does so in defiance of logic. The renaissance was accustomed to thinking of shifting places for God's location—in residences such as the enclosed garden (a figure for Mary in Jesuit iconology), the book of creatures, and various hieroglyphic shapes. Herbert here includes the womb as the smallest and most human of enclosures and therefore the most startling demonstration of God's compression of everywhere into one place. The fruitfulness of the well-laden tree, the prolific bearing of poems, and the tree-housing of singing birds are imperfect variants of both Mary's capacity to house the Lord and her name's capacity to encompass the celestial host. The key here is "presentation." No one doubts God's capacity to dwell everywhere at once in seventeenth-century theology, but by what runic magic is the poet's wordcraft to achieve the equivalent of a sacramental union? By petitions and prayers that seek presence as voice? Or simply by witty recognition that letters falling into the right order suddenly reveal and present?

Whatever we may think of the actual powers of presentation that the letters M–a–r–y have, the poet is not always fortunate enough to stumble upon language that will lift citational or descriptive loads out of their specific locations. "Church-monuments," for instance, reveals another side of signs, their tendency to crumble. The body of writing can as well be dust as incarnate presence. All bodily things, in fact, are restless. They constantly disintegrate and recombine without repose, and that problem with transcience is only compounded by our erecting of monuments as supposedly permanent texts in which the body may read lessons:

>                  I gladly trust
>
> My bodie to this school, that it may learn
> To spell his elements, and finde his birth
> Written in dustie heraldrie and lines;
> Which dissolution sure doth best discern,
> Comparing dust with dust, and earth with earth.
> These laugh at Jeat and Marble put for signes,
>
> To sever the good fellowship of dust,
> And spoil the meeting. What shall point out them,
> When they shall bow, and kneel, and fall down flat
> To kisse those heaps, which now they have in trust?

The answer to the last question is that nothing will point out monuments when they fall because they themselves are the best signs that men can build. Beyond significance or intelligence (once the soul has left it), dust offers no further location. For the time being, however, the spelling and decoding that these signs make possible are useful for moral purposes. Here and now the body's lecturer cannot transcend them, but it can point to them and interpret them. Also, physical monument and prayer are opposite and complementary placements in their respective corners of the church, as nature and the abode of virtuous souls are in "Vertue." As one falls, the other learns to rise and chiefly live.

This opposition is too neat, however, to do justice to the ways the poet finds to assemble a visible world as his native setting and as one of God's places. Less mutually exclusive than dust-bound signs and spiritual "understanding," the goal of prayer, are two quite different kinds of expressive signs in "Peace." There the poet advances from certain ambiguous places to objects seated in biblical allegory, in much the same way the poet's ventures into hermeneutic demonstrations in "Heaven" and "H. Scriptures II" are corrected by sacred words from scripture and heaven itself. The cave, the rainbow, and the garden of the earlier stanzas of "Peace" are as unstable as "the trees and leaves" of "Heaven" and the "dispersed herbs" of "H. Scriptures II." The cave issues its admonition to the pilgrim in a voice like that of pagan oracles. The evidence against the rainbow is more damaging because a rainbow should suggest a covenant of peace but in this case breaks and scatters like other monuments and signs. Neither the reclusive life of the cave nor nature's beauty gives the pilgrim the right sort of peace, then, although they seem logical places to look. Also, where the right sort of garden (Marvell's, for instance), combines beauty and privacy, the garden to which Herbert's pilgrim turns has serious drawbacks. The best its "gallant flower" can do is lead toward the church as a different sort of garden wherein the grain of gospel grows. Not all these locations are totally without promise, but they are indefinable until they have been transposed into biblical typology. Dealing in more secure types and figures within the precincts of a church, the "rev'rend good old man" who narrates the last half of the poem places the pilgrim among a different order of symbols whose harvest is easily decoded:

> Take of this grain, which in my garden grows,
>   And grows for you;
> Make bread of it: and that repose
>   And peace, which ev'ry where
> With so much earnestnesse you do pursue,
>   Is onely there.

The surface of the parable becomes distinctly unimportant once such translations are provided. As St. Augustine remarks about metaphors, they are sweet and enticing to the intelligence, but "Hardly anything may be found in these obscure places which is not found plainly said elsewhere."[6] What counts is the temple's founding and the peace it provides in doctrine and sacrament. Although in one sense the seeker cannot really possess that peace even in communion until end things arrive, the definition is complete enough for a foretaste. He at least knows that he cannot seek anywhere else for it: it is *only* here, where the reverend man indicates. As the search concludes, the substance of peace is the same as the substance of joy, love, redemption, life, bliss, gladness of the best, and other Herbert abstractions: all these meet at the end, and their realized definitions guarantee lyric celebration in the space that God fills. Herbert's endings combine a finished definition of place with a rising movement toward that something still further off. Stopping short of Crashaw's exclamatory outbreaks at that point, Herbert does not push poetry to the next phase, which in some ecstatic extremity would stretch language beyond its capacities.

Similar to "Peace" in its providing of sure signs in a middle state of biblical typology (between nature's disintegrating placements and sacramental union) is "H. Scriptures II," which emphasizes both the certainty of scriptural language and one's need to interpret it skillfully:

> This verse marks that, and both do make a motion
> Unto a third, that ten leaves off doth lie:
> Then as dispersed herbs do watch a potion,
> These three make up some Christians destinie.

As so often in Herbert, the purpose is to realize something about the final placement that constitutes bliss. Among biographical events, the interpreter finds his directions very scattered; but a totality of places and moments is fully transcribed in sacred writing. Despite their diverse authors and scattered locations, the scriptures are bound within a single cover where a knowledgeable interpreter can find all the matters that concern him. The secret lies in connection: as herbs from here and there are unrelated until the chemist provides the recipe that makes a potion, so statements and events in scriptural history lie sprawling, as poems do in *The Temple,* until an act of interpretation combines them. That same act *dislocates* each passage also, as herbs must be plucked from the field to serve in a healing formula and the reader must be drawn out of personal circumstances to find his destiny among scriptural types.

Herbert demonstrates a final type in the courtship of the sinner by Love in "Love III." As his most noteworthy sacramental poem, "Love III" closes the volume disarmingly. It implicitly provides the chair of grace the poet has asked for earlier and resolves the discrepancy between the rootedness of the mortal poet and the desire for transcendence. It allows no riddles of the kind that forestall the divine-human union in "Affliction I" or the theological formula of "The Temper I." It brings negotiations between sinner and love quickly to a point on the model of a quiet drawing-room talk. The exclamations and apostrophes that might ordinarily signal the speaker's identification with a transcendent other (or a Petrarchan enamorata) are entirely absent, even though it is nothing less than the union of God and man that the poem approaches. In contrast, the union of romantic poets with transcendent powers through objects comes with the fervor of spiritual effort, which is sometimes evident from the outset of the poem. For instance, in the first lines of Keats's odes, the poet has already risen to the high pitch of "Thou still unravish'd bride of quietness" and "O Goddess! hear these tuneless numbers." Wordsworth begins with an address of some intensity in "Oh blithe New-comer" ("To the Cuckoo") and "Stern Daughter of the voice of God!" ("Ode to Duty"). Shelley begins "Ode to the West Wind" with "O wild West Wind, thou breath of Autumn's being" and "To A Skylark" with "Hail to thee, blithe Spirit!" Given the nature of the romantic ode, such addresses are perhaps not very comparable to Herbert's conversational mode, but they underscore the tranquillity with which Herbert's divine being enters the poet's presence and makes gaps crossable and dislocations curable. The poet's own earlier extremities of fervor and agitation derive from motives that usually prove to be reproachable. The ambitious romantic in him must be disciplined. When a way out of the world's labyrinth does appear, as in "The Pearl," it turns out to be simple enough to preclude strain. In any case the poet's other dramatized roles and petitions for place collapse into the one he stages in "Love III." If Herbert does not look elsewhere in that final moment for landmarks in biography or social position, as he does in "Affliction I," it is because a single gesture suffices to place him at table.

No other poet in the renaissance offers so condensed a placement for lyric as Herbert's in *The Temple* in general and in "Love III" in particular, in a locality that transcends the court's versions of love and courtship and even Donne's private room while absorbing their intimate relations-of-two into dialogue form. The enactment of these relations quiets all previous yearnings, which derive from the sinner's unworthiness and sense of lost paradise. But it also avoids the ecstasies of "a true hymn." The key moment is not the ascension after crucifixion but the human supper before. It is still a historical moment that requires the acknowledgement of sin and betrayal and a sacramental miracle. The poet's response is not an "imping" of his wing on Christ's but the ritual enactment of breaking bread. The two parties stand simultaneously on earth and in paradise. Actually, we see no specific setting; the table could be set in the wilderness, as of old, in one's private chambers, or in the church. The poet blends into Everyman, whose voice is paradoxically both choral and personal; as though in answer to "Affliction I," service is love and love is service. Both seek ritual form and suggest the bending of the poetic office to a simple narrative allegory that recreates in one time and moment a relationship that has always been intended.

Since that relationship is paradigmatic and the personality of the poet is put in abeyance, Herbert in a sense finds a place for the divine presence in a *common* identity committed to ritual. The food of the repast may be an individual possession, since each of those at the doorway must decide to enter and accept it, but it is also a general gift, the taking of which abolishes all minor distinctions and cancels accidents of self. In this very unequal union of divine and human parties—but also very ordinary act of taking a place at table—Herbert has upped the admission requirements of Jonson's initiated circle and further mystified Donne's relations-of-two. His redefinition of love here and in other poems of *The Temple* and his rethinking of what makes a closed circle prove in subsequent sacred lyricists the less settling the greater the poet who heeds them. Nothing quite like his balance of self-concern and self-abasement, his enlivening of plain style with wit, or even his contained book of lyrics concluded by "Love III" is evident in Vaughan despite Vaughan's attraction to him. Milton of course never wished a priestly sacramental or ritual conveyance for the word so long as celestial light purges and disperses darkness inwardly. Herrick in *Noble Numbers* reverts to a simpler piety and in *Hesperides* forges his own selective receptions of Donne and Jonson (seldom of Donne, often of Jonson), prompters of a book as various as Herbert's is single-minded.

*Ile shew thee that capacious roome*
*In which thy Father Johnson now is plac't,*
*As in a Globe of Radiant fire.*

H-575

# HERRICK'S BOOK OF REALMS AND MOMENTS

## CHAPTER SEVEN

### TAKING INVENTORY

The seventeenth-century folding of existing kinds seemingly left very little as simple and intact as it was, as, for instance, in the Jacobean drama's subversion of comedy and tragedy, the stretching of love poems and sonnets in Donne, Herbert, and Marvell, and Milton's modifications of the masque, pastoral, epic, and tragedy. Almost a second Alexandrian movement in this respect, the poetry of Herbert, Vaughan, Milton, and Marvell turns in upon itself to question the functions of poetry. Herrick at first glance appears to be an exception. Of all seventeenth-century poets, he has perhaps the most casual tolerance of variety and the most unsustained fits of self-examination. He ranges easily from metaphysical wit to the simple piety of *Noble Numbers,* and from Jonson's assumptions about a cultivated small circle to a sense of the poet's near isolation. That he betrays so little concern for the national traumas marching and countermarching before him over a long career suggests that he could stay afloat. Yet he has the tetchy good sense to rid himself of the warty "Dean-bourn" and its churlish generations when they become intolerable.

A similar casualness is evident in his relations to readers. In what may be the last of his yearly holidays with a group of them, for instance, he bids farewell without commotion:

> Loth to depart, but yet at last, each one
> Back must now go to's habitation:
> Not knowing thus much, when we once do sever,
> Whether or no, that we shall meet here ever.
> As for my self, since time a thousand cares

> And griefs hath fil'de upon my silver hairs;
> 'Tis to be doubted whether I next yeer,
> Or no, shall give ye a re-meeting here.
> If die I must, then my last vow shall be,
> You'l with a tear or two, remember me,
> Your sometime Poet; but if fates do give
> Me longer date, and more fresh springs to live:
> Oft as your field, shall her old age renew,
> *Herrick* shall make the meddow-verse for you.
> "The parting verse, the feast there ended." H-355

These are not very close friends or the encounters would be more than yearly, but they are stable, and the poet can claim a special place among them, not as a center or a key educator but as simply one of them. Out of gatherings small commemorations grow, and out of the permanent departure of the poet a stronger feeling is to be allowed for a moment. So spring seasons come to a natural end for the individual, while the group continues to balance renewals and continued aging. In between occasions, each has his separate domesticity to occupy him and whatever tribulations that may mean.

It is for this reasoned tone and coupleted accounting that Jonson appears chief among Herrick's poetic company and brings "manners" into lyric compass. But the similarity serves mainly to underscore a difference and mark Herrick's place among the others of that Alexandrian turn: before society, whether rural and given or urban and to be cultivated by the poet, come the objects of place and occasion, and these are not as easily administered as Jonson's or as reducible to domestic possession. Although set forth without metaphysical complexity in poems of some formal regularity and definition, they can indeed be elusive to the critical touch. What counts about them is not merely their surfaces but their uses in the community and their emanations and affinities with the observer and with predecessors, who lead in several directions. Yet unlike the precisely etched objects of poets like William Carlos Williams and Marianne Moore, they do not stand alone but serve as emissaries, often from realms of lesser mythology—of faery or pagan gods, for instance. The messages they bring are cryptic and unsystematic and often not very earth-shaking, and so the poet is not expected to make important announcements at those yearly "re-meetings." Despite Herrick's commitment to epigram and sententiousness at times, they elude abstraction and moral urging, which offer interpreters such satisfying paraphrases of other seventeenth-century poets. Although they may stand as specimens and types—these Maypoles, wassails, custards, "ductile Codlin's skins," and trout-flies curious wings—we are not meant to reduce them to shadows or make them into signs and emblems, as we are encouraged to do with the landscapes of a Herbert or a Vaughan.

That our placement of them must be so tentative is largely due to Herrick's preference for contrast and variety in place of idea and arrangement. Certainly he provides decoration and furniture not merely for one but for several places, as *Hesperides* introduces us to many kingdoms in turn without mapping their connections or their mutual influences. Where he does decide to bring landscapes and their objects into some sort of order, he depends more upon custom and ceremony than upon rational principle. Neither Platonism nor Christian doctrine figures consistently in his poetry, for instance, and where one or the other does it is likely to ornament an occasion and appeal less to the devotional spirit than to the aesthetic sense.

Lacking a map of realms or exact calendar of moments, what does Herrick offer by way of guidance to interpret his objects and their settings? The introductory poems of *Hesperides* provide some early indications if not very conclusive answers. "To the Most illustrious and Most hopeful Prince, Charles," for instance, touches upon several realms—the book, nature, and the state—and gives them the special aura of sanctioned, important orders. The poet is to transport the fires of inspiration into those morning and evening stars, the volume's individual poems. Their source, the prince, preserves them even as they preserve him—permanence and glory being so entwined that one cannot exist without the other. The difficulty is that the volume does not pursue the prominence Herrick assigns either the prince or the state, which as it turns out, is true of nearly everything: whatever holds the stage at a given moment may be flattered with thematic weight and dignity, but in the way of a variety show. We have no reason to think that Herrick takes his large claims for Charles seriously, given the flat style, the conventional imagery, and the quick diversion of his attention to other matters.[1]

If from the dedicatory poem we are led momentarily to expect a book of royalist apologies, we are relieved to find a quite different list of subjects in "The Argument of his Book." As the term "argument" suggests, these other subjects are systematized to a degree, if not as rigorously as logical argument would require. The poetic site shifts from court to countryside, from sovereign to folk and to fairyland royalty. Although the sestet rises to full voice before it ends, the poem is relaxed in its inventory. The items it lists are predominantly natural, outfitted for celebration, and humanized by custom. The catalogue progresses from country items to a higher vision, but it does not really constitute a program or suggest an itinerary for the poetic sensibility among increasingly sophisticated matters. Where Milton's progress through joy and pensiveness in "L'Allegro" and "Il Penseroso" pits one set of assets against another, Herrick enumerates without much contrast except for heaven and hell. And where Milton's realm of fairy is clearly for the folk and stands somewhere between country song and visionary dream, Herrick's as it turns out serves primarily to enlist the eye with detail and to put common objects in a foreign light. It restricts mythology to household matters of mealtime, love, and furnishings. He accepts both his rural and his fairy realms for what folkways have made of them and concentrates on the description and on the genius of place.[2] Nor does he suggest the sort of optical illusions that Marvell works with in "Upon Appleton House"; despite the delight in disorder that "The Argument" suggests and several poems explore, he does not cause appearances to shift so confusedly as to throw the venture of seeing and assessing entirely into doubt. We recognize none of the experiments in perspective or anamorphic painting in him that we do in Marvell. He forgoes any dialectical use of realms to interrogate each other or to raise doubts about human citizenship in them.

What sort of organization does Herrick propose for the catalogue of topics that "The Argument" and *Hesperides* give us?[3] Does the movement toward the final couplet, for instance, really give it the scope it claims in its otherworldly expansion?

First, technically, Herrick manages a certain order by likenesses in rhythm, sound, and principles of adjacency. The surfaces of words and their phonic network, always important to him, make up a large part of the poem's sense of arrangement as well as its playfulness, which is vital to its sense of ease. Wassails and Maypoles are an impedimenta for holidays, with histories and symbolic dimensions. Second, the list of subjects is highly selective: the months and the ceremonial elements are a springtime concentration, and the balms and spices are obviously not plain but special fare. The relative certainty of seasonal things coming around in course is undercut by a questioning of origins, since roses had to have beginnings and thus a time when they were surprising. It is as a mythological poet concerned with fictions of origin that Herrick stresses ovidian metamorphosis: that both times and things "transshift" urges us toward the realm of faery—and ultimately behind it to the greater mythology of heaven and hell.

On one hand this carries argument and explanation toward absolutes. On the other hand, the introduction of the sacred, which has the apparent effect of encircling the poem with outer limits, is more pausal than definitive. As the poem opens a door upon the stock and surplus of *Hesperides* and its loosely assembled topics, heaven and hell in that context are not really binding even among the list of subjects they conclude. They do not gather up the rest or subordinate them—merely cast suspicion upon some of them. Although the minister in Herrick no doubt sees them as ultimates, the poet does not apply them to a scaling down of all other matters in proportion. In any case "The Argument" takes no particular notice of the potential dangers of sensuous revels and epicurean excesses, and just how the poet plans to sing of hell and what importance it will have remain mysteries both here and in the rest of the volume. Nonetheless, what seems at first familiar and easily definable in the daily or seasonal terms of the octave now becomes more elusive. The introduction of far different realms makes the reader pause as he steps through the doorway.

Even so, it is important to see that Herrick's catalogue of topics and the volume's subsequent miscellany are also far from random. The gaps between items are not an indication of confusion or an indefinable universe. The difference is evident if we think of the neutralized miscellany of Moore or Williams, especially in the latter's excursions into a happenstance world in poems like "Term." For Herrick, randomness has no great appeal, although disorder of course does. Where Williams takes delight in the "anarchy of poverty" ("The Poor"), for instance, Herrick's disorder is almost decorative. Heaven and hell bring the encompassing framework of "The Argument" to bear upon its miscellany somewhat tentatively but with sufficient force to conclude the sonnet. The final declaration climbs to higher ground from which creation's panorama may be seen, even as the poem begins to ask for a kind of explanation that requires a visionary poet, or an epic, and thereby leaves the lyricist suspended between realms. The balance between anticipation and the formal rounding off of the inventory is nicely maintained.

What "The Argument" announces about its subjects is both their particularity and the kind of access the poet will take to them. He will in fact sing "piece by piece," which means that he plans to act not as an epic poet gathering a cosmos into a single structure but as a poet of isolated moments and glittering images. The volume's multiplicity of surfaces promotes a seeing-in-parts that increases the observer's wealth "by subdividing it finely." Just so Robert Harbison describes Francesco Colonna's *Hypnerotomachia,* and although Herrick may not be a Poliphilo—a lover of "too many Polias," whose parts are multiplied by her wardrobe, as Harbison suggests of that more distracted lover—he is nonetheless a great "lover of many." He "manufactures series . . . feeds himself with course after course," until such a surfeit suggests that "there is no end to the succession of ascending thoughts we can have."[4] Anyone who reads Herrick's collection of small pieces consecutively sees this variety long before he locates any principle of order or recurrence. Even the volume's most expansive moments are in a sense belittled by the casualness of attitude that marks the movement from piece to piece. What counts is the poet's performance on each occasion, in each place, hallowed or profane.

CLOTHES AND THE FURNISHINGS OF FAIRYLAND

> A sweet disorder in the dresse
> Kindles in cloathes a wantonnesse:
> A Lawne about the shoulders thrown
> Into a fine distraction:
> An erring Lace, which here and there
> Enthralls the Crimson Stomacher. . . .
> Doe more bewitch me, then when Art
> Is too precise in every part.[5]
>
> "Delight in Disorder" H-83

By comparison to such far-ranging allegories of clothes as Swift's top notches and laced coates in *A Tale of a Tub* and Professor Diogenes Teufelsdröckh of weissnichtwo's eccentric philosophy in *Sartor Resartus,* Herrick's clothes are limited—almost to the dandy's enthrallment with charms. Clothes in all three, as in Jonson, are analogous to language; they are idiom, and fall generally under what these days we call semiotics. For Swift's heirs to religious heritage, they stand for doctrines, and for Teufelsdröckh, for outward forms in which all "habilatory endeavours, an Architectural Idea will be found lurking."[6] Herrick is ordinarily more interested in the enthusiast's sentiment. But on occasion he anticipates Carlyle's habilatory resplendence, and in "The Transfiguration" may be remembering Herbert's resurrected souls wearing "their new aray":

> Immortall clothing I put on,
> So soone as *Julia* I am gon
> To mine eternall Mansion.
>
> Thou, thou art here, to humane sight
> Cloth'd all with incorrupted light;
> But yet how more admir'dly bright

> Wilt thou appear, when thou art set
> In thy refulgent Thronelet,
> That shin'st thus in thy counterfeit?
>
> H-819

This is to say nothing of course against the counterfeit itself, with which Julia prefigures her paradisal self. But all things must be seen in proportion, and even the celebrator of Julia's petticoat realizes that some degrees of splendor reduce one's earthly enthrallments.

More characteristically, what Herrick pursues are ratios of revelation and concealment, art and nature, barely hinted in the "counterfeit" and balanced in a quite different way by Jonson in *The Silent Woman:*

> Still to be neat, still to be dressed,
> As you were going to a feast;
> Still to be powdered, still perfumed,
> Though art's hid causes are not found,
> All is not sweet, all is not sound.
>
> Give me a look, give me a face,
> That makes simplicity a grace;
> Robes loosely flowing, hair as free:
> Such sweet neglect more taketh me
> Than all the adulteries of art:
> They strike mine eyes, but not my heart.

Jonson's well-dressed lady is unsound and counterfeits something besides her immortal image. Both Herrick and Jonson find the concealment giving rise to paradoxes of clothing-as-language, then: clothes are both revealing and concealing. What catches the eye in Herrick's observer is their movement, not inner soundness or taste. Julia's petticoat, for instance, attracts the eye and holds it without suggesting much concern with the person within:

> Thy Azure Robe, I did behold,
> As ayrie as the leaves of gold;
> Which erring here, and wandring there,
> Pleas'd with transgression ev'ry where....
> And all confus'd, I there did lie
> Drown'd in Delights; but co'd not die.
> That Leading Cloud, I follow'd still,
> Hoping t'ave seene of it my fill;
> But ah! I co'd not: sho'd it move
> To Life Eternal, I co'd love.
>
> H-175

The petticoat is not only errant but capricious, sometimes one thing, sometimes another, which is why it must be watched so closely. Its "brave expansion" and conjuring of a star-filled sky give it magnitude and a touch of transcendentalism even as it remains closely attached to its owner. Its metaphoric alliances lead Herrick as interpreter into history and theophany without suggesting that its real interest lies in anything beyond itself. It is not merely a symbol, as it might be for Teufelsdröckh. We may be reluctant to believe that Herrick will maintain this high tone without a conversion of the surface into something else, but if we expect an ironic countermovement along the way or a sleight-of-hand that replaces it with something more pontifical, we are surprised: he gives himself completely to the wild fling and the swoon. The conjuring object sends the imagination into distances and beckons the onlooker as the Lord drew the Israelites and pointed the way to paradise; yet it clings to Julia and remains, after all is said, merely itself.

Such an object has perhaps more of Marvell's metaphoric riot and exaggeration than it has of Jonson's restraint. Its blazing and abating excites an aesthetic response and in effect makes up its own realm. If heaven and hell linger in the vicinity, they do not detract from its moment. The power that petticoats have resembles, if anything, that of wine and the muses. Whatever is to claim the moment must bewitch and urge the imagination toward some equivalent of fairyland, as though a hovering lyric enchantment were searching for a place to alight, whether in Oberon's, Charles's, or Julia's realm. Herrick gives just enough focus and direction to the description here and in related clothing poems to prevent scattering. Something similar happens in "Upon Julia's Clothes":

> When as in silks my Julia goes
> Then, then (me thinks) how sweetly flowes
> That liquefaction of her clothes.
>
> Next, when I cast mine eyes and see
> That brave Vibration each way free;
> O how that glittering taketh me!
>
> H-779

We would be justified with most other poets in thinking these clothes expressive primarily of Julia, as one of her many attractions. (It is after all she who makes them move.) But Herrick finds clothes, even so provocatively filled, leading relatively independent lives, like objects in Dickens that take it upon themselves to move without a visible force to propel them. Human purpose is not sufficient to explain their behavior, yet no gods or goddesses linger in the vicinity.

In such observations of lively thingness, the texture of images has ascendancy over their expressive purposes. Even while he makes verbal action a turnstile of denotation, he exploits additional dimensions of image, sound, and rhythm to stir an interest beyond strict accounting, as liquefaction and vibration do here. As Julia's silks move, the peripheral qualities of words mount up. Emotion climaxes in the "Oh how" and in the exclamation mark, without debt to or hindrance from maxim. Herrick is less interested even in the silks themselves, finally, than in their flowing and shaking. The attributes of clothes take over the priorities of substance and action, as "flowes" is recast in the heftier "liquefaction." Herrick announces this enshrinement of quality in a noun as a fuller discovery of something that has been tentative in "me thinks." The reiterated "then, then" in imitation of Julia's pace crystalizes the perception of movement. But then flowing itself gives way to the still greater vagrancy of "brave vibration," in a movement that, in being "each way free," liberates flashy qualities from their materials.

Herrick shares with Jonson another value of costuming, its implications for role-playing, ornamentation, "insincerity" and glamor—or in Jonson's view, more often false glamor. Yet no poet could be further from Herrick in the value of surfaces than Jonson, unless Donne in the *Satyres*. Like Donne, Jonson usually prefers the inner man and his undisguised honesty to any equivocations of the eye as in "Still to be neat." He scorns appearances and decoration, especially if they suggest a wavering faddishness, or again as in an Englishman dressed French:

> Would you believe, when you this monsieur see,
>   That his whole body should speak French, not he?
> That so much scarf of France, and hat, and feather,
>   And show, and tie, and garter should come hither
> And land on one whose face durst never be
>   Toward the sea, farther than half-way tree?
> That he, untravelled, should be French so much,
>   As Frenchmen in his company should seem Dutch?[7]

Jonson notices motion as Herrick does, but it is the cartoonlike motion of the costume sailing through the air and landing on one who is himself untraveled, and the puppet motion of the Monsieur walking about town as a mannikin or sidewalk advertisement. His emphasis on this detachability of appearances underscores the imposture of someone who is ignorant, English, unstylish, and un-French in everything except costume. The discrepancy between interior and exterior is as maddening to the moralist in Jonson as the excess of scarf, hat, and feather is to the aesthetician. Both prefer a plain answerability of inside to outside, the linguistic equivalent to which is attention to the strict meaning or inner essence of words rather than to mere sound and texture.

Herrick's tendency in dealing with objects is more often to rid them of moral and philosophical definition, and it is often the muses who grant him leave to do so as they push him toward frenzy, as wine does in making him "full of God." In "Master Herrick's Farewell unto Poetry" (S-4), the poet in his transcendence of local situations and modest settings converts virtually the whole world into motion:

> And in that mystic frenzy, we have hurled,
> As with a tempest, nature through the world,
> And in a whirlwind twirl'd her home, aghast
> At that which in her ecstasy had passed.
>
> S-4

This expansive mood exceeds Herrick's usual tempest in a petticoat and delight in disorder; he is normally not apocalyptic (needless to say), nor does frenzy provide access to higher realms. But at the margin of tangibility where change and motion prevail, rules relax and materials begin to vibrate and glitter. Paradoxically, to look upon them too directly would be to deprive them of bewitchment. The tyranny of the eye, like that of defining rationality, must be broken by a cultivation of disorder, by trans-shifting.

Herrick does sometimes return to the solid object itself to counter these flights of imagination. Several unclothing poems that remove lawns and veils point up substances that lie more or less inert and stable before us. In "To Perenna" he limits our contact with embodied beauty to light glances and concentrates on appraisal:

> When I thy Parts runne o're, I can't espie
> In any one, the least indecencie:
> But every Line, and Limb diffused thence,
> A faire, and unfamiliar excellence.
>
> H-16

The implication is that a roving eye would be quick to catch any indecencies if any were there. But the object is chaste and the eye fully satisfied by it, even though the desire to possess must hold off a little. The key words "diffused" and "excellence" suggest that vision requires the assistance of mind and imagination, since nothing is blatantly obvious even here. If we nearly catch up to excellence in "fair," we relinquish part of it again in "unfamiliar." The parts can be seen well enough for "love," which closes the distance and brings something resembling possession. In effect Herrick manages a well-defined indefinability: the poem makes a reasonably clear statement without actually producing an embodiment of excellence. "The Vine" does something similar in a dream state in which a catalogue of parts is tangible but has the remoteness of ideal visions.

Pleasures in Herrick are often either anticipatory or fleeting like those of "To Perenna" or again in "Corinna's going a Maying." Actually more satisfying to the eye *because* more teasing is the simultaneous stalling and realization of bits of vision in "To Anthea Lying in Bed":

> So looks Anthea, when in bed she lyes,
> Orecome, or half betray'd by Tiffanies:
> Like to a Twi-light, or that simpring Dawn,
> That Roses shew, when misted o're with Lawn.
> Twilight is yet, till that her Lawnes give way;
> Which done, that Dawne, turns then to perfect day.
> 
> (H-104)

We do not come upon such an insistant and acute placement of objects often in Herrick, and at that all but the last line here renders distances and postponements.

One of Herrick's most successful poems of elusiveness, "The Lilly in a Cristal," extends that half-vision through more complex situations than this and at the same time sustains an argument on behalf of concealment behind clothing that is itself paradoxically explicit and open:

> You have beheld a smiling Rose
>    When Virgins hands have drawn
>       O're it a Cobweb-Lawne:
> And here, you see, this Lilly shows,
>    Tomb'd in a Christal stone,
> More faire in this transparent case,
>    Then when it grew alone
>       And had but single grace.
>    . . . . . . . . . . . . . . . . . . . . . .
> Thus Lillie, Rose, Grape. Cherry, Creame,
>    And Straw-berry do stir
>       More love, when they transfer
> A weak, a soft, a broken beame;
>    Then if they sho'd discover
> At full their proper excellence;
>    Without some Scean cast over,
>       To juggle with the sense.

Nature screened through art is soliciting, as lawns and silks flow and a white cloud divides "Into a doubtful Twi-light." That such an extended discourse on the aesthetics of concealment should come down to practical advice on how to dress does not trivialize the observation for Herrick, although it demystifies it. The juxtaposition of burial rites and innocent vestal play in the first stanza of the poem suggests an intensity of beauty and a distinction between things seen and things unseen. The phrase "juggle with the sense" suggests that the courting of perceptions risks spillage even though the poet manages his lecture without obscurity.

"The Lilly in a Cristal" is remarkable partly for its avoidance of potential defenses of other sorts of artistic arrangement and ornament. Herrick's concentration on the arranger's manipulations and the viewer's reaction to them is unusual in renaissance aesthetics, although it has precedents in Castiglione's emphasis on the courtier's artful masking. In effect he proposes aesthetic delight as a kind of moveable feast gathering affairs of moment and place without regard to connection. Thus where one might expect a lilly enshrined in glass to suggest permanence, arrangement, and order, Herrick makes no use of these qualities, nor does he exploit the capacity of such objects to serve as emblems. Arranging them behind veils changes only our perception of them. It puts the viewer in a permanent proleptic state—always anticipating, never arriving at hermeneutic satisfaction. The poetic site is virtually the eye itself, and behind it the imagination. Any white dish of cream tinctured with color, with a strawberry in it, may capture the poet's attention, as Julia's petticoat or fairyland may.

Herrick never seems to doubt that what lies gauzed over will sooner or later be perfectly clear, the corollary of which is that teasing language delays but also names something recognizable and will not hurl endless enigmas at the ghost of Jonson. It was after all on Jonson's leathery plain truth that Herrick stropped his epigrams. His compression and eye for preserved essence coexist with his love of concealment. They are nicely captured by flies made into neat artifacts:

> I Saw a Flie within a Beade
> Of Amber cleanly buried:
> The Urne was little, but the room
> More rich then *Cleopatra's* Tombe.
>
> H-817

Herrick is sure that what the small bead shows is just what is there to be seen, ambered in its enclosure. (He nearly places Father Jonson himself in such a place in the "Globe of Radiant fire.") The richness is contained entirely in the color, not in any multiplicity of meanings, and of course not in any litter of crowns, gold plate, and jewels that Cleopatra's mourners might have sent off with her. No sleight of hand whisks away the fly and installs a fable in its place. "Cleanly" sets both the edge of the image and the value of the perception. It is the precision that grows into the richness, as small replaces great.

The mythology of Herrick's realms gives more attention to glittery costume than it does to placement—the *lesser* mythology reflected from scattered places and almost-sealed-off kingdoms. Thus the kingdom of faery, his most detailed and remarkable place, is separated from ordinary pastures, farm houses, and kitchens. The Oberon poems not surprisingly contain some of his best pure description. Their adjectival qualities and adverbial movement find a whole realm of charm to give them company. They defy translation into either pure familiarity or intellectualized equivalents or emblems. Unlike previous fairylands, for instance, Herrick's is not an extended conceit or kingdom wherein Britons may discover ideal images of a queen of glory or gentleman perfected in virtuous discipline; nor is it a Jonsonian masque realm of symbolic personages clothed in splendor. Rather, it arranges objects from the natural world in a special light, altering proportions and displaying articles pulled loose from their native habitat:

> A little mushroome table spred,
> After short prayers, they set on bread;
> A Moon-parcht grain of purest wheat,
> With some small glit'ring gritt, to eate
> His choyce bitts with; then in a trice
> They make a feast less great then nice.
>
> H-293A

And so on with the sounds of puling fly, piping gnat, fuzz-ball puddings, hornes of papery butterflies, the eggs of emits, stewed thighs of newts, a bloated earwig or two, moths, mole's eyes, and other dainties reminiscent of Drayton's *Nimphidia*.

Although the list also contains some of the familiar consumables of rural feasts, Oberon's fare is not that of an ordinary holiday. Herrick plays with niceties of size and holds down our disgust with a sense of elfish difference: we are never too immersed in the details of the cuisine to be nauseated by it, as we are by Gulliver's proximity to similarly overpowering things. Again in "Oberon's Palace," he scales down the size and calls attention to minutiae. The narrative is primarily a pretext to itemize such things as the shine of snails, the neat perplexity of the path, and "mites / Of Candi'd dew in Moony nights" (H-443). Fairyland has a built-in charm that moves its objects as by an invisible thread—in the way creatures from it upset a bowl of milk or spoil a party-frock without putting in an appearance. The eye is drawn into its pursuits of "disparkling" fires and jewels by lines of force as strong as the influence of stars and as hard to trace.

Where "The Lilly in a Cristal" withholds the direct perception of the things that it causes to "dance in the eye," Herrick is precise here with items lifted from the common world and left in moonlit paths and bowers. But he can delineate those items more exactly precisely because the groves of fairies are already distanced by estrangement. He is also careful not to allow fairyland to become overly nice, which would make us superior to it, as children to toys. It may be small but it is also crude and poses a resisting disorder or contingency, which as Herrick elsewhere insists should prevent art from prevailing too easily. The paving of the cave's floor is made from squirrels' and children's teeth. Diseased fingernails, warts, and a mole stolen from a virgin's neck provide exterior decoration, the latter decking the "holy entrance" of love's bower. The interior of Mab's residence resists any conversion of nature's particles into precious artifacts, as Herrick again makes the task of decoration more difficult by collecting a good many unsightly particles:

> within
> The roome is hung with the blew skin
> Of shifted Snake: enfreez'd throughout
> With eyes of Peacocks Trains, and Trout-
> flies curious wings; and these among
> Those silver-pence, that cut the tongue
> Of the red infant, neatly hung.
> The glow-wormes eyes; the shining scales
> Of silv'rie fish; wheat-strawes, the snailes
> Soft Candle-light; the Kitling's eyne;
> Corrupted wood; serve here for shine.
>
> H-443

The lighting is important to the reassembling of these dismembered articles, because it softens an otherwise stark discreteness. These anatomized eyes, warts, teeth that the fairies have secretly gathered are droppings from the precincts of a domestic world we both recognize and find transfigured here. Thus if we are a little taken back to see such things, we are also attracted to them as specimens in the glow of candlelight and rotting wood:

> No glaring light of bold-fac't Day,
> Or other over radiant Ray
> Ransacks this roome; but what weak beams
> Can make reflected from these jems,
> And multiply; Such is the light,
> But ever doubtfull Day, or night.

In that curious light, the viewer is stayed in his approach, as in the prolepsis of "The Lilly in a Cristal." He is forbidden to repossess what fairyland has stolen. And yet for all its dim light, fairyland puts into view a good deal of the ordinary. If Herrick leaves it undefended by intellect, resemblances to the human realm are nonetheless unavoidable. Oberon hustles off to Mab possessed by a recognizable lust, though we are not obliged to judge him for it. In his imperious bearing, he is a pompous little monarch, "this great-little-kingly Guest." His dream of Mab and the bearing of "her Elvish-majestie" atop her downy bed of "six plumb Dandillions" remind us of the pomp and circumstance of real courts and perhaps Drayton's faery equivalents, but it is a familiarity that we see through the wrong end of the telescope.

PURFLING THE MARGENTS AND
HARVESTING THE BOUNTY

For all his ventures into flickering light, disorder, and things behind the veil, Herrick does not suggest a dispossessed spirit or poet without a realm. He revels in both the variety of *Hesperides* and its tangible temptations. To counterbalance the perpetual tease of the proleptic mode, he likes to invoke such certainties as the seasonal round and the consummation of marriage, in revels of harvest and festivity.[8] These can be seen in two different sets of poems that concern rural bounty and the poem itself as a concrete object, or book of them enacting certain graces. "The Argument" of course combines both in a prefigurative way. "The Apparition of his Mistresse calling him to Elizium" does also, offering a typically hallowed meadowlike place for the reception of poets. Herrick has one of his mistress figures serve as a muse to beckon him toward a company of poets that includes Musaeus, Homer, Pindar, Anacreon, Virgil, Ovid, Catullus, Jonson, and others. Such a meeting place is intriguing for the quality of its light and its clarity, as though in dream—as in fairyland—the final veil could be lifted and one could arrive at a satisfying conclusion:

> Come then, and like two Doves with silv'rie wings,
> Let our soules flie to'th'shades. . . .
> This, that, and ev'ry Thicket doth transpire
> More sweet, then Storax from the hallowed fire:
> Where ev'ry tree a wealthy issue beares
> Of fragrant Apples, blushing Plums, or Peares:
> And all the shrubs, with sparkling spangles, shew
> Like Morning-Sun-shine tinsilling the dew.
> Here in green Meddowes sits eternall May,
> Purfling the Margents, while perpetuall Day
> So double gilds the Aire, as that no night
> Can ever rust th'Enamel of the light.
>
> H-575

Had Herrick provided a map of Hesperides, he would surely have placed these meadows near the center. Situated outdoors, the poets that his mistress names for his enticement do not require household goods, and coming before agriculture, the soil is fruitful without tilling. And yet the beauty of May is very formal, double gilded, enameled, and even booklike in its decorated margins—

which is to say that the scene the visionary imagination presents is coincidentally nature's and the poet's. Poets of course do appear in books with decorated margins, not precisely threaded, as *perfilare* suggests, but leaf-fringed, like Keats's urn, and since they have invented Hesperides and its fragrant apples to begin with, it is fitting that they should live there and welcome Herrick as one of their number. Anacreon is his special host, and the harvest of grapes for "bowles of burning Wine" prepares for the rapture of his greeting. Love itself, always so much a matter of unconsummated substitutions of playfulness and flirtation in Herrick, conducts the poet into his vision, as though the muse were not an impersonal or idealized grace but a specific mistress who appears to give not herself but a vision permeated with delight. Gordon Braden remarks with respect to Herrick's epithalamion that it converts a bedsheet into a flurry of snowflakes, as the sexual drive "at the crucial moment suddenly transforms itself into a swarm of objects."[9] Something similar happens here, except that it is paradise itself that spills out in all its shrubs, "tinsilling" sunshine, and purfling of margents, and then a considerable population of poets beheld "in a spacious Theater" full of glories. As we would expect, Jonson reigns here as a surrogate God, resplendent among the chief prophets of the ages:

> Ile shew thee that capacious roome
> In which thy Father Johnson now is plac't,
> As in a Globe of Radiant fire, and grac't
> To be in that Orbe crown'd (that doth include
> Those Prophets of the former Magnitude)
> And he one chiefe.
>
> 56–61

Unfortunately, the vision breaks off at the coming of day and much remains unsaid. Like Milton's blind poet beckoned by his late espoused saint, Herrick presumably returns to a day that is like night by comparison. But he spares us such an awakening and the framing of imagination's lucid tableau by the obscurities of ordinary sight. The Hesperidean paradise has radiance, magnitude, potential poetic wildness or frenzy, and personal invitation. Its harvest images in the midst of spring compress the best of youth with the fruition of maturity and the evolved products of time with eternity. It is just such a vision that Keats longs for and Yeats sails to Byzantium to locate. But it comes by means of escape from quotidian reality, in a realm of sleep. In that respect, despite its clarity, it remains just out of reach—again as vision rather than consummation.

As "The Apparition" indicates, Herrick shares with Herbert as well as with Jonson a sense of the book as a special place presiding over and presenting its parts, if presiding much more loosely than *The Temple* and not claiming the incarnate Word as a divine presence. The book of poets, enshrined in that decorated border, does not have a staged entry—an altar-shape in words or set of invitations and directions to the reader to initiate and guide his course to an inner sanctum or a mystical repast. But it is tangible enough, as it goes forth to voyage from house to house, to fall into the hands of virgins who blush over it and those who use it in ways the poet condemns. It is scratched by thumbnails and encounters sour readers and critics. In "When he would have his verses read," it also comes to those who are "well drunk and fed," who are better suited for it than those who are sober. The several prologue verses and the images of the book that recur throughout establish both book and poet as presences in a community that takes up poems mostly as interludes and goes about its business. Poems accompany the activities of alehouse and courtship that would be carried on without them. They not only cite piecemeal objects but dwell among similar things, consorting with cottages, courts, bedrooms, public houses, and the furniture, clothing, foods, and activities of those places. They thus dwell among the challenges that the orindary makes to poetic enchantment, just as it is mainly trivia that turn up in Oberon's realm. "The holy incantation of a verse" may be defeated by sober mornings, but it assists the rituals of wine, fireside, love, and marriage, all forms of consummation and possession. The authority of the poet derives not from the wisdom he offers for these occasions but from his presence as a participating guest and the service he offers in identifying the fleeting emanations of foreign realms and their almost invisible assistance at domestic events.

If any of Herrick's geographical realms, as opposed to the land of apparitions, overcomes the handicaps of evasion and suggests a home realm, it would be the rural estate, which combines the ordinary and the hallowed and treats assorted usable things with reverence. Such a place also has the sanctions of Horace and Jonson and hence seats the poet within a heritage that he both sustains and alters with his own light touch. Without taking leave of the familiar, the rural estate allows visitations from creatures of lower mythology and fosters hieroglyphs to go with its communal festivities, as "The Argument" suggests.[10] Again it allows the poet a place as a conductor of revels and genius of place. The wonders of the natural world are close enough to domestic routine to be absorbed into the orders of pantry and fireside. In that scheme of things, autumn means not so much parallels between deciduous nature and human mortality as hock carts and abundance:

> Come Sons of Summer, by whose toile,
> We are the Lords of Wine and Oile:
> By whose tough labours, and rough hands,
> We rip up first, then reap our lands.
> Crown'd with the eares of corne, now come,
> And, to the Pipe, sing Harvest home.
> Come forth, my Lord, and see the Cart
> Drest up with all the Country Art.
>
> H-250

A small piece of the Elizabethan social order survives here in the hierarchy of the country, which has a residue of the court. The landowner has transplanted elegance, which, as James Turner has pointed out, has little to do with the actual conditions of rural life.[11] The poet stresses decorum, ownership, and the master's place, as again in "The Country Life, to the Honoured M. End. Porter," where the bounty of nature is domesticated and issued under the customs of a rural holiday.

Even among these familiar places and rituals, disorder offers some variety to the revels. Indeed, confusion challenges ceremony on the estate as it does in fairyland and in the movement of Julia's clothes; another mask of the stager of revels is that of the truant. This is perhaps more evident still in "A Nuptiall Song, or Epithalamie," which qualifies careful artifice and wedding ceremonies with Dionysiac rout:

> 14. If needs we must for Ceremonies-sake,
> Bless a *Sack-posset;* Luck go with it; take
>   The Night-Charme quickly; you have spells,
>   And magicks for to end, and hells,
>     To passe; but such
> And of such Torture as no one would grutch
>   To live therein for ever: Frie
> And consume, and grow again to die,
>   And live, and in that case,
> Love the confusion of the place.
>
> H-283

The bridal bed is a "maze of Love" that "lookes for the treaders," cleverly woven with "Wit and new misterie." The wiles of love are intricate in the "hieroglyphicks" of kiss and smile. Sweet disorder challenges the sanctity of holy rituals, and life thrives on confusion.

A good deal of Herrick is summed up in that ritualized confusion of the bedroom and the country feast, with all their charms, their chantlike rhythm, and their passage to the borderlands of heaven and hell—reduced to human proportion. The erotic element is less attenuated and more clearly part of the cleanly wantonness of festivity and game than it is in the clothes poems. Threatened by a transience that urges us to seize the day, it implicitly contrasts the temporal setting of love's pleasures to the more lasting bliss that lovers might wish. Wedded love belongs more to the folk than to Christian sacrament and to the world of night charms and the colloquial diction of "grutch" and "frie."

In such matters, as in the country harvest poems, Herrick finds some Elizabethan continuities and some typical seventeenth-century replacements of poetry, but his invasion of so many realms with an effective striking capacity and quick retreat also has something modern about it. I suggested Williams and Moore earlier, but Herrick also makes appropriations of discrete items in another vein. Despite the shape-changing of nature's various things and the brevity of the poet's attention to anyone of them, enough of the stability of species clings to each inventory to prevent naming from becoming inappropriate; but the delight in disorder also uses philosophy to hold off philosophy. It is some such elusiveness in the geography of Herrick's work and overall wandering that prevents us from grasping the total Book of Herrick. Marvell's tour of the Appleton grounds and Vaughan's frequent pilgrimages encounter a similar resistance to readability and coherence but seek to do more with it. The closest thing to a rural ramble in Milton, in "L'Allegro" and "Il Penseroso," works through a Herricklike miscellany for a moment, in a dancelike rhythm Herrick would have approved, but realigns it in retrospect as preamble.

In Herrick the realms exist side by side—the rural estate, the far-off reaches of heaven and hell, the kingdom of strange metamorphoses and ancient poets discoursing in meadows. Things like maying are delightful, but when the poet urges his Corinna to come forth, it is for a momentary reprieve only. Other kingdoms and other moments will claim them. One resides not so much in an immortal book as in fading visions and ghostlike fables. The true lyric possession is of the moment, and such a possession is to be cherished in a falling rhythm:

> So when or you or I are made
> A fable, song, or fleeting shade:
> All love, all liking, all delight
> Lies drown'd with us in endless night.

Herrick's very assertion of this gives echoing, intangible return to classical precedents and reminds us that the present is both enriched and evaporated by them.

*You dwell, said he, in the City of Destruction, the place also where I was born: I see it to be so; and dying there, sooner or later, you will sink lower than the grave, into a place that burns with fire and brimstone: be content, good neighbors, and go along with me.—Bunyan,* The Pilgrim's Progress

# MILTON AND OTHERS WALKING, SOARING, AND FALLING

CHAPTER EIGHT

THE FALL OF KINGS AND GIDDY MEN

I want to insert another general commentary on seventeenth-century changes in topography at this point as though an interlude between chapters, partly as preparation for Vaughan and Marvell, partly as a resumption of some of the paradigmatic and historical uses I made of Milton earlier. The broadest point again has to do with the subversion of courtly settings and their presumed poet-audience relations, which as I've said gather up a large repertory of rhetorical devices. Those settings are thus often assembled from precut descriptive pieces, like the elaborately decorative elements of *Shepheardes Calender*. Of the wide range of rhetorical resources they rely upon, none is more important than periphrasis, which ranges from short epithets and metaphors to extended semi-allegories. By transcribing something into terms more elaborate than is strictly necessary, periphrasis sometimes realizes what might not show in a cleaner, simpler image—realizes, for instance, attitudes toward an object. At other times it is mostly adornment and a demonstration of poetic credentials before an audience of a certain training. When Spenser in *Shepheardes Calender* comes to November nearly at the end of his long task, the sun reflects Colin Clout's own discouragement over his poetic career. It is just such a figure as Sidney or Ralegh (Spenser's "shepherd of the ocean") would appreciate:

> And Phoebus, weary of his yerely taske,
> Ystabled hath his steedes in lowlye laye,
> And taken up his ynne in Fishes haske.
>
> 15–16

This is an elaborate way of course to say merely that in the late season (not Pisces late, however), the sun runs low on the southern horizon. The implications of the figure extend almost to allegory and drag in a history of myths and a residue of writers who have similarly set the sun charioting about the sky as a conscious force fit for Homer's or Virgil's busy commerce of gods and heroes. Phoebus is also Apollo driving steeds of inspiration above Parnassus, but here the pastoral variant humbles the "lay." The ambiguity of ystabled (which might as well have been ystalled) comes as a small bonus, since to be stabled is to be motionless when the poet would prefer a high-flying career. The modesty is evident also in the patronizing of small by great poets a few lines later: "The kindlye dewe drops from the higher tree, / And wets the little plants that lowly dwell" (31–32). In Spenser's further paraphrases, the twelve months and seasons get equated with styles and poetic moods; pipes of course become poetry; shepherds, fellow poets; wasted sheep, neglected trade; muses, capacities and talents; tears, verses; Tityrus, Virgil; ripe fruits and harvest, successful poems; weeds and chaff, failed outings; and so on. Weary Phoebus thus inhabits a consistent landscape-translation by which the craft of writing is artfully lowered into pastureland.

Whether lowered or elevated, adornment is a courtly demonstration of decorum among both poets and social ranks. A similar formal showing of place is what Lear has in mind, for instance, in having his daughters deliver their set pieces to him. When such ceremonial relations break apart and even the king is exposed to the bare elements, he discovers the quite different speech of unaccommodated man, which means man not only without a hundred attendants to go hunting and stir up a daughter's house but also without periphrastic avoidances of creaturely facts, men without polite fictions. In this respect *King Lear* is one of the most incisive of the renaissance rhetorical commentaries, and its targets I think are about equally the humanist expectations for eloquence and the assumption that nature—outdoors and human—will submit to demonstrations of status. In a moment I want to turn to the sense of clifftop falling that Shakespeare equates with the discovery of that stripped down truth.

Sixteenth-century humanist scholars were taught not so much to decipher enigmatic places as to deploy illustrative figures and images in support of rhetorical strategies. Handbooks such as Richard Sherry's (1550) elaborated those figures for teachers of composition and divided them into varieties of *rei descriptio* such as *topothesia* ("A fayned description of a place" that does not exist), *topographia* (description of an actual place), *chronographia* ("When we do plainely describe any time for delectations sake, as the morning, the evening, midnight"), *pragmatographia* (description of a thing by a gathering together of all the circumstances belonging to it), and *prosopopoeia* or personification (giving animation to senseless things).[1] Combined with enumeration, distribution, exclamation, apostrophe, narration, and the like, these schemes and tropes gave writers in both prose and verse the tools with which to generate the details of their topical maps, and they provided more or less conventional tones and accents.

Similar formulas appear in later poets as well, of course, but in abbreviated form and less prominently. Donne, as we have seen, avoids descriptive passages in favor of argument and dramatic monologues. Herbert views secular conventions and schemata with some distrust in the Jordan poems and in revisionary love poems, although he puts traditional Christian iconography and typology to frequent use. The relation of topography to readership is crucial in the sense that a remotely stationed poet such as Marvell in "The Garden" or Vaughan in "I walkt the other day" assumes the exclusion of any intermediary social or religious order between him and the truths he unveils. No one is addressed directly as the explicit subject of encomium and no one assumed implicitly as listener.

The reasons for this are no doubt personal in some cases, but they are also broadly social. Schoolmen, clergymen, government leaders, artists, and intellectuals in the seventeenth century loosened the controls that the court had earlier maintained as the audience of sophisticated literature, as in drama popular theater broadened the outlets of acting companies and playwrights. We have seen the nature of Jonson's group and Herbert's stationing of readers at the door of the temple; others appeal to different sets and exercise greater or lesser influence over them. Milton's fit few are expected to come prepared with Latin, Greek, and Hebrew traditions if they are to understand *Paradise Lost* without footnotes; sympathy for Puritan causes does no harm as well. Milton's training in rhetoric and composition was much like that of earlier young humanists, and as late as his Cambridge exercises he delivered rhetorical addresses that made considerable use of topics and figures from the handbooks. Yet the impression we get from the poems almost from the beginning is that he has an extraordinary concern for what the poet himself is doing in the landscape and very little for conventional periphrasis. Though he has ample precedents in the masque and in Spenserians for the conversion of place into tapestried symbol, the poet's assumed status as genius in attendance is what counts. The Nativity Ode establishes him as celebrant in a redefined landscape, as he marks Christ's transit between the majestic court and the stable. Sun, stars, sea, mountains, and shepherd haunts tune up for an altered harmony in tribute to the incarnate god.

In effect they learn a new placement, and the poet breaks free from the descriptive means that in classical poets kept nature in the hands of the old deities. As we have seen, even in the largely conventional tribute the Genius of the Woods offers the Dowager Derby in "Arcades," he claims attention himself as summoner of the shepherd throng. In "L'Allegro" and "Il Penseroso," the poet observes from a distance, more or less a figure of solitude despite the rural and village society around him. That joy and melancholy convert his surroundings into sites for poetry makes his solicitings of them compatible with reverie and solitude, which grow stronger and more productive as he proceeds.[2] Mirth has a greater range of festivities, which are attractive and blameless. The followers of Comus and the early cheerfulness and pastoral ease of the Cambridge shepherds of "Lycidas" will insist upon greater shortcomings in joy—as also in the long range will the Philistine festivities of *Samson Agonistes*. Here the Lydian airs that climax the poet's delights have an impressive gravity; and as critics have come to appreciate since Johnson, the two moods blend sufficiently to soften the contrast:

> Lap me in soft *Lydian* Airs,
> Married to immortal verse,
> Such as the meeting soul may pierce
> In notes, with many a winding bout
> Of linked sweetness long drawn out,
> With wanton heed, and giddy cunning,
> The melting voice through mazes running;
> Untwisting all the chains that tie
> The hidden soul of harmony.

Like a good deal about "L'Allegro" and "Il Penseroso," Lydian music is conditioned by its history among poets; the speaker implicitly has the company of muses who have traveled from Greece through roundabout to reach him. But Milton's attention is more on the internal experience and the melting voice than on any sharing of musical styles. The poet himself does not attempt to cultivate an audience and does not imagine doing so in the future. Unlike the Genius of "Arcades," he does not address a group or call others to celebrate his discoveries. No one is expected to overhear him except the fictive goddess of mirth herself. Melancholy raises objects seen from it to greater but also more lonely heights. The hermitage the poet thinks of seeking out is a place of esoteric study rather than monastic discipline or brotherly order. The speaker wishes not only to catalogue the gifts of melancholy but to resolve the contrast between choices, and to do so he needs to see how far each carries. He has no fear of falling and expresses no reservations about his mission, but we know in retrospect that a solitude presided over by mirth and melancholy can be deceptively peaceful. The poet of "When I Consider" and "Lycidas" discovers greater complexities in the calling.

When Milton rethinks mirth and melancholy in *Paradise Lost,* he gives them a quite different significance for sociality, the highest joy being the communal celebration of the angels, the gravest melancholy exile from the center. The solitary journey of Adam and Eve into the wilderness accompanied by providence blends the two. More importantly, however, the poem concerns communication as "L'Allegro" and "Il Penseroso" do not and considers explicitly the matter of privacy, aloneness, and the lyric address of helpmates to each other and to objects and their creator. It also concerns temptations, debate, and the need for accommodated dialogue and, as part of its reflections on its own making, stages the generating and reception of language in all quarters. These concerns are too vast for me to do much more with them than list them, but we need to take note of their relations to the pertinent matters here: the keying of lyric address to the isolation that comes of either soaring or falling and the straining of connections to an audience from remote extremes. Isolation is often accompanied by a psychology of falling and temptations to fall, when the lone self finds itself without outside support and far from desirable conclusions. The lady in *Comus* is separated from her brothers before Comus assails her. Eve moves apart from Adam to be tempted; Samson's betrayal of his trust comes when he is separated from his people and momentarily forgetful of them; Satan's first move in the rebellion is to draw off to the north of heaven. Isolation is such a natural preliminary to temptation that we might overlook it but for Milton's emphasis upon its contribution to the outcome. Christ of course reverses the implications of solitude in *Paradise Regained* by turning desert privations into advantages. His withdrawal is preliminary to the establishing of a moral paradigm to be sent abroad later.

Prefallen Eden has a privacy more in keeping with that of happy wanderers who represent the other side of solitude that Vaughan and Traherne among others associate with Eden. Unlike Marvell's version of the lone garden dweller, Milton makes Adam and Eve quite sociable. They also have no difficulty with remoteness, since all creatures about and above them are linked in a single order. When Raphael descends to them, he joins the celestial to the earthly paradise effortlessly, the downward spiral of his flight forming an almost geometric diagram of accommodation:

> Down thither prone in flight
> He speeds, and through the vast Ethereal Sky
> Sails between worlds and worlds, with steady wing
> Now on the polar winds, then with quick Fan
> Winnows the buxom Air; till within soar
> Of Tow'ring Eagles, to all the Fowls he seems
> A *Phoenix*, gaz'd by all, as that sole Bird
> When to enshrine his reliques in the Sun's
> Bright Temple, to *Egyptian Thebes* he flies.
>
> 5. 266–274

The vertical dynamic of such renaissance paintings as Raphael's "Michael Vanquishing the Devil" and Luca Signorelli's last judgment foreshortens similar journeys and prepares a similar linkage.[3]

In the fallen world, however, the reception of messages is likely to be traumatic even when the news is good. The narrator's appeals for divine help link soaring and falling and connect both to the great spaces and moral ups and downs of the story itself:

> Descend from Heav'n *Urania*, by that name
> If rightly thou art call'd, whose Voice divine
> Following, above th' *Olympian* Hill I soar,
> Above the flight of *Pegasean* wing.
> The meaning, not the Name I call: for thou
> Nor of the Muses nine, nor on the top
> Of old *Olympus* dwell'st, but Heav'nly born,
> Before the Hills appear'd, or Fountain flow'd,
> Thou with Eternal Wisdom didst converse,
> Wisdom thy Sister, and with her didst play
> In presence of th' Almighty Father, pleas'd
> With thy Celestial Song. Up led by thee
> Into the Heav'n of Heav'ns I have presum'd,
> An Earthly Guest, and drawn Empyreal Air,
> Thy temp'ring; with like safety guided down
> Return me to my Native Element:
> Lest from this flying Steed unrein'd, (as once
> *Bellerophon,* though from a lower Clime)

> Dismounted, on th' *Aleian* Field I fall
> Erroneous there to wander and forlorn.
>
> 7. 1–20

Since the first fall rejects the Father's wisdom, the poet must recover that wisdom to conduct us through the remainder of the epic.

Likewise, Herbert's version of invocation in "Easter-wings" appeals to Christ's pattern of ascent to cure one wasted by sin, and in "Prayer I" either God must descend or men must rise, though it is their nature to fall. Similar steeply up and down prospects threaten the poet's equilibrium in "Temper I." However, the fear of falling does not necessarily carry doctrinal definitions of peril; it can be simply part of a pervasive sense of individual vulnerability and slippery footing wherever egocentrism crops up. For that universal sense, Jay Appleton's *The Experience of Landscape* and Bert O. States's reading of the precipice speech of Edgar to Gloucester in *King Lear* (4.6.11–26) suggest other ways to gauge the hazards of topography.[4] Appleton bases relations between landscape and feeling on instincts for prospect, cover, and hazard; for States, steep places have a kinesthetic as well as a psychological impact. Both fit the portrayal in earlier renaissance texts of downfalls from high social position and subsequent exposure to the wild.

Edgar's clifftop prospect provides an index of the difference between those downfalls and the spiritual guilt of the metaphysicals and Milton. It warrants our scrutiny both as a remarkable inset lyric of place in its own right and as a contrast to the later giddiness. Edgar's description of the precipice for the blind Gloucester conjures a believable and detailed setting for Gloucester's proposed self-destruction:

> *Edg.* Come on, sir; here's the place: stand still. How fearful
> And dizzy 'tis to cast one's eyes so low!
> The crows and choughs that wing the midway air
> Show scarce so gross as beetles; half way down
> Hangs one that gathers sampire, dreadful trade!
> Methinks he seems no bigger than his head.
> The fishermen that walk upon the beach
> Appear like mice, and yond tall anchoring bark
> Diminish'd to her cock, her cock a buoy
> Almost too small for sight. The murmuring surge,
> That on th' unnumber'd idle pebble chafes,
> Cannot be heard so high. I'll look no more,
> Lest my brain turn, and the deficient sight
> Topple down headlong.
>
> (4.6.11–24)

Although States does not consider it, Edgar later gives us a matching view from the bottom upward:

> *Glou.* But have I fall'n or no?
> *Edg.* From the dread summit of this chalky bourn.
> Look up a-height; the shrill-gorg'd lark so far
> Cannot be seen or heard: do but look up.
>
> 4.6.56–59

Gloucester could not see if he did look up, but an absence of skylark song might seem to bear out Edgar's claim. More and more as he goes along, Edgar constructs his imaginary visions as a cure for Gloucester's self-destructive urge. The second passage, in fact, replaces the compulsive desire to fall with a defense against inhuman spaces and godless vacuums. It also reintroduces a mythic element reminiscent of the late comedies and their tragicomic falls and miraculous recoveries:

> *Edg.* Upon the crown o' th' cliff what thing was that
> Which parted from you?
> *Glou.*         A poor unfortunate beggar.
> *Edg.* As I stood here below methought his eyes
> Were too full moons; he had a thousand noses,
> Horns welk'd and wav'd like the enridged sea:
> It was some fiend; therefore, thou happy father,
> Think that the clearest Gods, who made them honours
> Of men's impossibilities, have preserved thee.
>
> 4.6.67–74

The spaces that Edgar conjures for the mind's eye now contain some of the wonders that genii loci perceive and interpret. He postulates a destiny to control one's will and gods to play with one's fate.

In States's reading of the first speech, the downward view arouses its vertigo by its sizing and spacing of items. Edgar conjures a world that is without "comforting gradations of distance," yet gives clarity to things that do not become vague with distance, like objects in a Breughel landscape that are "miniature within immensity." The same clarity reappears in the second speech, which, despite the distance that renders skylarks silent, finds small ridges on the horns of demons. In States's view the function of such optical devices is at least twofold: they demonstrate the powers of theatrical fantasy for an audience that (like Gloucester) literally sees nothing of the kind, and they raise a terrifying attraction of the mind's eye to things before the body can react with fear of injury: "In short, vertigo is not simple fear of falling; it is a peculiar collusion of the senses through which the body overextends itself and participates in space. It is primarily through the eye that we 'de-sever' the world, Heidegger says, and bring the world close, 'in the sense of procuring it.' Unfortunately, there is a frightful countermovement involved when you are procuring the world from a verge; for there is a sense in which the eye, grasping an object in space, takes the body along with it."[5]

What Edgar's visual prospect asks for in addition is some explanation as to why Shakespeare has these characters develop a father-son relationship of this sort at this particular moment. Edgar prepares for the verticality of both speeches upon first entering the heath, where being cast down is metaphoric for the loss of social position: "The lowest and most dejected thing of Fortune, / Stands still in esperance, lives not in fear" (4.1.2–3). Edgar refers of course to the wheel of fortune that makes one "dejected" in the Latin sense and assumes that from the bottom of the social precipice one can fall no further. Capitalizing upon that commonplace, he literalizes the metaphor in the prospect he conjures for his father, for whom he serves both as eyes and as moralizer. One must go through the experience of falling all the way to the bottom before "esperance" can cure despair (dejection in the English sense). When Edgar adds, "Welcome, then, / Thou unsubstantial air that I embrace" in the preparatory scene, he is already well on his way to the later vacuum that opens beneath his feet. It is true that "unsubstantial" means also a space before fallen beggars emptied of goods. Certainly it is not apportioned out to be possessed piece by piece in lyric blazon; it is a wilderness where all quarters are alike and one is blasted by every unobstructed wind. But if empty terrain has no impediments to break one's fall, it also sets none against hope.

As if to underscore that point, Shakespeare has Gloucester enter, led by an old man, and has Edgar point to a specific example of the fallen state in one "poorly led" (4.1.10), soon to be better led by being misled. Before that, Gloucester turns his own trope on the paradoxes of slates wiped clean and ledgers emptied of assets: "Our means secure us, and our mere defects / Prove our commodities" (4.1.20–21), which is to say that our goods tempt us with false security and sense of possession, but our flaws then prove to be our good. The power behind this conversion of superfluity into disaster—and then, if we are lucky, of poverty into an asset—is in Gloucester's view the capricious gods, to whom we are as flies to wanton boys. Edgar's answer from the bottom of the imaginary precipice is that the clearest gods also bring about miracles that preserve us. Gloucester may thus become again a "happy" father, blessed by happenstance in his son and (in Edgar's mythologized landscape of fiends and deities) by the tutelary powers of steep places. Demons, too, of course, are residents of Edgar's dreamlike vision; they are wild, with eyes like moons and horns wrinkled like the sea seen from a high eminence; and they are cagey in enticing old men to pitch themselves down. The abyss one falls through now has overseeing presences that cannot be visualized as samphire gatherers or diminutive larks can. We are led to guess at them by Edgar's fantasy, as from Lear's earlier talk of oaths, charms, and demonic curses. We might also remember the coincidence of Lear's wrath and the storm: the heath has uncanny collaborations with states of mind; spaces are permeated with spirits as well as crows winging "the midway air" no larger than beetles. Since some of these are full of malice in Gloucester's view, it may be tempting to them to nudge us over if we come too near the verge. And so the fear of falling has spiritual depths as well as bodily vertigo.

The experience of falling in that metaphoric sense involves the cancelling of identities based on status, retainers, and superfluity, and a reduction to something more essential that Cordelia and Lear take to be the bare forked animal. Gloucester realizes that phase of falling more clearly than Edgar, having gotten there quicker than most, thanks to Edmund. Edgar, too, however, instinctively poses as a beggar deprived of all comforts and social standing. And when the gods show themselves, they do so in providential bounty, as Gloucester seeks to right balances in rewarding his guide with a purse:

> that I am wretched
> Makes thee the happier: Heavens, deal so still!
> Let the superfluous and lust-dieted man,
> That slaves your ordinance, that will not see
> Because he does not feel, feel your power quickly;
> So distribution should undo excess,
> And each man have enough.
>
> 4.1.65–71

These sentiments are echoed by Lear and by the sense others have of overseeing but intangible deities who punish and sometimes reward. In the storm and in the curses of Lear, the gods suggest not an interpretable intent but mysteries that no one totally penetrates. Lear proposes to Cordelia that as they sit in prison they anatomize the cycles of power at court with the aloofness of sages:

> and we'll talk with them too,
> Who loses and who wins; who's in, and who's out;
> And take upon 's the mystery of things,
> As if we were Gods' spies: and we'll wear out,
> In a wall'd prison, packs and sects of great ones
> That ebb and flow by th' moon.
>
> 5.3.15–19

His emphasis is upon endurance and stability among a multitude of falls watched over but not prevented by the gods. Indeed, his implication seems to be that people damage themselves while spies keep count. In any case, as change governs all other things under the moon they will become immune to the common lunacy.

To return to Jay Appleton's terms: *King Lear*'s exceptionally hazardous landscape is without landing places, coverts, or comfortable plateaus; it is precipitous and slippery. Edgar does not suggest horizontal vistas to go with his views up and down but focuses on objects either made diminutive by distance or mythologized by fantasy. In such a world, men are puny and fragile even if no monsters rise out of fogs, approaching bigger and bigger. If the gods do not break their falls by miracle, they are destroyed by their own momentum. Nor does Edgar provide order and arrangement of emblematic objects in the landscape for the mind to escape the eye's dominance, as hieroglyphic worlds and medieval landscapes allow it to do. Close scrutiny does not produce security, only items scattered here and there to measure the gulf. The parallel to literal falling specifically with Lear is the loss of kingship. The gifts of the gods (if they exist) are position, power, social connection, the company of retinue. The giddiness Edgar raises in his listeners is not easily disconnected, then, from the contexts of hazardous rule of kings over subjects and of fathers over inheriting sons and daughters. It is I think specifically a courtly vertigo, similar to the one that Wyatt understood so well and that Sidney and Spenser identify in their versions of knights in and out of favor. To be cast out is to become not only socially isolated or debased but to be dejected. Shakespearean figures are not used to living on the margin and do not choose to do so, unless like Jaques they are chronically melancholy.

That courtly orientation becomes still more evident if we reconsider the vertigo of later figures for whom falling accompanies a spiritual precipitousness but not social ostracism. Also, pilgrims may have to go about and about to gain their eminences, but we know that mountains and their weather will be guiding signs and that the afterworld has a system of rewards, however postponed and misunderstood. Nothing essential depends on the social order for Vaughan, Milton, Traherne, or Herbert though blessings may be manifest through it. Mystery is associated with the comings and goings of providence; the rest of the pilgrim's confusion can be attributed to his own deficiencies or corrupted faculties. He does not entertain the possibility of wanton and destructive gods who might push him off an eminence.

The least visualized and social, the most moralized fall, is perhaps Herbert's in "Giddiness," which concerns the dizzy inconsistency not of powerful men but simply of man. It is unlike the giddiness of *King Lear* in every important respect:

> Oh, what a thing is man! how farre from power,
> From setled peace and rest!
> He is some twentie sev'rall men at least
> Each sev'rall houre.

Herbert's concern is not anyone's change of state or the way the gods torment the great. Man as a species brings whirlwind changes upon himself simply because his state is such and "His minde is so." The cure does not lie within himself, though the flaw does:

> Lord, mend or rather make us: one creation
> Will not suffice our turn:
> Except thou make us dayly, we shall spurn
> Our own salvation.

Changeable and unstable, we require a daily upholding lest we spin away into so many roles that our segments of the world return to primal chaos. As Donne is also wont to point out, everything would collapse every minute were it not divinely upheld. Or again, Herbert's church monuments under the "blast of Death's incessant motion" will soon "bow, and kneel, and fall down flat / To kisse those heaps, which now they have in trust." Vaughan is typical in imagining the day of judgment as a vast undoing of the six days' creation and at the same time a final cure geared to human worth, which paradoxically requires at that point both a reiteration of the fall and a final great ascendancy. First comes the unmaking:

> When thou shalt spend thy sacred store
> Of thunders in that heate
> And low as ere they lay before
> Thy six-dayes-buildings beate,
>
> When like a scrowle the heavens shal passe
> And vanish cleane away,
> And nought must stand of that vast space
> Which held up night, and day,[6]

—when these things are done it will be too late to ask "What shall I doe?" ("Day of Judgement"). But one can begin preparing early and can be assured of justice if not necessarily of mercy.

One of the things that happens both here and in Herbert's "Vertue," where the whole world turns to coal on that day, is the shrinking of real space to accommodate moral space and a sense of the ending as a resting place. In "Ascension-Hymn" the high heavens become the walks of those who have "gone into the world of light";

in "The World" eternity is reduced to a single vision moving "like a vast shadow." It is with eyes closed that we are to imagine the heavens rolled up like a scroll, or eternity "like a great Ring of pure and endless light." The removal of signs and stellar influences inscribed in the heavens may leave a vacuum, but it is not so immense as to defy crossing altogether. Vaughan expects a final court in their place, with records for human accountability. The day of judgment is thus preeminently a vertical day: a few ascend, many fall, but all are provided for. It is the interim that is cloudy and difficult. In Herbert's "The Temper I" the initial vertical ambitions of the poet remain extensive and extract an impassioned appeal for an end to those interim ups and downs:

> O, rack me not to such a vast extent;
> Those distances belong to thee;
> The world's too little for thy tent,
> A grave too big for me.

But flying with angels and falling with dust are ultimately one and the same, so that again the vast extent can be accommodated to human proportions if God so chooses.

The public fall that Shakespeare has in mind—the fall of kings and their counselors—is often supplemented in courtly poetry by the fall of lovers from grace. The two are comparable and sometimes closely linked. When Wyatt expresses his dread of falling and finds that it makes him "stand not fast," he is thinking not merely of the slippery footing of the court but the treachery of personal relations when trust is violated. In adapting the language of courtship and substituting God for the sovereign beloved, Herbert is mindful of the need to rethink those personal as well as the greater aspects of falling. As helpless to command his own fate as the forlorn lover, he hopes to limit the duration of his vulnerability and see past it. In that respect Herbert is typical of the metaphysicals in intensifying the frailty of the lyric speaker and universalizing his fall beyond local causes.

A similar giddiness crops up in others, sometimes where we least expect it. Marvell, for instance, is so much a poet of containment that sharp ascents and fear of falling might seem alien to him. But he associates falling with kingship in the Horatian ode and "The First Anniversary," in which Cromwell's spill from his coach has effects much like those that accompany the fall of Shakespearean kings:

> Thou *Cromwell* falling, not a stupid Tree,
> Or Rock so savage, but it mourn'd for thee:

> And all about was heard a Panique groan,
> As if Natures self were overthrown.
> It seem'd the Earth did from the Center tear;
> It seem'd the Sun was faln out of the Sphere.
>
> 201–206

That other versions of soaring and falling are also crucial to Marvell testifies to the inevitability of verticality among seventeenth-century poets. Containment predominates even in "On a Drop of Dew" only to a point. Although the soul refuses to spread out or take in the life into which it has plunged, it eventually exchanges self-enclosure for ascent and dissolves into the sun. The separability of body and soul both intensifies the panic of the fall and makes possible a conclusion as soaring closure. The vertical thrust of "The Definition of Love" is also extraordinary, although the state of love is not finished in this case but suspended. Hope cannot fly to its high object, and no union can take place "Unless the giddy heaven fall" and the world "be cramp'd into a *Planisphere*." Marvell nonetheless ends with a definition that establishes the union of minds against movements up or down, in effect locking the mind and its high object together at a fixed distance.

Distortions of scale in "Upon Appleton House" suggest a similar giddiness but a different attitude toward it. The tendency of all things to fall is countered by the Fairfaxes, especially by Maria:

> No new-born *Comet* such a Train
> Draws through the Skie, nor Star new-slain.
> For streight those giddy Rockets fail,
> Which from the putrid Earth exhale,
> But by her *Flames*, in *Heaven* try'd,
> *Nature* is wholly *vitrifi'd*.
>
> 683–688

Marvell takes advantage of rising fires and falling stars to gauge Maria's function as a local power. She is to trains of things following her as comets to their tails—or actually superior to such and to falling stars as well, since the comparison is denied even as it is offered. All such things fail or yield only partial light; she is suffused through all nature. If nature is clarified when she finishes working upon it, it is because she has brought down from heaven a spirit tested there and not itself subject to obscurities and deformities. Visual spaces are compressed in Marvell's close-up of earth's giddy rockets, and yet the heavens remain distant.

The effect is similar to that of the world as chaos later, with its contrast between earth's vast ruin and the smaller domain of Maria:

> All negligently overthrown,
> Gulfes, Deserts, Precipices, Stone.

> Your lesser *World* contains the same.
> But in more decent Order tame.
>
> 762–766

The short list of scattered regions and vacancies in the earth's surface is of places both extensively horizontal and vertical. (The "stone," since it is singular, does not give us discrete pieces with which to fill empty spaces, merely a material to go with sands of the desert and to hold up cliffs.) The list conducts a quick photographic journey over a terrain much larger than the tour of the Appleton estate but still visualizable all at once. The main point of the first two lines, however is the lack of relation among earth's parts and the miracle it takes to reduce them to "decent Order tame." If the lesser world of woods, streams, gardens, and meads that Marvell addresses does reflect overthrown things, they are reduced to miniature; no one will plunge from their precipices. Nor can deserts exist where the space is lacking; if gulfs do, they must be models only. For one who has played tricks with cattle as fleas, the visual manipulations come easily, as does the couplet which then transcendentalizes the entire microcosm of the estate: "*You Heaven's Center, Nature's Lap. / And Paradice's only Map.*" The distinctive thing about such a map is its reduction of distances to scale and of real things to symbolic counterparts. If heaven is truly centered here, it overcomes distances and their sense of isolation and leaves no place to fall.

Meanwhile, with the nation set aside, the family and the estate become the chief social unit. The fall that comes as a shock to an abdicating king and carries nature to ruin with him is avoided by the ex-general who has already resigned from high office but recuperates greatness in a private mode. Together with his daughter, he has the leverage to lift all local things under his jurisdiction to their fulfillment. England's fall is less lamentable because of that sturdy and holy household, where entering the door is so much like entering heaven's gate and prepares for doing so. This notion of a center returns to the geometry of the opening sections, where Marvell criticizes the high-thrusting ambitions of architects and thinks how to "immure / The Circle in the Quadrature." Perhaps better even than the holy mathematics of the house are the woods and streams that render the essence of heaven—better for the narrator, since nature is more his terrain and the experience is more available to lyric apostrophe. The poet's travels can remain horizontal because so much descends to the human plane in this highly privileged place. If leather boats are antipodes in shoes and the dark hemisphere is like those tortoiselike amphibians that carry them homeward, even fishers are maps of the heavens.

Variants of the fall and its cure are crucial to Milton, too, as we have seen, especially in the lyric passages and invocations of *Paradise Lost*. As though in answer to previous incidents of giddiness in the great and kingly, Milton magnifies Satan's fall severalfold, as Christ hurls him "headlong flaming from th'Ethereal Sky / With hideous ruin and combustion down / To bottomless perdition" (1.45–47). That hell is "bottomless" is itself an old figure intended to be more moral and metaphysical than descriptive. Without a sustaining creator, its inhabitants have no substantial being and hence no resting point, though they appear to rest. They also have no social foundation and no center for one, which leads to Pandaemonium's struggle for power. The sense of falling is intensified in Satan's plunge into chaos on the voyage to earth, which forecasts the poet's third invocation cited earlier:

> At last his Sail-broad Vans
> He spreads for flight, and in the surging smoke
> Uplifted spurns the ground, thence many a League
> As in a cloudy Chair ascending rides
> Audacious, but that seat soon failing, meets
> A vast vacuity: all unawares
> Flutt'ring his pennons vain plumb down he drops
> Ten thousand fadom deep, and to this hour
> Down had been falling, had not by ill chance
> The strong rebuff of some tumultuous cloud
> Instinct with Fire and Nitre hurried him
> As many miles aloft.
>
> 2.927–938

Edgar's imaginary cliff is diminutive by comparison, though more exactly realized. What Satan falls into is the least humanized realm of the poem, a place of confusion devoid of divine and demonic influence alike and incapable of conclusion or resting place because incapable of order or recognition. That it is not totally incomparable to human experience is established only later, by the high tower of Babel and man's fall into a similar hubbub, in repercussion from soaring pride and high climbing. Satan's sense of falling here is protracted of course and would be endless in panic and despair, Milton says, but for the intervention not of the clearest gods but of chance. Although his initial fall has overtones of the prince plunging from high place, Milton replaces the errors of a Lear with a sense of the ridiculous, since to break with God is to break with logic itself. Pity and fear are erased by that conversion of the tragic flaw into absolute terms and its removal from conditions with which we might identify.

These descriptive passages are seated in the midst of primarily dramatic and narrative actions that we cannot consider specifically lyric, but they produce interludes that offer commentary on events and attitudes toward them. It is primarily in such interludes that Milton explores the isolation of the fallen—in Satan's and Adam's soliloquies and in the narrator's invocations. When the narrator participates in the poem's soaring and falling and apostrophizes the powers responsible for it, he seeks to move from blindness and isolation into the company of the spirit that created the cosmos. That spirit established bonds between creator and creature, initiated a beginning, and pointed toward what followed from it. As his part of both the process and the ending, the poet seeks to join that hierarchical company whose members see and to a degree possess a common source. In the second invocation, he has escaped "the Stygian Pool" and been

> Taught by the heavn'ly Muse to venture down
> The dark descent, and up to reascend,
> Though hard and rare.
>
> 3.19–21

In the invocation to Book 7 cited earlier, he is less sure about the next phase. Urania dwells in the divine presence itself and contributes "Celestial Song" for God's entertainment. But if she does not guide the poet in his native element as well, he will repeat the fall and wander erroneous, without end.

The only truly secure pattern of descent into isolation and the periods of death for Milton is Christ's, the ending of which is known before the outset. Except for a brief prediction of the entire cycle (Book 3. 227–65), however, Milton does not dramatize that descent in *Paradise Lost.* The final cure for falling is reserved for *Paradise Regained,* where Christ reverses the fall of angels and men and the fall-of-great-men theme by refusing empire and secular power. That he makes a soft landing from the pinnacle is due to angels that

> in a flowry valley set him down
> On a green bank, and set before him spread,
> A table of Celestial Food, Divine.
>
> 4. 586–88

The renewed services of the host depend upon the emergence of a visible and active divine being. The only conclusive ceremony belongs to paradise, but one of the functions of such flowery valleys is to establish relations between the immediate place and that more distant one. Both lyric and the cure for isolation depend upon that connection.

> *He knocks at all doors, strays and roams,*
> *Nay hath not so much wit as some stones have*
> *Which in the darkest nights point to their homes,*
> > *By some hid sense their Maker gave;*
> *Man is the shuttle, to whose winding guest*
> > *And passage through these looms*
> *God order'd motion, but ordain'd no rest.*
> Vaughan, "Man"

> *I see them walking in an Air of glory,*
> > *Whose light doth trample on my days....*
>
> *Either disperse these mists, which blot and fill*
> > *My perspective (still) as they pass,*
> *Or else remove me hence unto that hill,*
> > *Where I shall need no glass.*
> Vaughan, "Ascension-Hymn"

# MOMENTUM AND THE SPIRIT'S PASSAGE IN VAUGHAN

CHAPTER NINE

DISCURSIVE LANDSCAPES OF PILGRIMAGE

Religious verse of the kinds that the metaphysicals, Milton, Ralph Knevet, Henry Colman, Mildmay Fane, and Christopher Harvey wrote was basically a post-Elizabethan and with exceptions pre-Restoration phenomenon. Although a number of earlier poets translated psalms and wrote poems of pious supplication, they did not go extensively into confessional or meditative verse. That Knevet did so only after circumstances halted his *Supplement of the Faerie Queene* indicates something of the impetus that civil disruption gave to meditational forms, together with the model that Herbert set for Colman's *Divine Meditations,* Harvey's *The Synagogue, or the Shadow of the Temple* (1640), Crashaw's *Steps to the Temple* (1646), and Vaughan's *Silex Scintillans* (1650). Vaughan did not take up the devotional verse for which he is chiefly remembered until what is usually described as a personal turnabout in the late 1640s. Seventeenth-century religious lyricists generally elected either to explore institutional affiliation (such as Herbert's with the Anglican temple) or to pursue independent spiritual guests. One of the significant developments in that devotional and meditational literature is passage "on the way" that converts religious experience into landscape terms, or landscape into expressive and revelatory form. The readability of setting becomes central both to lyric address and poet-God relations. As Vaughan indicates, such topographies and the spiritual wayfaring conducted within them can be equivalents to church and doctrine, to psychological states, to social conditions, or to some mixture. Which of these is primary is not so much at issue as the kind of metaphoric equivalency and progress that topographical juxtapositions make possible. Whatever analogous realms appear must be read first in objects and substances whose surfaces are matters for relatively copious description and interpretive concern. Meditational topics and terms of petition follow from the literal path.

It is less the rhetorical elaboration of setting, then, than prose traditions and homiletic literature that prepare for the plain way. Vaughan reflects that literature to some extent, but the most remarkable itinerants to grow out of it are Bunyan's. In Christian's dreamscape pilgrimage proceeds through psychological, social, and doctrinal states that exceed those of comparable journeys in their elaborate naming of characters and use of dialogue to expand and clarify placements. Actually, although Bunyan followed Vaughan by over a decade, the two bear comparison not only in their casting of spiritual states as topographical progresses but also as outsiders for whom the solitary journey has no exact institutional or social equivalents. Bunyan is more revealing than Herbert in this instance because of Vaughan's recurrent desire to allegorize nature as a "way" and to posit a first-person figure as pilgrim-poet through a succession of poems. Vaughan of course wrote from outside the Puritan regime of the 1650s, as Bunyan wrote from outside the restored church. The marginality of each may have contributed to his emphasis upon the hermeneutic conditions of pilgrimage and upon an implicit theory of signs embedded in place. Each sets up new ways of reading those signs even while he draws upon age-old biblical types and figures. Primarily, what links them is a sense shared with Milton and Marvell of the exploratory figure of solitude locatable by topographical keys. Despite Vaughan's recollection of a sizeable portion of Herbert's lexicon of images and themes, he could not find in Herbert so unchurched a journey, in which meditational and spiritual stages are marked by mountains, flowered graves, fountains, stars, and sun.

When Christian takes a few steps with By-ends, however, the language is very much like Vaughan's in converting incident "along the way" into spiritual planes. Bunyan heaps up an unusual number of titles for places and for those whose journeys, guided by convenience and ease, make up negative examples. We continue to be aware of all the circumstances of pilgrimage—the wicket-gate, the slough, valleys, palaces, overhanging mountains, and of course the polarizing ends of movement, the City of Destruction and Mount Zion. But the added terminological abundance of the By-ends episode complicates the straight way with easy ways. The secular world contains a multitude of mislabeled paths, each an outlook or a vocabulary of enticements and choices that in effect mark a mode of discourse. By-ends of course is from the well-populated town of Fairspeech and has "many rich kindred there." He is a fellow citizen of Lords Turn-about, Time-server, and Fair-speech, and of Messrs Smooth-man, Facing-both-ways, Any-thing, and Parson Two tongues—obviously none of them straight talkers. To solidify his family credentials, he has married the daughter of Lady Feigning, bred "to such a pitch" that "she knows how to carry it to all, even to prince and peasant." In case the reader should miss the point in all this, Bunyan has By-ends condemn himself from his own mouth, since where *he* comes from they never "strive against wind and tide" and are zealous only when religion goes "in his silver slippers" and walks in the sunshine. As the Christian world knows, this is no way to go on a pilgrimage. Undeceived, Christian leaves By-ends to the more fitting company of Mr. Hold-the-world, Mr. Money-love, and Mr. Save-all, as molded by the schoolmaster Love-gain in the arts of "getting, either by violence, cozenage, flattery, lying, or by putting on a guise of religion"—combinations of banking interests and social mobility that Bunyan knew had always ruled the world and assumed would continue to do so.[1] The regions that these and other backsliders and turnabouts inhabit become externalized maps of the wavering spirit, from corners of which desire to get ahead whispers to the will to relax and abide. At every turn of Bunyan's road, such enticements catch the eye and misdirect the vagabond feet. Dialogue turns concourse into discourse and makes advancement through doctrinal categories, psychological and social disorders.[2] Spiritual vacillation is associated with faulty doctrine and requires straightening out by characters like Interpreter and Evangelist. Thus at several stations, Bunyan takes the opportunity to reiterate and interrogate, to clarify, reaffirm homiletic truths, and finish Interpreter's work of expounding and teaching. The end justifies the metaphoric means by which "feigned words, as dark as mine, / Make truth to spangle and its rays to shine," as Bunyan remarks in his apology. Localities become special kinds of *loci communes* based not on the art of oratory but on Puritan teaching, with emphasis upon deeds.

Were it not for that emphasis, *The Pilgrim's Progress* might be accused of making too thorough a conversion of the way into a well-figured story and the conduct of an argument for its own sake. The extension of the tropes threatens to make a talkative demonstration, ornamented by fantasies. To purge it of excess in that line, Bunyan makes clear on several occasions the distinction between sincere, useful language and language as display. That distinction comes forward thematically in Faith's exposure of Talkative and the futility of talk by itself. Truly profitable dialogue may have the rhetorical graces of a Say-well but not with Say-well's motives or Talkative's spiritual weakness. Faith's truthfulness is accordingly blunt and provocative; it is designed to guide spiritual movement and its rejections of worldly motives, just as Christian's renarrations and wayside summaries are designed to keep straight the road he is actually walking.

Bunyan's proliferation of titles and places makes for a different topographical intricacy than that of other allegorical places of the renaissance, even of the protestant homiletic tradition. The multiplying of faces and names around By-ends and in Vanity Fair discredits all secular analogues to the celestial city and therefore a good deal that passes as valuable experience elsewhere. As soon as a representative of worldliness speaks he flies into a discrepancy. In effect, all profane discourse wanders in error, in a terrain where fallacies start up at every turn and are shot down by sharp-eyed quoters of scripture. By-ends' dialogue is an animated extension of a discourse he is obliged to carry on as the logic of his category of error. He cannot talk like Evangelist any more than Evangelist can talk like Parson Two-tongues. Like him, others tend to be simultaneously components of a theological argument and psychological locations or sources of motive, the terrain and its population being an externalizing map of mind and a social topography but above all a set of instructions. Bunyan stresses the functonal *graphia* of topography—the writing out of a realm inscribed everywhere for guidance.

That practice of emblematic sign-posting we discover also in devotional poetry, but as we might expect lyric is concerned less with narrative continuity and the construction of instructional stages than with the enigmas and interpretive prospects of particular places and spiritual states. Vaughan inherited the labeled regions and the otherworldliness of pilgrimage from sources in common with Bunyan, but his byways are less available to moral translation. The demand for an overall direction and an ultimate conclusion is equally strong but harder to convert into a storied progress. In "I Walkt the other day," for instance, Vaughan's pilgrim is puzzled by a discrepancy between the "face of things" and their truth. Destination is subordinate to the exploring of their evasions. The structure of the poem looks to be narrative and is indeed episodic, but it is also inconclusive and suspended, and physical movement gives way early to a meditational probing:

> I Walkt the other day (to spend my hour)
>   Into a field
> Where I sometimes had seen the soil to yield
>   A gallant flowre,
> But Winter now had ruffled all the bowre
>   And curious store
>     I knew there heretofore.
>
> Yet I whose search lov'd not to peep and peer
>   I'th'face of things
> Thought with my self, there might be other springs
>   Besides this here
> Which, like cold friends, sees us but once a year,
>   And so the flowre
>     Might have some other bowre.[3]

The flower's interpretability is complicated by an allusion to Herbert's "Peace," a poem that is itself concerned with ways of conducting a search for ultimate repose. Herbert transcends nature's instability in abandoning caves and gardens for biblical types, and once the search is keyed to the right doctrine, peace comes forward as its product. Here, Vaughan's pilgrim is more casual in his initial walk, and nature's store is somewhat random. The hard season puts out of sight the easier rewards of other occasions, and so the pilgrim must dig and pose "Many a question Intricate and rare." Actually, his first lesson is similar to Herbert's not only in "Peace" but in "The Flower," "Vertue," and other poems: nature's curious offerings and the speaker himself are very frail. First readings are in error. Only the dead are beyond the wintry state and the treacheries of bowers.

Were nature's bowers clearly of no value, however, their attractions would be less serious. As it is, whatever is fair and young extends glimpses of paradise, without which regeneration would lack a psychology and stages of growth. The creative spirit itself after all assumes topographical forms and is their source. An apt interpreter therefore finds it veiled in masques and shadows:

> O thou! whose spirit did at first inflame
>   And warm the dead,
> And by a sacred Incubation fed
>   With life this frame
> Which once had neither being, forme, nor name,

>         Grant I may so
>     Thy steps track here below,
>
> That in these Masques and shadows I may see
>     Thy sacred way,
> And by those hid ascents climb to that day
>     Which breaks from thee
> Who art in all things, though invisibly;
>     Shew me thy peace,
>     Thy mercy, love, and ease.

Vaughan's "O thou!" is typical of his personal lyric crossings, which seek to short-circuit the longer evasions of nature and the pilgrimage through it. The walk does not produce fine doctrinal distinctions of Bunyan's sort. The pilgrim as poet-interpreter or bard wishes to see further into the products of the sacred Incubation and make its breaking day his own awakening. As eternal day descends, it must somehow work free of topographical clues. To read mercy, love, and ease into "all things" invisibly is to translate those things, as doctrine springing "From a poor root" raises "it to the truth and light of things" and makes it less and less rootlike.

In generating the accelerated pace of that "O thou!" Vaughan transposes the music and cadence of the stanza. The casual narrative opening "I walkt the other day (to spend my hour)" has allocated moments of the itinerary to stanzaic parts with some exactness without over-running the lines to any great extent. Significance arises from such walks more or less as it will, and the formal unit accords with the moments. Even so, the opening stanza turns upon that casualness with a sense of irony in the first of the poem's several reversals ("But Winter now had ruffled all the bowre"). The contrast between wintry bleakness and what will "e'r long / Come forth most fair and young" disrupts the fabric of description and the leisure of narrative. The frequency of contrastive movements thereafter signals the unfolding of an ever more intense spiritual search until in the petition itself Vaughan turns measured stanzaic development into an on-rushing enjambment, gathering the last three-stanza section into a single crescendo. The difficulty is to translate one sort of movement and the lesser rewards of field walking into the "Light, Joy, Leisure, and true Comforts" of quite another movement. One way to link them would be simply to make one a proleptic sign of the other. But the pilgrim stands suspended between realms, capable of interrogating the places of his walk but not of bringing forth spiritual counterparts—hence the petitionary mode of the conclusion and the return to the careworn sense of exile.

By comparison to Bunyan's anxiety-ridden, unsteady, but true progress, Vaughan's way not only in "I walkt" but in other topographical progresses is less detailed, and the completion of the journey is more vaguely postponed. Vaughan is obviously less concerned with the familiar types of Vanity Fair and the attractions of the social order, nor does he line the way with specific enemies lying in wait to lure the pilgrim into ditches of folly or quagmires of sin. These differences in technique amount to a different discourse and different conduct of an investigation. They assume less confidence in the open teachability of doctrine and a significant residue of religious mystery in scripture itself. Vaughan's mode in "I walkt" is after all quintessentially lyric and is not instructional in the way of a gathered Puritan sainthood; it makes intensified personal approaches both to things and to the spirit represented obscurely in them, incubated in forms, hovering in names and substances. Settings like the fountain of "Regeneration" and the fields of "I walkt" do not offer the poet the hermeneutic aids of an Interpreter or Palace Beautiful, despite the questions "Intricate and rare" one might address to them. Whether we come from Bunyan, Herbert, or such earlier pilgrimages as Redcross's, then, we are struck by the spiritual trauma of Vaughan's pilgrim figures, the cause of which is a gap between realms and a difficulty in the messages that "hid ascents" permit. The suggestiveness of descriptive language cannot be separated entirely from that signifier-referent hiatus and the structural complexity that comes of the poet's going back and forth between the spirit "in all things, though invisibly" and the things themselves.

QUESTING WITHOUT REACHING AFTER FACT OR SYSTEM

Vaughan uses both Donnean conceits and Bunyanesque walking allegories, but his pathways and their figures are less cerebral. Unlike the Coleridge that Keats thought he saw, he does not try to coerce half-knowledge into enlightenment and thereby let escape "a fine isolated verisimilitude caught from the Penetralium of mystery." Not that he is entirely content with doubt, as Keats on occasion thought poets should be; but his best poetry assumes its inevitability and when it turns to direct address presupposes a considerable distance between speaker and object. Settings for the elusive spirit are difficult even from the vantage points of biblical typology. They are vague enough at times to suggest solipsism, although Vaughan as the swan of Isca is also the genius of a particular region. He is often a poet of halting and broken momentum toward the paradisal terrain he would prefer to inhabit and a constructor of structural irregularities, which go with being unsettled.

I do not mean to suggest that Vaughan has no use for reason, but he expects less of it than Donne and less of doctrine than Herbert. A sign of his restlessness in this regard is the proximity of wilderness and the forsaking of enclosures. As he views the apocalypse, for instance, it undoes all directions and locations, as in "Day of Judgement" a consuming fire rushes to all points of the compass almost instantaneously and makes further pilgrimage unnecessary,

> When through the North a fire shall rush
> And rowle into the East,
> And like a firie torrent brush
> And sweepe up *South*, and *West*.

The ascension series at the beginning of Part 2 of *Silex Scintillans* contrasts celestial soaring with the limitations of those who are not yet ready for deliverance. The pilgrim himself, in spirit at least, takes the loftier way:

> I soar and rise
> Up to the skies,
> Leaving the world their day.

To soar is clearly not a rational process. The abandonment of Herbert's enclosure and possession for wilderness is the topographical equivalent to impatience with plodding logic and its servant discourse. As the saved on the last great day run "in their white robes to seek the risen Sun," he imagines their impressive transformation. When the visionary company have departed in "Ascension-Hymn," he is acutely aware of the distance between his place and theirs:

> They are all gone into the world of light!
> And I alone sit lingring here;
> Their very memory is fair and bright,
> And my sad thoughts doth clear....
> I see them walking in an Air of glory,
> Whose light doth trample on my days.

Although walking and soaring both have the potential to solve heaven's mysteries, only death will completely unveil them. The pilgrim's central project may be to decipher his surroundings and locate the divine spirit within them, then, but he seldom builds bridges for the reader to cross between one kind of observation and another.

It would be a mistake to find Vaughan's experience of the semivagabond state too greatly different from that of other Christian pilgrimages, but economies of nature are more common elsewhere, and they are primarily that which provides bridges to providence, as in Herbert's itemization, for instance:

> Who hath the vertue to express the rare
> And curious vertues both of herbs and stones?
> Is there an herb for that? O that thy care
> Would show a root, that gives expressions!
>
> And if an herb hath power, what have the starres?
> A rose, besides his beautie, is a cure.
> Doubtlesse our plagues and plentie, peace and warres
> Are there much surer then our art is sure.
>
> "Providence"

That economy suggests human possession and home ground even if the poet lacks precise words to say just how, as Hakluyt's navigators and Purchas's pilgrims aim to possess and use what providence puts before them—one by mapping, the other by translating geographical features into allegory. Vaughan's pilgrims must forgo even the edenic remnants they find in nature if they are to discover the way to regeneration. As "Ascension-Hymn" explains:

> Dust and clay
> Mans antient wear!
> Here you must stay,
> But I elsewhere;
> Souls sojourn here, but may not rest;
> Who will ascend, must be undrest.
>
> And yet some
> That know to die
> Before death come,
> Walk to the skie
> Even in this life; but all such can
> Leave behinde them the old Man.

This rings with proverb assurance and clarity along a string of rhymes until metaphoric death replaces the real one and we find those who somehow walk the skies "Even in this life." Faith may fill in where reason falters, but even scripture sometimes recedes from reach. The lost Son can no longer be tracked in "The Pursuite," and again no Evangelist or Palace Beautiful makes a timely appearance to offer individual instruction. The single beam of light the sun leaves the pilgrim in "Mans Fall, and Recovery" serves mainly to remind him of the general dispossession of humankind.

In "Regeneration," which conducts Vaughan's most noteworthy pilgrimage, it seems doubtful that the viator ends much closer to his goal than he begins; the spirit's evasiveness is unceasing. The exterior world initially reflects the pilgrim's condition, and subsequently certain figures take up stations as though as signs for crossroads. But progress is notable for its abruptness and lack of distinct way-stations. When a second spring arrives, it reflects upon the first one's incapacity to thaw the heart and suggests something approaching the paradise that eye and ear find in accord with inner wishes:

> The unthrift Sunne shot vitall gold
> A thousand peeces,
> And heaven its azure did unfold
> Checqur'd with snowie fleeces,
> The aire was all in spice
> And every bush
> A garland wore; Thus fed my Eyes
> But all the Eare lay hush.

Splendor momentarily thrusts aside dissatisfaction, and presumably the speaker need not puzzle himself about significance when such blessings shower down and the sun gives a foretaste of paradise. But the spirit refuses to grant him personal applications of doctrine and indeed declares that its only statement is precisely this nondeclaration. It comes and goes as it pleases, whether in visiting the soul in exegetical acts that turn the letter into truth or in visiting poets as their muse.

Vaughan is especially anxious about the latter guidance. "Regeneration" follows a confessional preface that attacks secular verse (including presumably *Olar Iscanus*) and endorses Herbert as a model of sacred writing. The blasted infant buds of the opening stanza and the sin that eclipses the mind thus no doubt reflect both the usual errors of youth and a brief career of errant poems. "Regeneration" makes an opening demonstration of a new poetics as permeated with vital gold as the scriptural text, its unthrift sun, allows. The poem does in fact have moments of brightness and rained-down abundance and seems on the verge of discovering not only the transcendent paradise of gospel but a real presence in the worded here and now. The pilgrim listens to every sound and watches keenly every stirring leaf in hopes that the rushing wind heralds that presence. But the poem is equally given to sudden turns away:

> I turn'd me round, and to each shade
> Dispatch'd an Eye,
> To see, if any leafe had made
> Least motion, or Reply,
> But while I listning sought
> My mind to ease
> By knowing, where 'twas, or where not,
> It whisper'd; *where I please.*

It is at that point of greatest expectations that the baffling message comes and refuses to be a message. The colloquy it extracts, "Lord, then said I, On me one breath, / And let me dye before my death!" is a desperate one—despite the receptive state induced by the hushed silence and despite the unthrifty sun. The plenitude of scent and of signs only intensifies the absence of sound that might confirm some intent behind the snowy fleeces. The problem is to get from one spiritual plane to another and to finish the journey. Scriptural parallels offer assistance, but I find them less decisive here than other interpreters do.[4] Vaughan treats each turn of the spiritual work not as a stage in exegesis but as a personal trial. That passages in scripture are themselves written in metaphoric code appears to mean that they are intended to veil their secrets.

Vaughan's expectations in "Regeneration" are both keen and beyond fulfillment. By comparison, not only Bunyan but Traherne tends to stress the certainties of landscape and the reachability of its blessings, as in the simplicity of youth:

> All appeared New, and Strange at the first, inexpressibly rare, And Delightfull, and Beautifull. I was a litle Stranger which at my Enterance into the World was Saluted and Surrounded with innumerable Joys. My Knowledg was Divine. I knew by Intuition those things which since my Apostasie, I Collected again, by the Highest Reason....
> The Corn was Orient and Immortal Wheat, which never should be reaped, nor was ever sown. I thought it had stood from everlasting to everlasting. The Dust and Stones of the Street were as Precious as GOLD. The Gates were at first the End of the World, The Green Trees when I saw them first through one of the Gates Transported and Ravished me; their Sweetness and unusual Beauty made my Heart to leap.[5]

Traherne finds less to puzzle over and less to feel guilty about. If one encounters deceptions, these do not stem from inherent enigmas of place. In contrast, when Vaughan turns to search the shadows and listens intently for something to quiet desire, he is instructed in effect to wait: either preparation has not been complete or the receptacle is not sufficient for the burden. The spirit that whispers to him will not be invoked for visionary privileges, as Milton's will, and will not codify itself into rites of passage, as the poem has suggested it might at first. Even to institute a House of Holiness or Hill of Contemplation might be to lessen it by explanation. The best that Vaughan's pilgrim can expect is thus an intermittent divine presence that leads him on.

## THE CALENDAR OF PILGRIMAGE

The Christian calendar places the soul's research among objects in the differing lights that special moments cast. That calendar is set for Vaughan as for Herbert and the tradition largely by the events of Christ's life, which pilgrims use to mark their own stages. "Ascension-day," for instance, like other days of the Son, will bring divine force definitively into play, and the quickened soul thinking ahead to it can see its deliverance:

> Thy glorious, bright Ascension (though remov'd
> So many Ages from me) is so prov'd
> And by thy Spirit seal'd to me, that I
> Feel me a sharer in thy victory.

Or since that day is quite exceptional, the soul can turn to Sunday's foretaste of victory:

> 1.
> Bright shadows of true Rest! some shoots of blisse,
>     Heaven once a week;
> The next worlds gladness prepossest in this;
>     A day to seek;
>
> Eternity in time; the steps by which
> We Climb above all ages; Lamps that light
> Man through his heap of dark days; and the rich,
> And full redemption of the whole weeks flight.
>
> 2.
> The Pulleys unto headlong man; times bower;
>     The narrow way;
> Transplanted Paradise; Gods walking houre;
>     The Cool o'th' day;
>
> The Creatures *Jubile;* Gods parle with dust;
> Heaven here; Man on those hills of Myrrh, and flowres;
> Angels descending; the Returns of Trust;
> A Gleam of glory, after six-days-showres.
>
> 3.
> The Churches love-feasts; Times Prerogative,
>     And Interest
> Deducted from the whole; The Combs, and hive,
>     And home of rest.
>
> The milky way Chalkt out with Suns; a Clue
> That guides through erring hours; and in full story
> A taste of Heav'n on earth; the pledge, and Cue
> Of a full feast; And the Out Courts of glory.

Vaughan lists Sunday's attributes in a copious mode, gathering nearly three dozen figures from society, nature, and theology in a looseness that points up the sundry satisfactions of spirit. The differences from Bunyan and Herbert are again notable in that miscellany. Herbert's "Prayer I," which provides the technique of other Vaughan poems as well as this one, arranges its objects with much greater care. Although both octave and sestet mix concrete and abstract terms for prayer, the octave stresses physical measurements and movements from earth to heaven and back. The sestet, less active, pursues the placid results. So delivered, words have some of the stability and permanence of peace as well as the exalted style of men well dressed, heaven descended.

Although Vaughan mentions a similar seeking and climbing in "Son-dayes," his concern is weekly deliveries of the divine, and since Sundays are but a sample, a "Clue," he is simultaneously aware of an undelivered remainder. His images make a series of propositions, each dropped as the next appears, so that progress through them means continual displacement rather than a crossing from the temporal to the eternal. Although the opening theme is sustained, varied, and insistent, every metaphor comes as though a new term of praise. That Sundays have so many sides, all of them new contacts with God, testifies not merely to the poet's ingenuity but to the fullness of their gifts. Any structural development beyond amplification would violate the repetitive nature of those lamps that come regularly to light "man through his heap of dark days." To demonstrate its point, the poem need document only "the rich, / And full redemption of the whole weeks flight."

Vaughan's Sabbath makes certain contacts with eternity possible without speech—paradoxically best by "bright shadows of true Rest"—which is to say by a light revealed *as* shadow. The scent of spices, the smile of the day star, and the primrosed fields suggest a "posting intercourse and mirth / Of Saints and Angels" to clarify earth. But on ordinary days, the poet cannot expect such declarations, and the year obviously contains more of such than it does church holidays. Creatures in their sullen mysteries then refuse to speak. In one surprising stop, in fact, in "The Stone," the pilgrim finds even mute plants turning against man and serving as spies, which gives a new twist to the world's obscurity. Informing objects cannot be bribed as human witnesses can and do not consent readily to any gainful ill, as women do: "No gold nor gifts can them subdue." Instead, Vaughan finds a sinister truthfulness in them:

> They hear, see, speak,
> And into loud discoveries break,
> As loud as blood. Not that God needs
> Intelligence, whose spirit feeds
> All things with life, before whose eyes,
> Hell and all hearts stark naked lyes.

The very stones will accuse men, then, in the end, as scripture has said they will. God has them do so because "ev'n mans own eye / Must needs acknowledge" them to be just:

> Hence sand and dust
> Are shak'd for witnesses, and stones
> Which some think dead, shall all at once
> With one attesting voice detect
> Those secret sins we least suspect.
> For know, wilde men, that when you erre
> Each thing turns Scribe and Register,
> And in obedience to his Lord,
> Doth your most private sins record.

This goes beyond the passage from *Joshua* (24.27) that Vaughan cites, since Joshua intended merely to erect a monument in testimony to God's covenant with his people. Because everything bears witness here, not even savages are too remote to lack a confessional; "ev'ry bush is somethings booth." Nature becomes not a general book of types and symbols or a kind of church but a ledger of specific misdeeds; all lyric approach to it is choked off by the sins it must report.

The spirit is not totally capricious for Vaughan, however, or Sundays would not be so regular and the final judgment so certain. Like Herbert, Vaughan addresses a considerable number of confessional lyrics directly to God and to his representatives, including light. He also knows something of Traherne's uncomplicated communion of childhood and the delights of rendering daily tribute. Indeed, he finds morning birds more easily interpreted than we might expect and in awakening poems reinforces celebration with something close to certainty when the moment is right. As Jonathan Post has observed in noting the distinction between "The Morning-watch" and "The Evening-watch," Vaughan prefers the early hour and offers it an adamic hymn (p. 196). In "Providence" water and timely sustenance come by mysterious means, but by comparison to the wealth of states and powers of kings they are less subject to abrupt removal. This the birds themselves know:

> none can sequester or let
> A state that with the Sun doth set
> And comes next morning fresh as he.
>
> Poor birds this doctrine sing,
> And herbs which on dry hills do spring
> Or in the howling wilderness
> Do know thy dewy morning-hours,
> And watch all night for mists or showers,
> Then drink and praise thy bounteousness.

No doubt they have their kinship with poets as birds do elsewhere, and it is recurrence of new life in the face of wilderness deprivations that brings them to song. At a creaturely level, what appears to the senses is often interpretable; one humanized dimension of providence is its daily economy. Or as Vaughan remarks in "The Bird" concerning similar alternations of tribulation and blessings, hymns come forth more cheerfully for the good buffeting of sullen storms, which mark a special providential calendar:

> Hither thou com'st: the busie wind all night
> Blew through thy lodging, where thy own warm wing
> Thy pillow was. . . .
> And now as fresh and chearful as the light
> Thy little heart in early hymns doth sing
> Unto that *Providence*, whose unseen arm
> Curb'd them, and cloath'd thee well and warm.
>     All things that be, praise him; and had
>     Their lesson taught them, when first made.
>
> So hills and valleys into singing break,
> And though poor stones have neither speech nor tongue,
> While active winds and streams both run and speak,
> Yet stones are deep in admiration.

That deep admiration of stones should not be underestimated, nor should the more familiar heralding of dawn by a bird capable of exemplifying what Vaughan in "Cock-Crowing" calls a transplanted "seed":

> Father of lights! what Sunnie seed,
> What glance of day hast thou confin'd
> Into this bird? To all the breed
> This busie Ray thou has assign'd;
>     Their magnetisme works all night,
>     And dreams of Paradise and light.

The source of life is the same as the source of the clarity that enables one to interpret it. Daybreak is valuable not only for what it reveals directly but also for what it hints, as in "Rules and Lessons":

> *Mornings* are *Mysteries;* the first worlds *Youth,*
> Mans *Resurection,* and the futures *Bud*
> Shrowd in their births: The Crown of life, light, truth
> Is stil'd their *starre,* the *stone,* and *hidden food.*
>     Three *blessings* wait upon them, two of which
>     Should move; They make us *holy, happy, rich.*

However, birds of light "Chirping their solemn Matins on each tree" are likely to be counterbalanced by the heavy notes of "dark fowls." Enlightened moments, like Sundays, tend to appear as interludes in any fuller reading of Vaughan. Actually, a veil falls even between the poet and the crowing cock. It brings forth an urgent petition to the cock to cross to the perfect day that it heralds, which in "Cock-crowing" constitutes the poet's true destination and the end of calendar days:

> Onely this Veyle which thou hast broke,
> And must be broken yet in me,

> This veyle, I say, is all the cloke
> And cloud which shadows thee from me.
> This veyle thy full-ey'd love denies,
> And onely gleams and fractions spies.
>
> O take it off! make no delay,
> But brush me with thy light, that I
> May shine unto a perfect day,
> And warme me at thy glorious Eye!

Such apostrophes are exclamatory precisely because of the incompleteness of the journey.

Vaughan's alternation of dark and light moments shows in several brilliant metaphoric beginnings that trail off into doubts or into moralizing and make the structure of his poems appear disproportionate and the ends anticlimactic at times. His hold upon favorable moments is somewhat strengthened by the vocabulary of hermetic philosophy and alchemy, which interprets the indirect ways of providence working in a variety of nature's forms. But that vocabulary is closer to an intuitive dualism than to rational science.[6] In the hermetic way as a negative state or preparation, to take one phase of it, the soul moves toward light's purity only paradoxically, by way of dark, which is both a spiritual abandonment and an absence of signs. Although it is also a preparatory blank that disciplines the pilgrim's crossing, as Vaughan suggests in "Resurrection and Immortality," even resurrection takes the way of mortification, doomsday the way of destruction:

> a preserving spirit doth still passe
>   Untainted through this Masse,
> Which doth resolve, produce, and ripen all
>   That to it fall;
>   Nor are those births which we
>     Thus suffering see
> Destroy'd at all; But when times restles wave
>   Their substance doth deprave
> And the more noble *Essence* finds his house
>   Sickly, and loose,
>   He, ever young, doth wing
>     Unto that spring,
> And *source* of spirits, where he takes his lot
>   Till time no more shall rot
> His passive Cottage; which (though laid aside,)
>   Like some spruce Bride,
> Shall one day rise, and cloath'd with shining light
>   All pure, and bright
> Re-marry to the soule, for 'tis most plaine
>   Thou only fal'st to be refin'd againe.

This may sound at first like rhymed philosophy, as though from a spiritualist opposite of Lucretius translated from Latin. But it has a greater love of paradoxes to go with a touch of Bunyan in its animation. Its strong interactions of soul and matter, light and dark, sickness and health, falling and rising are less enigmatic in this case, thanks partly to the certainty of the hermeticism. "Resolve, produce, and ripen" is a surprising sequence when we realize the responsibility that bodies are being assigned for the development of their inmates. Even so, incarnation or its duration is still dangerous to the soul and undercuts the value of pilgrimage: long life is not really educative but degenerative. The "spruce" bride of the resurrection has some of Bunyan's awakening and upspringing energy after that prolonged crisis. In a typical Vaughan rhythm of visions that open out and close down again, the passage offers a sense of ascension before returning to the voice of epigram or proverb. Superimposed on this rhythm of realizations is a pattern of rhymed lines, the couplings of which toll off alternating longer and shorter phrases until a pair of iambic pentameter lines completes the narrative course and its summing up. Unevenness is thereby curbed more than usually as doctrine finds its voice, but of course only by way of a futuristic promise that leaves some dissatisfaction with the current life. Only when bodies are fully permeated with spirit will they conform to it.

The hermetic vocabulary of "Resurrection and Immortality" helps Vaughan assess the incarnation and the interpenetration of moments far apart by calendar measure but close at hand in vision. "Preserving," "untainted," "substance," "essence," and the release of light all have chemical implications in which the mysterious knitting of material and immaterial substances follows certain rules. Pursuing the course of those rules, the stanza wavers and then develops a crescendo of the kind that can make Vaughan's philosophical passages an adventure. However, the pilgrim's capacity to find allegorical significance in such mixtures of chemical and esoteric tropes is usually insufficient compensation for the persistent darkness of bodies, and Vaughan does not always seem to know the relative weight of the soul's trials or how they work toward the ends it desires.

Getting doctrine from objects to exploit for poetic purposes is not really at issue, except in a few hermetic poems like this one, nor is the dramatic sense that the poems often lack; rather what seems to be missing is a perception of depths that make the viator pull back from the spiritual edge and call upon intelligence. Ideally, his sustaining powers should dwell simultaneously in the wits and in the feelings. But the urgency of Vaughan's excursions onto mountainsides is somewhat blunted by a generalizing habit he shares with his times and its sententious capsules. Perhaps the best that such moralizing can produce comes in "Regeneration," which combines confession with emblem and uses both to fend off "cliffs of fall / Frightful, sheer, no-man-fathomed" (in Hopkins's words), as in the impressive mixture of mountainous extremity and introspective assessment in the initial disequilibrium that sets the question in motion:

> Storm'd thus; I straight perceiv'd my spring
>    Meere stage, and show,
> My walke a monstrous, mountain'd thing
>   Rough-cast with Rocks, and snow;
>   And as a Pilgrims Eye
>     Far from reliefe,
> Measures the melancholy skye
>    Then drops, and rains for grief,
>
> So sigh'd I upwards still.

Getting to the pinnacle quickly at the outset, Vaughan's speaker finds scales there that weigh smoky pleasures and late pains. They serve not as comforts but as a focal point that draws the mind from its internal state to an emblematic judgment before the poet proceeds to the next part of the landscape.

We might expect reinforcements by some stronger developmental principle at this juncture if Vaughan is to follow up the allegory of the mountain and its scale or make the process of regeneration something akin to that of Christian's journey. As it is, by turning to the "unthrift Sunne," he leaves hanging what has preceded. Without much elaboration he drops the idea of the false spring and the provocations of eclipsing clouds and storms that lead to it. But the dreamlike rapidity of movement and the abrupt transitions are effective in their own right, as are the economy of phrasing and the unexpected vistas. Vaughan changes scenes adeptly even where he does not propel one from another by any logic we can anticipate or paraphrase. One reason the intelligence cannot take the initiative or even keep pace is that the spirit places enigmas in every element, not merely in its whispering of "where I please." The questing soul is thus always in danger of being drawn too far into things that promise to be decipherable but turn out to be traps. In "The Tempest" even the hermetic mind may follow its chemical curiosity too ardently down quasi-scientific byways:

> Sure, mighty love foreseeing the discent
>   Of this poor Creature, by a gracious art
>   Hid in these low things snares to gain his heart,
> And layd surprizes in each Element.
>
> All things here shew him heaven; *Waters* that fall
>   Chide, and fly up; *Mists* of corruptest fome

> Quit their first beds and mount; trees, herbs, flowres, all
> Strive upwards stil, and point him the way home.

Such things are interpretable seeds, and "all have their *keyes,* and set *ascents.*" But man, "Though he knows these, and hath more of his own, / Sleeps at the ladders foot." Tricked into companionship with leaf and flower, "hugs he stil his durt."

Liberating men from the dictates of the body and from things converted into signs is one of the tasks of the negative way and the emptying moment. The answer in "The Night" to the abundance of clues is blankness, and to confusion, an act of faith:

> There is in God (some say)
> A deep, but dazling darkness; As men here
> Say it is late and dusky, because they
>     See not all clear;
> O for that night! where I in him
> Might live invisible and dim.

Such descents are practice for the greater obliteration that inspires the ascension poems and "Resurrection and Immortality." They are the reverse side of Sundays. The lingering doubts of "some say" are brushed aside by the wishful equivalent to apostrophe in "O for that night!" But nothing in the poem is more impressive than the visualizing of night's blocking of interferences and its own substantial gifts. Unlighted dew, soft calls, and the attachments of like things make up a network of catches for the soul. The regular returns of night are types of the cycle that will complete the course of natural forms; they assist hermetic wisdom's penetration to secret ties within and beyond mere chemistry, the more powerfully for their escape of reason and possession.

It is not always clear how we are to reconcile the expectation of blessedness with Vaughan's frequent indeterminacy, or abstractions like "The Crown of life, light, truth" with vestiges of the creator embedded obscurely in nature. But Vaughan is perhaps less inconsistent in addressing actual sites than he seems at first. Casual and idiomatic turns of phrase find a middle ground between visionary hope and the stock of unreliable things on which it feeds. His balancing of what lies at hand with panoramic sweep can sometimes have startling results, as in the opening of "The World," justifiably one of his most celebrated passages:

> I Saw Eternity the other night
> Like a great *Ring* of pure and endless light,
>     All calm, as it was bright,
> And round beneath it, Time in hours, days, years,
>     Driv'n by the spheres

> Like a vast shadow mov'd, In which the world
> And all her train were hurl'd.

This surpasses anything that previous allegorists venture and puts in succinct terms Vaughan's blend of temporal and visionary lyric loci. Perhaps a habit of solitude on the margins without the prospect of an intimate audience was necessary before this blend could be found. Certainly in moving from the Jonsonian poet of the small circle in *Poems* (1646) to the poet of a shattered courtly community surrounded by what he considered to be the madness of warrior saints, Vaughan felt more keenly than most the poet's isolation and reduced public role, though he made a virtue indeed of adversity. It helped to have Herbert's ease with common language as a model, just as the satiric portions of what follows the opening vision of "The World" benefit from Donne. The first line has the casual tone almost of a report of an evening's outing, but the vision itself appears to come from no particular occasion or predictable time.

The transition from lyric to irony and to Bunyanesque types who ignore such visions suggests something of Vaughan's flexibility and skill in the unfolding of a capacious stanzaic unit. He rarely attempts to combine wit and lyric as Donne and Jonson do once he assumes the vatic voice of *Silex*, but the main body of "The World" consists of an incisive rendering of the complaining lover, statesman, miser, and "down-right Epicure." The view from eternity encourages some such estimation of "time in hours, days, years," but only the capacity to portion out the dramatic movement of the vision in the idiomatic voice of the down-to-earth prophet makes the marriage of levels possible. The contrast of tones and attitudes is perhaps even more Blakean than Bunyanesque in the address to fools:

> Yet some, who all this while did weep and sing,
> And sing, and weep, soar'd up into the *Ring,*
>   But most would use no wing.
> O fools (said I,) thus to prefer dark night
>   Before true light,
> To live in grots, and caves, and hate the day
>   Because it shews the way,
> The way which from this dead and dark abode
>   Leads up to God,
> A way where you might tread the Sun, and be
>   More bright than he.
> But as I did their madnes so discusse
>   One whisper'd thus,
> *This Ring the Bride-groome did for none provide*
>   *But for his bride.*

Nothing about eternity can be fully vocalized, but the speaker carries the spiritual crossing into lecture, in an address that he *can* make. Within the cave, one cannot walk or soar, and yet in nearly all the ordinary days of the year one is confined there. Favored ones who walk grandly may "tread the Sun," but they must be chosen to do so. The final whispered message eludes all those who persist in their madness.[7] The poet himself is not yet delivered, and that postponing of completion we come to expect: as the desire for conclusion pushes ahead, the interpretive process lingers.

The encounters of Vaughan's pilgrims with places and special moments are more intense for the presence-absence of the spirit in masques and shadows and, paradoxically, in prodigious gifts of nature as well. Those pilgrims find fewer sure footholds to prevent falling than Christian does; tenor and vehicle are less securely joined than a name like Worldly Wiseman joins them. Consequently, surfaces call attention to themselves. But Vaughan is less fully aware of the implications for metaphor of the evasiveness of objects than one might expect, especially by comparison with Marvell in poems like "A Dialogue between the Resolved Soul, and Created Pleasure" and "On a Drop of Dew." Sometimes wavering between lyric apostrophe, confession, and elegy, sometimes combining all three, as in "I walkt," Vaughan feels the enticements of the spirit's near presence and yet knows too the great distance to paradise. That the spirit shatters its gold into a thousand pieces is both prodigal in generosity and disunifying. If the various modes are not always coherently sorted out and logically sequenced, his better lyrics nonetheless make passage through what he believes to be parts of a single realm. They create their own topographical blend of concrete image and suggestive symbol shading into allegory. No one balances lyric possession and celebration with quite his sense of their limits and their local recollections of the sacred incubation that feeds "with life this frame." His sense of end things is also his own. As the concluding poems of both *Silex* I and *Silex* II indicate ("Begging" and "L'Envoy"), the search goes on. If "The new worlds new, quickning Sun" remains certain, the end draws off. The interim yields some social and religious programming but no reformation progress or Herbertlike communion. Corruption will grow until the sickle of *Revelations* thrusts in. The poet meanwhile expects some transfers of authority and insight directly to him, but mainly he must cope with postponement. Things that will appear in eternity's "cloudless glass" without "blemish or decay" are observable beforehand only behind "This long worn veyl." The function of the text is to juxtapose, cross back and forth, and ultimately to petition, in the one kind of apostrophe that means most to Bunyan and Herbert, too: "Dear Lord, do this!"

*The viscous Air, wheres'ere She Fly,*
*Follows and sucks her Azure dy;*
*The gellying Stream compacts below,*
*If it might fix her shadow so;*
*The stupid Fishes hang, as plain*
*As* Flies *in* Chrystal *overt'ane;*
*And Men the* Silent *Scene assist,*
*Charm'd with the* Saphir-winged Mist.
                "*Upon Appleton House,*" *673–80*

# MARVELL'S FLIES IN CRYSTAL

CHAPTER TEN

One of the seventeenth century's more ambitious and eccentric poems, "Upon Appleton House" touches upon several of the century's concerns with lyric settings, sometimes in oblique and unexpected as well as important ways. Without making too fine a point of it, one can see pieces of Jonson's country house modeling of propriety and taste, Donnean wit, and, in the woodland scene, traces of a Vaughanlike hermeticism. Something akin to Milton's genius of place appears momentarily in the speaker in that same scene and in Maria Fairfax later. Like Milton, Herbert, and Vaughan, Marvell gauges topography by likeness to paradise insofar as it can be imagined, though he is less direct and single-minded in doing so, both here and in other poems. He finds chaos beyond the estate but "decent order tame" within it. He puts lyric apostrophes to several uses from parody to praise, mixing them with narrative, descriptive, and proverbial or epigrammatic segments. Like Bunyan and Vaughan, he explores the nature of signs and the limits of clarity and order among them. The woodland offers a discourse of mosaic leaves and divining birds, though nothing so explicitly allegorical as Bunyan's Interpreter or Vaughan's waterfall. "Upon Appleton House" goes beyond juxtaposition and topographical sequence in fitting one thing to another, its concern being partly with representation and fitness, or with how one thing is represented in another, large in small, for instance. It thus works through metonymy to metaphor and through description to encomium.

In orchestrating all of this, the wandering philosopher who conducts our tour of Appleton takes an unusual and uneven passage among specific scenes and objects, subjecting them to devices of perspective. He superintends our perception of the likenesses he gathers in a spectrum of settings, natural, familial, national. These are not uniformly serious devices, as most readers have acknowledged; in its many-faceted genre mixing, the poem is not hesitant to mix moods.[1] In the woodland nature's expressive mode opens to bardlike perceptions, for instance, but then yields quickly to self-effacement. Although some skepticism about a persona who changes from moment to moment is in order, Marvell does not extend the poem's irreverence to the household itself, at the nominal center of the poem, or to likeness between the estate's topography and paradise. He builds upon the soundness of the family and the promise of its youngest member.

METAPHORIC MAPPING

When Maria walks through the meadows of "Upon Appleton House" at evening, she has a surprising impact upon both objects and the poet's figures. Let us begin with that transmission of an influence and conversion of proximity into likeness. Thanks to the speaker's enthusiasm and outbreak of thematic explicitness, we have no difficulty appreciating the fact that from both her and her emblem, the kingfisher, Appleton's creatures borrow their best qualities; the question is just how. Answers require both metaphysical considerations and attention to the nature of the magic and the charms that genii loci claim. As souls command bodies and as heavenly influences descend to earth, so special agents exercise authority over nature. But we also recognize a good deal of poetic license in Marvell's exaggeration of Maria's impact and realize that it is just such license that signals the generation of lyric enthusiasm from description. To go from a juxtaposition of objects to encomium requires that Maria bring into play both heavenly powers and a chemistry visibly at work on objects, as the thinner substances of water and air, for instance, thicken to hold the kingfisher's "azure dy" and shadow.

In the simplest terms, this is a way for a panegyrist to say merely that everything is struck by her; but even so, the behavior of things is unusual and the description extended. Marvell notices the corporeality of objects and parallels between their wonderment over her and an increasingly viscous verbal medium. Before introducing the thickening of the air, for instance, he comments generally on nature's power to pull its miscellany into order: "See how loose Nature in respect / To her, it self doth recollect" (657–58). That recollection is again almost chemical, as though elements once scattered in chaos begin to bond and find their proper mixtures only when Maria appears. The word "recollect" links that gathering of elements with memory's casting back to their origins, in a paradise that once was. The sun, earth, clouds, and streams all offer tribute as a phase of the estate's mapping of paradise. Struck by her presence and by the halcyon ("And each an horror calm and dumb, / *Admiring Nature* does benum," 671–72), air and water compact; fire and earth change places and generate new vitality in each other. If comets and falling stars that have been exhaled "from the putrid Earth" (687–88) perish quickly, in their place Maria draws all earth into her train and makes it light or glass.

Praise is based here on a transumptive carrying of large powers into local ones. Vitrification is not exclusively a lighting process or an interior inspiration; it is also hardening, in keeping with the other thickenings of substance. If Maria's flaming implants the glow of stars in nature, it also compresses what it influences, as the "Saphire-winged" mist, which charms those who look upon it, thickens air. Some testing of lower elements by fire has already taken place in the woodland's "light Mosaic" from which fancy weaves its prophecies, and something similar is perhaps suggested in the divinations of bird song, which the speaker links with fire upon his entry into the woodland (511–12). Water is no longer merely water but a receptacle for images, earth no longer putrified substance sending off sparks but a glassy mirror. Everything recollects itself in something other as crude nature advances a degree toward celestial emerald and gold. The relationship of symbols to ultimate referents in this topographical mirroring is similar to that of history to myth, or map to higher reality: it stresses the gap and the difference but also the workability of the connection. Given that gap, however, the poet must step back and get a run at lyric. Description does not automatically work toward it.

As Marvell sets relations between the greater order and Appleton on sound footing, he allows nothing to fly hauntingly out of range. No voices from the depths of the forest remind him of a mortal's inability to follow; he needs no visiting powers or romantic avatars since Maria is fully before him. Even so, verbal containers never quite fit their contents, any more than the stream can really catch the kingfisher or its shadow. Nature's reaction to Maria and the legendary halcyon suspends the more normal associations of kind, size, and function—with some strain on metaphoric logic. He emphasizes that yoking of unlike things by paying attention not only to their unusual thickness but to color and arrangement. Textured qualities constitute an expressiveness-in-stillness, as he suggests in "Admiring Nature does benum" and in "stupid Fishes." The speaker does not distort to the point of deformity, to be sure, or he would find no access to paradise even through this extraordinary map; but odd associations continue all the way to the end. Flies associated with fish become all the more oddly flies. It is their customary nature to buzz and be inconsequential; made ornamental in crystal and rendered very quiet, they testify to the power that vitrifies. The portrait of the meadows infolded by the snakelike stream is similar in visual oddity. The stream licks its own muddy back and becomes clear. All told, the poem presents a good deal of such, sometimes ostentatiously: herons dropping young from trees, bloody Thestylis pouncing on wounded rails, cattle that look like fleas, eels that bellow in oxen, boats that sail over bridges, inverted trees, grasshoppers laughing from tall grass like giants overhead, and brambles that pin down and wrap up the speaker.

Some of these explorations of the near-grotesque may be intended to appeal in an Alice-in-Wonderland style to a young Maria herself. But the assault on decorum begins long before she appears in the poem. In the opening stanzas, the speaker violates the moral and aesthetic discriminations he claims to value and raises the problem of scale and proportion. That initial assault indicates the poem's distrust of media and prepares for Maria's correction of lumpish and deformed things. In finding mysteries in nature's meadow and woodland forms and complications in their interpretation, Marvell proceeds to a second phase of "unproportion'd dwellings" and gives containment and fenestration epistemological implications, at the same time preparing for the clearer descent of the divine to Maria, Appleton's best window onto paradise. When she is not in the vicinity he notices the babble of things and calls of one thing to another in a variety of voices. All efforts at coding and decoding are subject to disruption. Birds with their heavenly dialects and grasshoppers with their squeaks sound strange to human ears:

> And now to the Abbyss I pass
> Of that unfathomable Grass,
> Where Men like Grashoppers appear,
> But Grashoppers are Gyants there:
> They, in their squeking Laugh, contemn
> Us as we walk more low then them:

> And, from the Precipices tall
> Of the green spir's, to us do call.
>
> 369–76

Whether one understands what these creatures say or not, or what the sentinel bee means when it asks "the word," the likeness of their sounds to language is unmistakable, as again with the nightingale that makes "tryals of her voice" and reminds us of figures for the lyricist staking claims and lamenting. The poet takes the call of doves more especially for his own and as an "easie philosopher" claims success in deciphering and imitating other birds as well, though he never tells us what they say.

In any case gestures toward lyric are not sustained more than a moment until later. They become stronger in the woodland's light mosaic and its infiltrating sense of the divine:

> Already I begin to call
> In their most learned Original:
> And where I Language want, my Signs
> The Bird upon the Bough divines;
> And more attentive there doth sit
> Then if She were with Lime-twigs knit.
> No Leaf does tremble in the Wind
> Which I returning cannot find.
>
> 569–76

But even here a persona who has imagined himself a bird and an inverted tree undermines seriousness to some extent. From reading in nature's book, he quickly passes to chance's better wit, embroidery in oak leaves, a languishing on moss while the wind winnows his thoughts, and from there to his strangest entanglement in nature in the poem (stanza 77).

Actually, the visual oddities of "Upon Appleton House" and the speaker's ranging from near vagabond to orphic bard are of a piece with the spirit of holiday outing and truancy, beginning with Lord Fairfax's retreat from involvement in national affairs to make garden forts and proceeding to fishermen whose heads are shod with their canoes. That truancy is not necessarily subject to correction in the speaker. Paradoxically, here as in "The Garden," byplay is serious, and imagination thrives on oddities and the indirect way. Where Herrick works with harvest, Maying, epithalamia, praise of country life, and public ceremonies that formalize and sanctify revels, Marvell avoids these or overturns them. "Upon Appleton House" is not his only excursion into festivity, but he is usually more critical of it. The Resolved Soul is bent upon removing all created pleasures between it and its celestial destiny, and in a comparable pastoral translation of truancy, Damon answers Clorinda's invitation to love in a moralistic tone toward enticing "baits." The Mower chastizes the meadows for pursuing their "gawdy May-games" and vows that "Flowrs, and Grass, and I and all, / Will in one common Ruine fall." In "The Coronet" the gathering of flowers for shepherd queens has already been abandoned in favor of the rich chaplet the poet weaves for his savior, and even that is spoiled by the "serpent old" twined within. In "Upon Appleton House," the subtle nuns' temptation of the Virgin Twates with "brighter Robes and Crowns of Gold" is similarly perverted. With balms and other "baits for curious tastes," they stress too much the ornaments of altars and shrines and make the life of retreat an extended epithalamion.

One recurrent factor in these images of ruined and dangerous festivity is superfluity and the poet's awareness that both festivity and excessive art distort the natural order and obscure its already difficult messages. This does not prevent Marvell from celebrating a retreat from social obligations and moral concerns in "The Garden" and the woodland section of "Upon Appleton House," but even there the surplus of things runs counter to simplicity. Thus in "The Garden," harvest fecundity is for bodily appetites; the mind searches for nature's kinds repeated in a finer tone, and it is happier still to escape to worlds and seas of its own invention.

Marvell appears distrustful both of art and of natural bounty in these instances. More strikingly, in "Upon Appleton House" he has the speaker approach briars and brambles as though in a holiday letting go turned upside down:

> Bind me ye *Woodbines* in your twines,
> Curle me about ye gadding *Vines,*
> And Oh so close your Circles lace,
> That I may never leave this Place:
> But, lest your Fetters prove too weak,
> Ere I your Silken Bondage break,
> Do you, *O Brambles,* chain me too,
> And Courteous *Briars* nail me through.
>
> 609–16

People frequently wear garlands and wrap up in Mayday greenery, but here the abundance and strength of the wrappings put the speaker on the way toward complete vegetable metamorphosis. Marvell is again aware of the density and interference of bodies, whose materiality stands between the mind's desire to be at one with paradise and any actual fulfillment of that desire. A moment spent imagining such fulfillment is not enough; only permanent habitation and the complete removal of distance will do.

Such absorption into things in defiance of bodily forms carries the truant away from both sociability and logic. The forest from the moment he enters it is a refuge from beauty's arrows and implicitly from the shepherd lovers and other masks of courtship, although ceremonies are still evident in the decorum of address and the emphasis on silken touch and courtesy. Here the rhymed couplets and rearranged syntax suggest an almost chanted speech. A similar playfulness is evident in the speaker's putting aside of human intelligence earlier:

> The Oak-Leaves me embroyder all,
> Between which Caterpillars crawl:
> And Ivy, with familiar trails,
> Me licks, and clasps, and curles, and hales.
>
> 587–90

If streams capture halcyon shadows, why should plants not reach out to capture men? It is almost logical to think they can embroider, and pleasurable to the speaker to think they might. In any case, he suspends his tribute to the Fairfaxes momentarily and follows his own inclinations without, however, exercising orphic power over nature's wildness.

## FROM LOCAL MAP TO CHRONICLE AND ODE

The retreat from empire-making in "Upon Appleton House" leaves Marvell without some of the traditional grounds for panegyric and encourages a view of the estate, in compensation, as itself the possessor of inflamed or vitrified assets beyond any envisioned in "To Penshurst." Elsewhere, Marvell is less inclined to exclude the nation in looking for maps of paradise. For a moment I want to take a roundabout way to other sections of "Upon Appleton House" in order to situate Marvell among texts considered earlier and to suggest his view of the private and public aspects of lyric address. He tempts us to such recapitulation by the odd angles he takes on the ideas and conventions of his predecessors. For him as for others, an earthly or celestial paradise provides the best opportunities for the poet's crossing, but he is less sober than Vaughan or Milton in proposing that. As "The Garden" suggests, one can rise by natural inclination of mind and soul to proleptic glimpses of "far other worlds and seas" partly on the initial promptings of curious peaches and fair trees; but while the speaker says such things he also counters the exaggerations of amorous tree-carvers. The name of the tree *on* the tree makes literal the common association of topos (or emblem) with place, or the collaborations of words and things in producing an enclosed poetic paradise, but of course it does so humorously and ironically. Hence, though Marvell is "metaphysical" in removing courtship as the purpose for enumerating the bird consorts and decorative streams of the garden and in seeing the trees themselves as both the delights of solitude and the representations of an ultimate "Fair Quiet" and "Innocence," he is less inclined than Milton, Vaughan, or Herbert to look for an actual divine presence in the garden topography. Even where providence is clearly in evidence as it is in the island paradise of "Bermudas," the address of the pilgrim-singers is happy rather than intense, and the poet himself reports on their thanksgiving song as from a distance. In contrast, Vaughan's quest through the several scenes of "Regeneration" is to submerge the self in the right topic-place, the dwelling of the spirit; Milton finds Christ himself "publishing" his father's image in the desert in *Paradise Regained*.

The idea of paradise in Marvell serves in part to scale down whatever lesser felicities an earlier, more sociable lyric stationed there for the amorous users of gardens pursuing their Daphnes. It not only challenges the hyperboles of lovesick shepherds and sonneteers but mocks the joining of lyric and heroic in the encomium of great men. At the same time, Marvell is also aware that nature is at best an oblique representation of paradise. On one hand Clorinda and Damon take pastures, caves, and fountains to be Pan's voices and thus sublimate passion in artistic motives; their duet swells the slender oat of conventional pastoral. On the other hand, Thrysis and Dorinda dwell on the discrepancies between Elizium and the meadow periphrase of it. The analogy between these only whets their appetite and tempts them with an opium-softened flight from the lesser world. Likewise, for the soul in "On a Drop of Dew," dissolving and running to the glories of its native realm requires its divorce from the body. Even though his periphrastic "coy" figures are expressions of heaven, the poet who projects that flight must also escape metaphoric imprisonment in emblemized topoi; certainly paradise is not *adequately* mapped by its tropes and figures.

Where the poet's reading of the Appleton estate as paradise's best available map is assisted by Maria's remaking of gardens, streams, and meadows, Marvell has a more difficult task with Cromwell as go-between and the entire nation as his panorama. From "The First Anniversary" we know how assiduously he labored to make Cromwell too a vicegerent "Learning a Musique in the Region Clear, / To tune this lower to that higher sphere." Indeed, much of "The First Anniversary" suggests a return to masque applications of classical and Christian symbols to encomium. In the Horatian Ode, that surrogate authority receives its severest test in the displacement of the old order and parallels the reluctant emergence of the poet himself into public affairs. Since the course he takes in some respects is a return to the laureate figure of courtly encomium, it is crucial for Marvell to juxtapose the claims of the king and this new delegate.

I am less concerned with the scope of the poem's historical vision and other thematic matters, however, than with the lyric means by which Marvell imposes odic form on chronicle materials and enables the speaker to cross from his more usual metaphors for paradise to civil struggle. Where topographical description generates its paradisal likeness on more or less traditional and logical grounds, he works here with a paradoxical narrative arriving at a troubled climax. The attention he gives to Charles's beheading is a sign of his having come to a kind of interpretive clearing and odic intensity, but that reading perhaps requires explanation and defense. It gains some credence I think, at least indirectly, from Marvell's identification of the craft of politics with artful performance and the purging of the feeling for Charles that comes from his stoic resignation.[2] The conversion of civil violence into theatrical art parallels the passage of narrative into ode: both are keyed to the precise moment when one age gives way to another with maximum violence. That violence, though not pretty, is a spectacle of tragic dimensions and a sacrificial cleansing:

> And *Hampton* shows what part
> He had of wiser Art.
> Where, twining subtile fears with hope,
> He wove a Net of such a scope,
>   That *Charles* himself might chase
>   To *Caresbrooks* narrow case.
> That thence the *Royal Actor* born
> The *Tragick Scaffold* might adorn,
>   While round the armed Bands
>   Did clap their bloody hands.
> *He* nothing common did or mean,
> Upon the memorable Scene:
>   But with his keener Eye
>   The Axes edge did try:
> Nor call'd the *Gods* with vulgar spight
> To vindicate his helpless Right,
>   But bow'd his comely Head
>   Down as upon a Bed.

Having concentrated on Cromwell's austerity and valor in preceding passages, Marvell attributes subtlety to him here as a first step in softening the portrait and institutionalizing his raw force.

The word *wiser* has a peculiar ring even so. The insights that have come to Cromwell in private must be converted into public policy, but the latter stresses stagecraft rather than wisdom. Marvell drops Cromwell from view momentarily in concentrating on the spectacle of regicide itself. In conceding that Charles was born to royalty, he recalls the ancient rights of the preceding passage, but Charles's keener eye presumably finds in Cromwell's wiser art something deeper than trickery, and his performance both gains stature from and is embittered by that discovery. The stage is after all a scaffold and the audience composed of bloody-handed enemies. But executions and tragic falls are not meant to be delicate. This abruptly wrong event, like the unexpected and unnatural matters of "Upon Appleton House," is precisely what reveals; in great disorder one finds the access road to a higher order.

Marvell follows the course of events that deliver this harrowing realization with a tonal transition from the semi-comic image of Charles fleeing ghosts through the complicated grammar of the statement on clapping hands (which brushes aside the make-believe of the stage metaphor momentarily), to the calm of Charles's resignation. His alternation of tetrameter and trimeter couplets works changes of pace, scale, and tone formal enough to call further attention to the relations between art and raw event. The second or shorter couplet performs sometimes a retrenchment or shrinkage, sometimes an epigrammatic summary. The last two sets of shorter lines in the beheading passage work in opposite directions: "But with his keener Eye / The Axes edge did try," and "But bow'd his comely Head / Down as upon a Bed." As Charles veers away from meanness and cowardice and reclaims himself from the momentary confusion that led him to prison, all commonness leaves him. The trial winds up to a pitch at precisely the point at which eye meets cutting edge. Since the ax will sever not merely muscle and bone but one age from another, this cannot be a time of easy transition; nor can its poetry be a poetry of logical explanation and ordinary rhetorical persuasion. The "keener eye" presumably sees that nothing could be more arbitrary to a neck than a falling ax and matches wiser art with a wariness of its own.

But the gods, Charles realizes, are not to be called upon even by one so painfully enlightened. If he represents right in their eyes, it is obviously now an abandoned right. Since the lucid reality of the ax forestalls illusions and rules out vulgar revenge, his only course is to lie down and confirm the script. The last of the trimeter couplets manages to suggest this not only by the softening image of

Charles going calmly but also by falling rhythm, an enjambment that emphasizes "down," and a reinstatement of make-believe that carries forward the artful conversion of the crude event into theatrical terms. What Charles accomplishes is the dominance by performance and vision of revolutionary change, which requires a shift of settings, loyalties, and (as we are seeing demonstrated) poetic forms and vocabularies. The new script enables a performer who is not going to get up and play the role again to assist in the birth of a harsh new reality and in the defusing of its impact. So the king comes down, and Cromwell and a new republic rise up.

The poet who converts chronicle to Horatian lyric is an implicit party to this final softening of regicide. He serves both as a rhetorician guiding the sympathies of his audience and as a kind of elegiac therapist who brings feelings into conformity with necessity. From "And Hampton" to "Foresaw its happy Fate" he pursues the displacement of the old order through a subtle and varied movement that reaches a crescendo in eighteen lines and then ebbs away. After a pause he picks up a new phase of narrative and interprets its key moment with an assurance that reflects his identification with it and celebration of it. Praise now springs forth directly from the events themselves and joins lyric to epic statesmanship:

> This was that memorable Hour
> Which first assur'd the forced Pow'r.
> So when they did design
> The *Capitols* first Line,
> A bleeding Head where they begun,
> Did fright the Architects to run;
> And yet in that the *State*
> Foresaw it's happy Fate.

That expansiveness carries through six additional lines that draw out the parallel with Roman empire and deliver a sort of reprise, as the speaker gets further elevation and lets the tragic scene recede.

Nowhere does Marvell intrude noticeably as a dramatic presence in this crucial passage, which renders the conviction not of a personality (as a Miltonic passage might have) but of an observer responding ambivalently to events and gaining sympathy with the king's poise through a sense of history's inevitability. His salutation of the new power marries lyric to advice-giving as well as to chronicle and binds all these up in its affirmation. The nation's crossing to its ordained new form is thus matched by the speaker's negotiated course from private gardens and ambivalent reservations to an open odic platform.

## STANZAIC PLACEMENT

I have emphasized a selection of technical aspects in the Horatian ode partly because Marvell so inextricably entangles art and statement. The poet's deciphering of chronicle requires a conversion of events into tangible signs of progress. It is as agents of providence that Charles becomes eligible for elegiac commemoration and Cromwell warrants praise. As the courtly world dies and is replaced by parliamentary rule, Cromwell must remain armed, but like a disciplined falcon he must also submit to rule. Interpreting both of them is akin to the speaker's translation of objects in "Upon Appleton House" into representations of heaven's design. Marvell is confident that in Maria, for instance, as in Cromwell, the most effective instrument of providence is tuned in heaven before working transformations on a lower plane. The sense of finality that hovers about both her and Cromwell is crucial to the lyric crossing. They are makers and therefore models for his own fashioning of metaphors from the palpable materials of estate and nation. His architectonic skill also draws upon their mastery of arrangement. Descending to minutia, it draws our attention to matters of diction and phonic system, which is part of the atmosphere of play and festivity that we detect even in Charles's execution. His structural skill in "Upon Appleton House" is evident not merely in well-devised stanzas and divisions of the poem, however, but in a roughness or purposeful awkwardness that acknowledges the distance between raw materials and the order buried within, or between media and their meanings.

Critics have paid less attention to the smaller units of that mixture of finesse and verbal disturbance than to the large-scale problem of hiatuses between segments of the poem; but the poem is nearly as noteworthy for its couplet wit, epigrammatic statement, and calculated sharp turns as it is for its overall construction and its play with optical devices and unusual imagery. The lyric place, finally, is not the settings of Appleton but the couplets of Marvell's photograph album, and the topics are after all worded and imaged things. The stanza moves forward by measured, finely divided steps that usually coincide with enclosing sentences; but far from being seamless and easily unified, both the stanzas and larger segments of the poem display their divisioning as a measure of what it takes to control the diversity of the country estate and the potential chaos of the outside world. Where everything runs to disorder and surprising transformation, all the more credit must go to the restorers of harmony—to Maria foremost but secondarily to the poem's arranger and commentator. His disarming irony and his criticism of deformities fit neatly into those small packages, especially their antitheses.

In the first stanza, for instance, Marvell approaches praise for Fairfax by circling around the central object, the house, with a combination of praise and satiric dispatch:

> Within this sober Frame expect
> Work of no Forrain *Architect;*
> That unto Caves the Quarries drew,
> And Forrests did to Pastures hew;
> Who of his great Design in pain
> Did for a Model vault his Brain,
> Whose Columnes should so high be rais'd
> To arch the Brows that on them gaz'd.

The first two lines forestall an expectation that Marvell supposes in the reader: the poem will concern not grandeur, which can be achieved only by self-indulgence and laughable waste, but disciplined modesty. In praising *Paradise Lost,* Marvell will later realize the difference between Milton and himself in this regard. Milton's project is grand, and the music must accord with it. Meanwhile, Marvell gets along in rhyme:

> Well mightst thou scorn thy Readers to allure
> With tinkling Rhime, of thy own Sense secure;
> While the *Town-Bays* writes all the while and spells,
> And like a Pack-Horse tires without his Bells.
> Their Fancies like our bushy Points appear,
> The Poets tag them; we for fashion wear.
> I too transported by the *Mode* offend,
> And while I meant to *Praise* thee, must Commend.
> Thy verse created like thy *Theme* sublime,
> In Number, Weight, and Measure, needs not *Rhime.*
>                 "On Mr. Milton's *Paradise Lost*"

Setting forth to read *Paradise Lost* for the first time, he has been apprehensive about its "vast design" and its "*Messiah* Crown'd, / Gods Reconcil'd Decree, / Rebelling *Angels,* the Forbidden Tree, Heav'n, Hell, Earth, Chaos, All." Milton's skill in blank verse is partly what reassures him. However, for himself, rhyme will have to suffice. In "Upon Appleton House," its playfulness helps expose the absurdity of a greatness that has far less substance than Milton's. To conceive some grand projects to begin with requires a huge emptiness of brain remindful of caves that architectural ambition has carved out, and in the hollow palaces that result the bardic winds that should winnow one's thoughts get totally lost. That each of the couplets illustrates the excesses they criticize underscores the rarity of tasteful performances. Although they are hooked together loosely, the syntax and diction are taut in individual sentences, and each illustration stands as a building block under its overarching thesis. As an epigram each sets a standard of compression before proceeding to expanded terms of praise.

In the second stanza, Marvell encloses similar epigrammatic illustrations with two general statements of principle, the first exacting its judgment by asking a leading question, whose tortured syntax again breaks the rules the sentence promotes:

> Why should of all things Man unrul'd
> Such unproportion'd dwellings build?
> The Beasts are by their Denns exprest:
> And Birds contrive an equal Nest;
> The low roof'd Tortoises do dwell
> In cases fit of Tortoise-shell:
> No Creature loves an empty space;
> Their Bodies measure out their Place.
>                                              9–16

The odd emphasis of the rearranged sentence suggest a jerry-built construction whose pieces fall together at odd angles. The third line prepares a general category for the specific examples with a similarly turned-around syntax, and the examples, although straightforward in arrangement, release several small surprises in imagery and diction. "Contrive" gives to birds a slightly labored craft in nest-building, and "low-roof'd" is a childlike way to see a tortoise shell and a peculiar image to apply to a great lord's house. The snugness of a place reduced to the exact size of its dweller's skin exaggerates more than a little the kind of modest dwelling that "To Penshurst" praises. Despite this Marvell manages to counter human unnaturalness with well-expressed beasts. The final couplet expands to the governing rule of all creation. The second stanza advances over the first in positing an appropriate site and a set of common laws that chastize ambitious man as an anomaly among creatures. All the more praiseworthy, then, someone who keeps to proportion and observes the principles of good householding. The very awkwardness of the couplets lets us see the labor of fitting Fairfax among dwarfish confines and narrow loops, in small miracles of shapely dwelling. Judgment in the long run serves praise, as description does also. Both emphasize the exactness of ownership when ambition is properly curbed and things are by their dens expressed.

Not until this groundwork has been well laid and several such sequences have been set in place with their mortar visibly spilling over does Marvell allow outright praise for Fairfax, and even then the speaker is limited to the dimensions of the house—not its decorations, design, beauty, social implications, or such elements of courtly praise as survive in previous country estate poems. Constraint and satiric observation prepare for another sort of homecoming, which Marvell glimpses early and develops later with greater intensity:

> But all things are composed here
> Like Nature, orderly and near:
> In which we the Dimensions find
> Of that more sober Age and Mind,
> When larger sized Men did stoop
> To enter at a narrow loop;
> As practising, in doors so strait,
> To strain themselves through *Heavens Gate*.
>
> 25–32

After the unflattering "stoop" and "loop" and after the spatial limitations of the house and embodiment generally, the expansion of "Heavens Gate" comes as a mild surprise and makes a first gesture toward the perspective that comes with lyric intensification later. But Marvell keeps solid contact with tangible bodies and their sizes even here, as in the pun on "strain" and the reduction of paradise to its entrance, which heads off any overly hasty progress to the estate as heaven's map. The perspective is visually concrete and humorous, the tone even and judicious, at least through the first half of the stanza. The interplay of wit and potential crescendos of praise are reminiscent of Donne's combinations of lyric and irony, but more coy, less cerebral, and harder to decipher.

Nothing in this opening section quite prepares for translation to the plane that the word "holy" occupies in its unusual conjunction with "mathematicks." Through these openings, Marvell reveals another side of epigram when it is assembled in an unfolding thematic and descriptive order—its usefulness to a metaphysical structure with philosophic backgrounds and its capacity to open onto range upon range of implications. For both Marvell and the reader, texts like the *Timaeus*, in which Pythagorean numbers are given holy tasks and share in the rule of creation, have presumably made some of the necessary connections between the human realm and the governing order. Although Lord Fairfax's small model is not allowed to take great advantage of that tradition, confirmations of its compatibility with the greater scheme of things come forward when the poem reaches out to constellations, the sun, and all that Greece and Rome have said. Actually, the poem expands and contracts simultaneously in its small-large comparisons and shifting perspectives: each stanza is a small site of praise that looks minutely into details; yet windows open upon increasingly large prospects until the culminating stanza on heaven's map.

One effect of Marvell's building couplets into stanzas is a hesitation in the movement toward lyric when it does come forward, which until Maria permits greater access to paradise is usually at pausal or preparatory moments. Much on the poet's mind as a standard throughout, paradise is largely what generates that movement. But because the way is obstructed by both natural and manmade deformities, lyric pauses must come partly as escapes of time and place or as recollective and plangent moments—two versions of paradise being the lost Eden and the ruined England:

> Oh Thou, that dear and happy Isle
> The Garden of the World ere while,
> Thou *Paradise* of four Seas,
> Which *Heaven* planted us to please,
> But, to exclude the World, did guard
> With watry if not flaming Sword;
> What luckless Apple did we tast,
> To make us Mortal, and The Wast?
>
> 321-28

The development of this stanza contrasts with the epigrammatic style of the opening section as Marvell submerges its subdivisions in the affective curve of an apostrophe sustained through eight lines. The loss of England's privilege is not dated, but civil war is evidence of it. The question the stanza comes to is not meant to be answered; it points up a contrast and makes more remarkable the preserved order of the estate as sanctuary.

Marvell performs a similar fusing of units in narrative and descriptive passages, although analytic epigrams can be seated among these as well. Couplets are useful not only for metaphoric wit but for defining, identifying, assessing, and relating, and all these activities can be inserted into loco-descriptive movements toward lyric. Because he is more interested in seeing concretely than in celebrating through much of the poem, he gives couplets several kinds of descriptive tasks, sometimes as juxtaposed snapshots, at other times as tests of shifting perspective. The account of grazing cattle, for instance, takes up several striking points of view side by side, to no apparent end except to play with perspective and therefore with the instruments of seeing:

> They seem within the polisht Grass
> A Landskip drawen in Looking-Glass.
> And shrunk in the huge Pasture show

> As Spots, so shap'd, on Faces do.
> Such Fleas, ere they approach the Eye,
> In Multiplying Glasses lye.
> They feed so wide, so slowly move,
> As *Constellations* do above.
>
> 457–64

Where couplets elsewhere tend to compress judgment or praise, here they slice up and organize description and play one perspective against another. The likeness of pastures to the heavens is a lowly, tentative version of the same synecdoche that brings paradise down in Maria's governance. But the narrator, absorbed in microscopes and telescopes, holds back any awareness of general laws of resemblance and juxtaposition. Each shift works a small triumph of wit, until the viewer becomes not a neutral or even necessarily an accurate observer but the owner of an eye, marveling less at the thing itself than at its appearances. Once he has set out to multiply those appearances, the speaker stops only at the boundary of the stanza itself, which makes up his picture frame and a containment for lyric's small affective sweep.

Other descriptive stanzas are more like animate emblems, paradoxically both mechanical in their make up and fluid in changing shapes and perspectives, as in the description of the nightingale:

> The *Nightingale* does here make choice
> To sing the Tryals of her Voice.
> Low Shrubs she sits in, and adorns
> With Musick high the squatted Thorns.
> But highest Oakes stoop down to hear,
> And listning Elders prick the Ear.
> The Thorn, lest it should hurt her, draws
> Within the Skin its shrunken claws.
>
> 513–20

Marvell's exaggerations in this case are in the interests of praise for the hushed atmosphere of the woodland, which he has compared earlier to that of a temple. The main device in both that comparison and the nightingale description is again paradoxical overstatement: the bird is very low on its squat thorn but its voice reaches very high; the elder trees and oaks are very high and stately but bend very low. Thorns that retract their needles suggest the roses of paradise or of folk ballads in which the pierced breasts of birds are emblematic of tragic love. The end-stoppage and the wit keep the stanza sufficiently bemused in tone to disarm the exaggeration.

In his manipulations of metaphor, stanza, and couplet, Marvell urges the reader to see double—to see the site of the vagrant wanderer in all its levels and its topographical range from the local to the cosmological, and at the same time to see the words, meters, and other tangible materials out of which a poem is constructed. The place of lyric is neither strictly those verbal materials and the attitudes housed in them nor any set of particulars and universals dressed to advantage in loco description; it is rather a dynamic combination of poetic devices and emblems extending from the local setting outward to England and upward toward paradise. Its impulse for celebration is checked by the awkwardness of the presentation and the deficiencies of media, but praiseworthy ideals nonetheless emerge from the world's deformities and the materials of language. The poem finds and commemorates a principle of householding and poetic image-making that conforms in spite of everything to universal rule. In the final analysis (if there can be such a thing), "Upon Appleton House" is about approaches to a perfect form that, although beyond doubt itself, is so difficult to achieve that it puts all poetry's devices and all perspectives under strain and brings the speaker forward as the poem's first character. A given setting may contain clues to that perfection and a Fairfax may endorse it and build upon it, but the poet appears more impressed at times with the defects of expressive forms and the limits of all ways of seeing. The mind knows what will suffice, but words and images seldom pass through sudden rightness—unless fish really are so like flies in crystal, or distant cows so like fleas, or leather-boated heads like antipodes in shoes, that we experience no comic stumbling in crossing from one to the other. The poetic fit is rough and yet strangely apt at the same time; its incongruities direct our attention to substances not quite malleable enough for ordinary craft to shape them as classical propriety requires but nonetheless subject to tactful coercion and a verbal maneuvering that establishes metaphoric logic in odd juxtapositions. The passage into lyric hangs upon attractions to such things as ambered flies; when the medium clears, what the eye sees is a small, marvelous image of another world compressed into something one would not have expected to be so revealing.

## CONCLUSIONS AND SPECULATIONS

Marvell's sense of place and tactics in moving from description to lyric address while making landscapes into expressive forms are the most sensitive and variable among poets of mid century with the exception of Milton, and certainly the most unpredictable. The Mower (in "The Mower against Gardens") prefers an unspoiled naturalness and is upset by love's intrusion. But in a voice more his own, Marvell also praises Lord Fairfax for regimenting his garden and responds enthusiastically to Maria Fairfax. Woman threatens the outdoor sanctuary of "The Garden," and the speaker of "Upon Appleton House" professes to be hiding from beauty's arrows, yet Marvell rejoices in Maria's improving of gardens and woods and in "To his Coy Mistress" makes courtship the point of the hypothetical stroll from the Ganges to the Humber. "A dialogue between the Resolved Soul, and Created Pleasure" expresses distrust of nature, which also harbors the serpent of "The Coronet," and both poems are inclined to treat all things temporal as traps for the unwary. Yet both "The Garden" and "Bermudas" present landscapes presided over by providence. The pilgrims in "Bermudas" make rocks and shores a sounding board for joyous notes that reach toward heaven and rebound across the new world.

Some of these variations in the reading of landscapes can be explained by the dramatic speakers who voice them, but others appear to stem from moral and philosophic changeability over a period of years. Certainly Marvell is one of the more imaginative and experimental poets of the times. "Clorinda and Damon" and "To his Coy Mistress" are particularly important to any assessment of that variability because they go impressively against Marvell's frequent preferences for solitude. In the latter, if the lovers are to prevail over deserts of vast eternity (the spirit's final legacy), they must compress passionate experience into the few moments they have. Such compression is perhaps a synecdoche or an epitome, but rather than reducing a world to love as Donne does in placing it in his chambers, Marvell's speaker has no desire to reconstitute a broader setting, merely to control his own. Clorinda and Damon work through several aspects of place on their way to an encompassing view of Pan's realm. Although lyrics could conceivably emerge from Clorinda's interpretation of shepherdom as well as from Damon's, they would be only tinkling accompaniment to embowered love; so they devise their greater hymn according to his view of Pan.

Experimenting with such differences in the placement of lovers, new-world pilgrims, mowers, and the poet himself, Marvell takes excursions abroad that predict the exile of the romantic poets if not their states of mind or their preoccupations. When we think of these and other typical Marvellian situations, we are struck by the prominence of uprootings and relocations in them, not merely in the changing of sites but in the mind's restless shifting of positions among Neoplatonist, Christian, Stoic, and pagan alternatives, which Marvell often entertains in debate. He is concerned enough with the loss of hospitable locality and common value to return to it frequently. The Mower, displaced from his formerly easy relationship with the meadows, seeks revenge on "Unthankful Medows" for carrying on as though Juliana had not wreaked havoc. Like Juliana's torture of the Mower, Clora's distraction of the speaker of "The Gallery" complicates the settings of the soul. In his tour of its impressions of Clora, the speaker has each picture present her in a different posture. None is final, but one—a conventional Arcadian pose of the innocent shepherdess—he finds preferable, perhaps because it is diffused into the attractions of hillside, flowers, and sun. Despite these variations in topography, Marvell's lyric addresses tend to come forth at points at which something suggests a paradise, glimpses of which are more likely to occur in solitude than in the busy companies of men.

Although it is not my chief purpose to periodize such lyric locations beyond the basic contrast I have pursued between courtly poetics and radical seventeenth-century departures from it, some of the avenues one might take from Milton and the metaphysicals to later modes warrant further speculation. The ideological and historical distance from these poets to later lyricists is obviously considerable, but one imagines seeing in the underbrush at least the remnants of a path. Without doubt seventeenth-century lyric loci set new conditions for loosened connections between poetic vocation and social setting. This is less true for the cavaliers of course. With the courtly center under question, such poets as Suckling, Lovelace, Cotton, Carew, and Herrick salvage fragments of a system of codes and remnants of attitudes and tones. They accept relatively narrower limits than the metaphysicals and Milton and do not explore comparable displacements or the adventures of wandering. Nor do they claim to be guardians of place who can establish conduits from above to them, as Milton's Genius of the Wood does. As a group seventeenth-century lyricists discard a good deal of earlier concerns with secular power and claim other kinds of authority for their personas. No important seventeenth-century poet seems to have felt that he sacrificed anything of value by doing so. The private places of Donne, Herbert, Vaughan, Milton, and Marvell turn out to be not provincial in their views but universal and central.

Dryden, Waller, Cowley, and even Marvell at times may seem exceptions to this abandoning of public provinces, or to the lack of regret over it, and to a degree they are. Marvell praises Fairfax and Cromwell in ways that keep Old Testament figures and the founding of governments in sight. But Fairfax is commendable primarily after he has left public service; and although as a type of military hero and statesman Cromwell maintains Roman connections in "An Horatian Ode," in "The First Anniversary" Marvell praises him for bringing latter days nearer and moving beyond mere empire toward final kingdom. Dryden links biblical types to empire in "Astrea Redux," *Absalom and Achitophel,* and "Threnodia Augusta" and returns to a revised courtly panegyric reminiscent of Daniel and Jonson. However, his interweaving of biblical and current events in Absalom is more analytic, judicial, and moral than lyric.

One of the questions that shift in genre raises is how to transfer the panegyric of earlier progresses and triumphs to restoration subjects. Some of the symbolism of masques and mythological narratives still shows in Dryden's association of song and ode with end things in "A Song for St. Cecilia's Day" and the ode to Anne Killigrew:

> Whatever happy region is thy place,
> Cease thy celestial song a little space;
> (Thou wilt have time enough for hymns divine,
> Since heav'n's eternal year is thine.)
> Hear then a mortal Muse thy praise rehearse,
>     In no ignoble verse
> But such as thy own voice did practise here,
> When thy first fruits of poesie were given,
> To make thyself a welcome inmate there;
>   While yet a young probationer,
>   And candidate of heav'n.
> . . . . . . . . . . . . . . . . . . . .
>   When rattling bones together fly
>   From the four corners of the skie;
> When sinews o'er the skeletons are spread,
> Those cloath'd with flesh, and life inspires the dead;
> The sacred poets first shall hear the sound,
> And formost from the tomb shall bound:
> For they are cover'd with the lightest ground;
> And streight, with inborn vigor, on the wing,
> Like mounting larks, to the new morning sing.
> There thou, sweet saint, before the choir shalt go,
> As harbinger of heav'n, the way to show,
> The way which thou so well hast learn'd below.
>                                              12–22, 184–95

However, the facility of this and its narrow escape from comedy in the "rattling bones" flying from the four corners of the sky suggest strain. The translation from the funereal place of elegy to the visionary place of sacred verse lacks the conviction of Vaughan's and Herbert's doomsdays or even of Marvell's postponed Latter Day in "The First Anniversary."

More convincing is the relationship of the sacred and the mundane in "Mac Flecknoe," where the poet's lute is to be handed to Shadwell rather than to heaven's probationer and Dryden can exploit a sense of exploded lyric for satiric purposes. This is a familiar idea but is perhaps worth reiterating here. The cosmic setting is useful primarily to gauge folly's growing pretensions. Shadwell will abuse the poet's calling shamefully by warbling the glories of stupidity in which, according to Flecknoe, he already outdoes very illustrious predecessors:

> Heywood and Shirley were but types of thee
> Thou last great prophet of tautology.
> Even I, a dunce of more renown than they,
> Was sent before but to prepare thy way.
>
> 29–31

Flecknoe-John-the-Baptist thus recognizes a son whose divinity he proclaims as his own last great calling, making known talents that have heretofore languished in the desert. Dryden returns to the courtly setting in establishing biblical parallels to coronation and acknowledging satire's urban throng. He thus gives Dulness the worst of the ancient and modern worlds: its tautology reduces to mindless copying what should be inspiring divine images in historical incarnations; its coronation parodies earlier triumphs. Thus Shadwell perpetuates Roman empire, but only as a deformed or defective son perpetuates family features:

> The hoary prince in majesty appear'd,
> High on a throne of his own labours rear'd.
> At his right hand our young Ascanius sate,
> Rome's other hope, and pillar of the state.
> His brows thick fogs, instead of glories, grace,
> And lambent dullness plaid around his face.
>
> 106–11

The potential lyricism of the couplets and the flashes of glory that Flecknoe suggests are quickly turned around. Thick fogs and lambent dullness would obviously not have the impact they do were it not for the enthusiasm they play upon and the grandeur that might attend authentic panegyric.

The London audience for stupidity's triumph stands no less condemned than its leaders:

> Th'admiring throng loud acclamations make
> And omens of his future empire take.
> The sire then shook the honors of his head,
> And from his brows damps of oblivion shed

> Full on the filial dullness: long he stood,
> Repelling from his breast the raging god;
> At length burst out in this prophetic mood.
>
> 132–38

The mock-epic echoes of *Paradise Lost* that serve Pope so well in "The Rape of the Lock" and *The Dunciad* help expose dullness' service to chaos here. Among other things it is the logos that perishes—the same that filters into earlier lyric and epic settings to bring intelligible connection and governing purpose. For Dryden as for his immediate predecessors, lyric is often generated by a perception of analogues among created objects or by the sense of the total harmony they express; but these perceptions, to be reused, must be liberated from pretenders. The result is a quite different satire-lyric balance than Donne's or Marvell's. In *Songs and Sonnets*, critics and meddlers are held at arm's length by a wit that predicts and disarms them but does not get in the way of love's approved hymns; here misguided lyric commemoration sets up an overturning of fools and knaves caught in the act of spreading their verbal inflation. Enthusiasm of all sorts has grown so suspect for Dryden that rather than come when it calls Shadwell would be well-advised to write acroustics and anagrams, where (in debasement of Herbert's wit) Flecknoe suggests,

> thou may'st wings display and altars raise,
> And torture one poor word ten thousand ways.
> Or, if thou would'st thy diff'rent talents suit,
> Set thy own songs, and sing them to thy lute.
>
> 207–10

Dryden is able to draw in "Mac Flecknoe" upon the same universal values and epochal thought that Spenser once believed to be disseminated through Troynovant by its queen and her poets. But his point is that contemporary scribblers in all the forms they have debased—comedy, tragedy, lyric, epic—have violated the Roman heritage and broken the continuity of genres in their passage to the provinces. If the logos is to reign anew, it must have more than nature's remote corners for its resident symbols; it must have a new Augustus and a reborn classical poetics. It is less clear from "Mac Flecknoe" and *Absalom and Achitophel* than from the ode to Anne Killigrew that Dryden might wish to add to classical standards the hallowed places of his immediate predecessors and their privileged authority.

Whatever its resituations after Milton, Marvell, Cowley, Dryden, and others at mid century, lyric could not easily be coaxed back from the margins to public affairs as Spenser, Sidney, Jonson, and others once understood them. It has since become the instrument of primarily individual experience that Hegel assumed it was inherently, but without the potential unity of ideas or crossings of the subject to a central authority that romanticism often wished, thinking nostalgically of Milton. Instead, lyric in its postromantic forms typically places before us relatively discrete environments at some distance from both a center and an audience. In A. R. Ammons's words:

> I look and reflect, but the air's glass
> jail seals each thing in its entity:
>
> no use to make any philosophies here:
>   I see no
> god in the holly, hear no song from
> the snowbroken weeds: Hegel is not the winter
> yellow in the pines: the sunlight has never
> heard of trees: surrendered self among
>   unwelcoming forms: stranger,
> hoist your burdens, get on down the road.[3]

Somewhere down such roads the poet assumes that another such pause will be in order, during which another setting will beckon with sufficient urgency to extract an address. Certainly his vocation depends primarily upon that calling rather than upon the sorts of duties or moral injunctions Sidney would have the poet obey, or for that matter, upon the seeing of wholes in parts.

To stop with that I know is more to fizzle than to conclude, but I resist the temptation either to seek out a better landing place in the territories opened and mapped for us this century by Stevens, Frost, Eliot, Roethke, Williams, and others, or to return once again to Milton for a kind of retrospective summary. It would take an Olympic record in hop, skip, and jump—taking off from Marvell, skipping to the romantics, and landing somewhere in the vicinity of Yeats—to get where it would be most interesting to go, and would open more questions than could be settled in reasonable space. I have already made enough short-landings to know better than risk it, or as Spenser surely would have put it (in a better figure), even wherry craft does make us wheeze and feele the muscle's weery waite.

It is also true that I have followed throughout, silently for the most part, the premise that individual poets of any stature require whole chapters and a searching out of critical, representative poems. What count most, even in our gauging of the interplay of genre and influence, are individual, transforming minds. Authorial practice over a career tells us more about a given performance—and about literary history, too—than any other single source. If that authorial presence proves to be as illusory as the circle or the paradise that hangs in the offing for the group I have selected, it nonetheless gives us the most interesting accompanying illusions of stylistic variation and nuance and the wherewithal to make up individualized lexicons of symbol, image, and diction if we want them. The chief value of history, genre, and theory, all important in their own right, then, is their use to us in catching the distinctive voice of a Herbert or Milton, or what we each think is that voice. To consider any further poets that extensively at this point, though it might incidentally help to define the renaissance turn I have posited, would require more than anyone would want and would do very little to get a better sense of those distinctively mapped places we have explored. Accordingly, I dodge the matter of concluding and plan instead to take up separately the most intricate of the inner workings of that turn, in Milton's Shakespeare, or Shakespeare's Milton, and the relations of poetry to drama—relations of lyric placement to social dialogue. That path from Bottom's woods to Comus's is too long and twisty for anything but its own map.

# NOTES

## ABBREVIATIONS

| | |
|---|---|
| ELH | *English Literary History* |
| ELR | *English Literary Renaissance* |
| JEGP | *Journal of English and Germanic Philology* |
| MLN | *Modern Language Notes* |
| MLR | *Modern Language Review* |
| PMLA | *Publications of the Modern Language Association* |
| PQ | *Philological Quarterly* |
| SEL | *Studies in English Literature* |
| SP | *Studies in Philology* |
| TSLL | *Texas Studies in Literature and Language* |

## PREFACE

1. *Hakluyt's Voyages*, ed. Irwin R. Blacker (New York: Viking Press, 1965), p. 17.

2. Richard Wilbur, *Responses: Prose Pieces 1953–1976* (New York: Harcourt, Brace, Jovanovich, 1976), p. 155.

3. *Hakluyt's Voyages*, p. 17.

4. The contrastive halves of renaissance lyric that I propose bear a resemblance to pieces in Harold Bloom's "Tessera" pattern of belatedness in *The Anxiety of Influence* (New York: Oxford University Press, 1975), pp. 49–76, but I do not intend similar psychological implications or look for examples of "family romance."

## CHAPTER ONE

1. A. R. Ammons, *Collected Poems, 1951–1971* (New York: W. W. Norton, 1972), pp. 318–19. Possession for poets, through poetry, is at best indirect and attenuated, since what they possess is a poem's reflection of objects that can be named also by others, changing hands and conceptual frameworks through the realms of dis-

course. But lyric address nonetheless explores the grounds on which strong personal relations with objects are vocalized. Even when a prized object draws off or withholds itself, like Keats's nightingale or Grecian urn, it may leave behind redefined attitudes and feelings and altered possession of other things. For lack of better words, then, I use *possession* and its synonyms for the poet's verbal impounding of things. Such terms should be understood to differ fundamentally, of course, from legal, physical, even spiritual possession: though they do not necessarily designate a weaker grasp, they always imply a countermanding dispossession in the escape of *res* from *verba*.

2. See Jacquetta Hawkes, *A Land* (New York: Random House, 1951) and Paul Shepard, *Man in the Landscape: A Historic View of the Esthetics of Nature* (New York: Knopf, 1967).

3. John Crowe Ransom, "What Ducks Require," from *Selected Poems* (New York: Knopf, 1974), p. 90.

4. Thomas Hardy, "Shelley's Skylark," from *Collected Poems* (London: Macmillan, 1952), p. 92. For an interesting commentary on Ransom, Hardy, and Keats's "Ode to a Nightingale," see Robert Pinsky, *The Situation of Poetry* (Princeton: Princeton University Press, 1976), pp. 29–55.

5. Michael Riffaterre, *Semiotics of Poetry* (Bloomington, Indiana: Indiana University Press, 1978), pp. 4–5. See also Jonathan Culler's discussion of this portion of *Semiotics* in *The Pursuit of Signs* (Ithaca, New York: Cornell University Press, 1981), pp. 80–99. I have also found Culler's comments on apostrophe enlightening, pp. 135–54.

6. Martin Heidegger, *Poetry, Language and Thought*, trans. Albert Hofstadter (New York: Harper & Row, 1971), pp. xv, 64. The poem in the epigraph to this chapter is taken from this translation.

7. Morse Peckham, *Man's Rage for Chaos: Biology, Behavior, and the Arts* (New York: Schocken Books, 1967).

8. Emily Dickinson, *The Complete Poems*, ed. Thomas H. Johnson (Boston: Little, Brown and Company, 1960), p. 485.

9. Wallace Stevens, *Opus Posthumous* (New York: Knopf, 1969), from *Adagia*, pp. 164, 166, 175.

10. John Crowe Ransom, "Poetry: A Note in Ontology," in *Critical Theory Since Plato*, ed. Hazard Adams (New York: Harcourt Brace Jovanovich, 1971), p. 873.

11. Martin Heidegger, *An Introduction to Metaphysics* (New Haven: Yale University Press, p. 61.

12. Graham Hough, *A Preface to The Faerie Queene* (New York: Norton, 1963), p. 107.

13. Jerome Mazzaro, *Transformations in the Renaissance English Lyric* (Ithaca: Cornell University Press, 1970), p. 1.

14. *Englands Helicon*, ed. Hugh MacDonald (London: Routledge and Kegan Paul, 1949), p. 54.

15. John Donne, *The Elegies and The Songs and Sonnets*, ed. Helen Gardner (London: Oxford University Press, 1965).

16. See Ernest B. Gilman, "Words and Image in Quarles' *Emblemes*," *Critical Inquiry* 6 (1980):358–410. Drawing upon Northrop Frye, Andrew Welsh puts lyric elements under the headings of *melos*, *opsis*, and *lexis*, or musical principle, visual principle, and logical principle. In that format, which my discussion also reflects, emblems would fall under forms of visual dominance, although Frye considers riddle the radical of *opsis*, as charm is of *melos*. See *Roots of Lyric* (Princeton: Princeton University Press, 1978), pp. 47–66; Frye, *The Anatomy of Criticism* (Princeton: Princeton University Press, 1957), pp. 251–302.

17. The Milesian philosopher remarks, "The reality of the world is in living things" and "all things are full of Gods," which identifies the philosopher, theologian, and poet. See Albert L. Hammond, *Ideas about Substance* (Baltimore: Johns Hopkins Press, 1969), p. 14.

18. George Herbert, *The Works*, ed. F. E. Hutchinson (London: Oxford Univeristy Press, 1941).

19. I've selected the most common version of sonnet 129. Another text would produce a slightly different reading.

20. For Marotti's view of Elizabethan sonnets and their demise see "'Love is Not love': Elizabethan Sonnet Sequences and the Social Order," *ELH* 49 (1982):396–428. Similar analogies between amorous and social affairs are evident also in pastoral. See Hallet Smith, *Elizabethan Poetry* (Cambridge: Harvard University Press, 1952), pp. 1–63; Louis Adrian Montrose, "'The Perfecte paterne of a Poete': The Poetics of Courtship in *The Shepheardes Calender*," *TSLL* 21 (1979):34–67 and "'Eliza, Queene of shepheardes,' and the Pastoral of Power," *ELR* 10 (1980):153–82, and my *Pastoral Forms and Attitudes* (Berkeley: University of California Press, 1971), pp. 63–81.

21. Fulke Greville, first Lord Brooke, *Poems and Dramas*, ed. Geoffrey Bullough (New York: Oxford University Press, 1945), Sonnet 7 of *Caelica*.

22. Sir Thomas Wyatt, *Collected Poems*, ed. Joost Daalder (London: Oxford Univeristy Press, 1975).

23. Heidegger, *Metaphysics*, p. 60.

24. Heidegger, *Poetry, Language, Thought*, p. 81. On the notion of the poet's being called forth, see also Gerald L. Bruns, "Intention, Authority, and Meaning," *Critical Inquiry* 7 (1980):297–310, partly in answer to Herbert F. Tucker, Jr., "Browning's Lyric Intentions," pp. 275–96.

25. John Donne, *The Divine Poems*, ed. Helen Gardner (London: Oxford Univeristy Press, 1952).

CHAPTER TWO

1. See Terry Comito, "Beauty Bare: Speaking Waters and Fountains in Renaissance Literature," from *Fons Sapientiae: Renaissance Garden Fountains*, Fifth Dumbarton Oaks Colloquium on the History of Landscape Architecture.

2. On chaos and hell see Robert M. Adams, "A Little Look into Chaos," in *Illustrious Evidence*, ed. Earl Miner (Berkeley: University of California Press, 1975), pp. 71–92; Walter Clyde Curry, *Milton's Ontology, Cosmogony, and Physics* (Lexington, Ky.: University of Kentucky Press, 1957); Merritt Y. Hughes, ed., *John Milton: Complete Poems and Major Prose* (New York: Odyssey Press, 1957), pp. 179–94; Roland Muschat Frye, *Milton's Imagery and the Visual Arts* (Princeton: Princeton University Press, 1978), pp. 43–148.

3. See Janet Adelman, "Creation and the Place of the Poet in *Paradise Lost*, in *The Author in his Work*, eds. Louis L. Martz, Aubry Williams (New Haven: Yale University Press, 1978), pp. 51–69. Sin's first "lyric" to Satan and other combinations of hymnal and heroic language I have considered in "Complicity of Voice in *Paradise Lost*, *MLQ* 25 (1964):153–170; "The Splinter Coalition," in *New Essays on Paradise Lost*, ed. Thomas Kranidas (Berkeley: University of California Press, 1969), pp. 34–57; "Symbol-Making and the Labors of Milton's Eden," *TSLL* 3 (1976):433–50.

4. See William A. Oram, "Nature, Poetry, and Milton's Genii," in *Milton and the Art of Sacred Song*, eds. J. Max Patrick and Roger H. Sundell (Madison: University of Wisconsin Press, 1979), pp. 47–64. To Oram's listing of the many genii loci in Milton, Adam should be added as both a culminating one and their chronological predecessor.

5. Arnold Stein, *The Art of Presence: The Poet and Paradise Lost* (Berkeley: University of California Press, 1977).

6. John G. Demaray, *Milton's Theatrical Epic* (Cambridge: Harvard University Press, 1980), pp. 57–72.

7. Tension between the orphic poet and the civil laureate is not new, of course. John van Sickle finds it in Virgil's *Eclogues,* for instance, where it is past-engaged in the sense that encounters between poet, state, and nature are reinterpretive and the poet's authority derives partly from predecessors. For Virgil, figures of growth and innovation prevail, however, in both the new age the fourth eclogue celebrates and the poet's own innovations. By bringing the ponderous globe and all ages to exalt the "magnum Iovis incrementum," the poet can be simultaneously herald to a political power and a Tracian Orpheus or Pan. See John B. van Sickle, "Studies of Dialectical Methodology in the Virgilian Tradition," *MLN* 85 (1970):921–22; cf. Michael C. J. Putnam, *Virgil's Pastoral Art* (Princeton: Princeton University Press, 1970), p. 165. Virgil's balancing of the orphic and laureate roles was no doubt closely assessed by both Spenser and Milton, Spenser in the higher mood of Colin's praise of Eliza in *Shepheardes Calender* and Milton beginning in the Nativity Ode, his first run at preempting secular panegyric and cancelling what he considered various idolatrous majesties.

8. See George Steiner, *Heidegger* (Sussex: The Harvester Press, 1978), p. 63.

CHAPTER THREE

1. Kenneth Burke, *A Grammar of Motives* (Berkeley: University of California Press, 1969), pp. 21–58.

2. See W. T. MacCaffrey, "Place and Patronage in Elizabethan Politics," in *Elizabethan Government and Society,* eds. S. T. Bindoff *et al.* (University of London: Athlone Press, 1961), pp. 95–126.

3. Paul Alpers, "Lycidas and Modern Criticism," *ELH* 49 (1982):468–96. See also Anna K. Nardo's comments on the idea of a community in "Lycidas," *Comus,* and Milton's sonnets—a godly community through which the individual passes on his way toward "divine circumferences." *Milton's Sonnets and the Ideal Community* (Lincoln, Nebraska: University of Nebraska Press, 1979), p. 21.

4. Isabel G. MacCaffrey, "*Lycidas:* The Poet in a Landscape," in *The Lyric and Dramatic Milton,* ed. Joseph H. Summers (New York and London: Columbia University Press, 1965), pp. 67–68.

5. See James Turner, *The Politics of Landscape* (Cambridge, Mass.: Harvard University Press, 1979), p. 19; and Raymond Williams, *The Country and the City* (New York: Oxford University Press, 1973), especially pp. 1–54. See also Ruth Nevo, *The Dial of Virtue* (Princeton: Princeton University Press, 1963), pp. 3–47.

6. Thomas Hobbes, "Answer to Davenant's Preface to *Gondibert,*" in *Critical Essays of the Seventeenth Century,* ed. J. E. Spingarn (London: Oxford University Press, 1908), pp. 54–56.

7. See Daniel Javitch, *Poetry and Courtliness in Renaissance England* (Princeton: Princeton University Press, 1978); Stephen Greenblatt, *Renaissance Self-Fashioning from More to Shakespeare* (Chicago and London: University of Chicago Press, 1980); A. C. Hamilton, *Sir Philip Sidney: A Study of his Life and Works* (Cambridge: Cambridge University Press, 1977); Richard Helgerson, *The Elizabethan Prodigals* (Berkeley: University of California Press, 1976); Walter Oakeshott, *The Queen and the Poet* (New York: Barnes & Noble, 1961), a literary biography of Raleigh; Arthur Marotti, "'Love is not love': Elizabethan Sonnet Sequences and the Social Order," *ELH* 49 (1982):396–428; John W. Moore, Jr., "Colin Breaks his Pipe: A Reading of the 'January' Eclogue," *ELR* 5 (1975):3–24; Helgerson, "The New Poet Presents Himself: Spenser and the Idea of a Literary Career," *PMLA* 93 (1978):893–911;

Louis Adrian Montrose, "Celebration and Insinuation: Sir Philip Sidney and the Motives of Elizabethan Courtship," *Renaissance Drama*, n.s. 8 (1977):3–35; and Russell Fraser, *The War Against Poetry* (Princeton: University of Princeton Press, 1970).

8. In Helgerson's reading Sidney's *Defence* does not resolve even Sidney's own doubts about the literary calling, and it seems unlikely that Sidney managed to reconcile love and honor, wit and judgment, pleasure and profit to his satisfaction. See *Elizabethan Prodigals*, p. 125.

9. Drayton's *Poly-Olbion*, for instance, can be found to maintain the courtly centrism of *The Arcadia*, historical chronicles, Daniel's *Civil Wars*, and *The Faerie Queene*. The most conspicuously geographical poem of the renaissance, it is concerned with the entire realm of Britain—its forests, groves, oceans, winds, vales, hills, rulers, villages, crafts, trades, homey country matters, Dryads, nymphs, water gods, wood goods, flora and fauna, and primarily river systems. It interweaves historical anecdotes and some of the nationalist aims of Hakluyt's travel literature and Spenserian romance without of course the sustained action of princes and heroes or interest in chivalry, idea, or argument.

10. I have considered country house poems separately in "Householding and the Poet's Vocation, Jonson and After," forthcoming in *English Studies*.

CHAPTER FOUR

1. Concerning Donne's nearly lifelong struggle with preferment and the court, see R. C. Bald, *John Donne: A Life* (New York: Oxford University Press, 1970); Edmund Gosse, *The Life and Letters of John Donne*, 2 vols. (Gloucester, Mass.: Peter Smith, 1959); John Carey, *John Donne: Life, Mind and Art* (London: Faber and Faber, 1981), pp. 60–93.

2. *Ben Jonson: Poems*, ed. Ian Donaldson (London: Oxford University Press, 1975), p. 209, 1. 52. Subsequent references are to this edition unless otherwise noted.

3. See Ian Donaldson, "Jonson and the Moralists," in *Two Renaissance Mythmakers: Christopher Marlowe and Ben Jonson*, ed. Alvin Kernan (Baltimore: Johns Hopkins University Press, 1977), p. 161.

4. *The Poems of Thomas Carew*, ed. Rhodes Dunlap (Clarendon: Oxford University Press, 1949), "To Ben Jonson," p. 65. The comment from Howell is from *Epistolae Ho-Elianae*, ed. Joseph Jacobs (London, 1890), p. 403. It is cited by Dunlap, p. 247. For the relationship between Carew and Jonson, see Edward I. Selig, *The Flourishing Wreath* (New Haven: Yale University Press, 1958), pp. 152 ff. See also Esther Cloudman Dunn, *Ben Jonson's Art* (New York: Russell and Russell, 1963), first published 1925, especially on Jonson at court, pp. 1–27; John Palmer, *Ben Jonson* (Port Washington: Kennikat Press, 1967), first published 1934, on the Apollo Room of the Old Devil Tavern and other meeting places of the Jonson circle, pp. 109 ff.; and Rufus A. Blanshard, "Carew and Jonson," *SP* 52 (1955):195–211.

5. Arthur F. Marotti, "All about Jonson's Poetry," *ELH* 39 (1972):208–37; see also Richard C. Newton, "'Ben. / Jonson': The Poet in the Poems," in *Two Renaissance Mythmakers*, pp. 165–95; George Parfitt, *Ben Jonson: Public Poet and Private Man* (London: J. M. Dent, 1976); "The Poetry of Ben Jonson," *Essays in Criticism* 18 (1968):18–31, and "Ethical Thought and Ben Jonson's Poetry," *SEL* 9 (1969):124–34; William V. Spanos, "The Real Toad in the Jonsonian Garden: Resonance in the Nondramatic Poetry," *JEGP* 68 (1969):1–23; L. C. Knights, "Ben Jonson: Public Attitudes and Social Poetry," in *A Celebration of Ben Jonson*, eds. Wm. Blissett, Julian Patrick R. W. Van Fossen (Toronto: University of Toronto Press, 1972), pp. 167–87; and Earl Miner, *The Cavalier Mode from Jonson to Cotton* (Princeton: Princeton University Press, 1971), especially on the social mode and the good life, pp. 3–99.

6. *Timber, or Discoveries*, in *Ben Jonson*, eds. C. H. Herford, Percy and Evelyn

Simpson (Clarendon: Oxford University Press, 1947), vol. 8: *The Poems and the Prose Works*, p. 620.

7. *Volpone*, Ben Jonson, eds. Herford, Simpson, vol. 5:24–25.

8. Dyer risked his status as counsel and compromised his ambassadorial mission to Bohemia in conducting experiments under the tutelage of the professional con man, Edward Kelley.

9. For commentary on the Charis sequence, see Paul M. Cubeta, "'A Celebration of Charis': An Evaluation of Jonsonian Poetic Strategy," *ELH* 25 (1958):163–80; Judith Kegan Gardiner, *Craftsmanship in Context: The Development of Ben Jonson's Poetry* (The Hague: Mouton, 1975), pp. 104–8; Richard S. Peterson, "Virtue Reconciled to Pleasure: Jonson's 'A Celebration of Charis,'" *Studies in the Literary Imagination* 6 (1973):219–68; Wesley Trimpi, *Ben Jonson's Poems: A Study of the Plain Style* (Stanford: University Press, 1962), pp. 210–28.

10. L. A. Beaurline, "The Selective Principle in Jonson's Shorter Poems," *Criticism* 8 (1966):64–74; W. David Kay, "The Christian Wisdom of Ben Jonson's 'On My First Son,'" *SEL* 11 (1971):125–36. See also J. Z. Kronenfeld, "The Father Found: Consolation Achieved through Love in Ben Jonson's 'On My First Sonne,'" *SP* 75 (1978):64–86.

11. Richard S. Peterson, "Imitation and Praise in Ben Jonson's Poems," *English Literary Renaissance* 10 (1980):267, also in *Imitation and Praise in the Poems of Ben Jonson* (New Haven: Yale University Press, 1981). See also Trimpi, p. 77.

12. Cited from John Hollander, *Vision and Resonance* (New York: Oxford University Press, 1975), p. 182.

13. On the Cary-Morison ode, see Paul H. Fry, *The Poet's Calling in the English Ode* (New Haven: Yale University Press, 1980), pp. 15–30; Peterson, pp. 195–232; Trimpi, pp. 198–200; Edwin Honig, "Examples of Poetic Diction in Ben Jonson," *Costerus* 3 (1972):56–58; Ian Donaldson, "Jonson's Ode to Sir Lucius Cary and Sir H. Morison," *Studies in the Literary Imagination* 6 (1973):139–52; John Lemly, "Masks and Self-Portraits in Jonson's Late Poetry," *ELH* 44 (1977):258–63; Mary I. Oates, "Jonson's 'Ode Pindarick' and the Doctrine of Imitation," *Papers in Language and Literature* 11 (1975):126–48.

14. The lack of recognition for Jonson's originality must be qualified, however, given the recent claims made for it by several critics in Claude J. Summers's and Ted-Larry Pebworth's edition of essays, *Classic and Cavalier: Essays on Jonson and the Sons of Ben* (Pittsburgh: University of Pittsburgh Press, 1982). Some of those claims seem exaggerated, but Richard C. Newton's argument for Jonson's assimilation of the coherence of a printed text, the bound authorial opus, supports my own sense of the integrity of the work as a whole and *therefore* (can one say?) its independence— its ownership by the author and centering of the circle in the poet's well-provisioned mind and signed works. See pp. 31–55.

Further support can be gained by careful mining from Alexander Leggatt's *Ben Jonson: His Vision and His Art* (London: Methuen, 1981). See especially "False Creations," pp. 1–44. If a false image is a departure from nature, as Leggatt suggests, a true image must appropriate "appropriately" one or more of nature's ready-to-be-cooked fish, and so the topography is mapped by an apportioning of its parts to this or that function of the poetic order and order of the estate, which distributes of course not just food and fire but all the "mysteries of manners, arms, and arts."

## CHAPTER FIVE

1. Quotations from Donne are taken from the following editions: *The Satires, Epigrams and Verse Letters*, ed. W. Milgate (Clarendon: Oxford University Press, 1967); *The Elegies and The Songs and Sonnets*, ed. Helen Gardner (Clarendon: Oxford University Press, 1965); *The Divine Poems*, ed. Helen Gardner (Clarendon: Oxford University Press, 1952).

2. The criticism of the satires is particularly variable in its views of the speaker. For a useful sampling of those readings, see N. J. C. Andreasen, "Theme and Structure in Donne's Satyres" and Thomas O. Sloan, "The Persona as Rhetor: An Interpretation of Donne's Satyre III" in *Essential Articles for the Study of John Donne's Poetry*, ed. John R. Roberts (Hamden, Conn.: Archon Books, 1975), pp. 411–23, 424–38; M. Thomas Hester, "The Satirist as Exegete: John Donne's *Satyre V*," *TSLL* 20 (1978):347–66; Richard C. Newton, "Donne the Satirist," *TSLL* 16 (1974):427–45; Wilbur Sanders, *John Donne's Poetry* (London: Cambridge University Press, 1971), pp. 34–39; John R. Lauritsen, "Donne's Satyres: The Drama of Self-Discovery," *SEL* 16 (1976):117–30.

3. M. Thomas Hester in "'Zeal'" as Satire: The Decorum of Donne's *Satyres*," *Genre* 10 (1977):173–96, allies the satires with the lamentations of Jeremiah. Donne's satiric muse is zealous as well as cankered. Compare Alvin Kernan, *The Cankered Muse: Satire of the English Renaissance* (New Haven: Yale University Press, 1959), pp. 117–18. See also Hester's booklength expansion of the argument in *Kinde Pitty and Brave Scorn; John Donne's Satyres* (Durham, N.C.: Duke University Press, 1982).

4. Alexander Pope, *The Poems*, ed. John Butt (London: Metheun, 1963). In an excellent lining up of three versions of the courtier in Horace, Donne, and Pope, Howard Erskine-Hill finds Pope falling into self-righteous complacency and snobbery at times in his translation of Donne. The key matter in my view, however, is his sociability and his implied allies, which make that snobbery possible. See "Courtiers out of Horace" in *John Donne: Essays in Celebration*, ed. A. J. Smith (London: Methuen, 1972), pp. 273–307. Pope is also more topical than Donne, which suggests a complicity between reader and writer that Donne does not assume. See Maynard Mack, *The Garden and the City* (Toronto: University of Toronto Press, 1969), pp. 89–90, 164–65; Ian Jack, "Pope and 'The Weighty Bullion of Dr. Donne's Satires,'" *PMLA* 66 (1951):1009–22, also in *Essential Articles for the Study of Alexander Pope*, ed. Maynard Mack (Hamden, Conn.: Archon Books, 1968).

Wyatt, too, strikes me as a more sociable satirist than Donne. He follows an itemization of the practices of court in the first satire with an invitation to John Poyntz to join him in Kent. His distaste for the pretensions and dishonor of Henry's court resembles Donne's view of the masquerading that dominates Elizabeth's, but the tone is softened by the epistolary address and particularly by the confessional nature of his comments to a friend.

5. Oliver Wendell Holmes, *The Autocrat of the Breakfast Table* (Philadelphia: Henry Altemus, 1897), p. 297.

6. Ralph Knevet, "The Habitation," from *A Gallery to the Temple* (Pisa: Libreria Goliardica, 1954), p. 47.

7. John Carey, *John Donne: Life, Mind and Art* (London: Faber and Faber, 1981), p. 47.

8. *Devotions upon Emergent Occasions*, Meditation X.

9. In its subordination of the life to the works, my view of Donne's response to the pursuit of a career diverges from that of some biographers. Donne's courtly ambitions come foremost for Arthur Marotti, for instance. This is not the place to debate the relations of symbolic actions to life struggles, but Marotti's reading has the disadvantage of reducing such poems as "The Canonization" and "The Sunne Rising" to "unsuccessful," ironic, "recreational" attempts to justify the marriage to Ann More and relieve the pain of a "placeless, hopeless state." They are surely more than that. I see no contradiction between Donne's anxiety over a'living and his witty severing of courtly ties in the lyrics, nor between his satirizing of the court earlier and his recurrent overtures to it. The relationship of his poetry to it seems to me different in kind from that of his predecessors. Where Wyatt, Gascoigne, and Sidney associate amorous failures with "sociopolitical failure and frustration," as Marotti has argued convincingly, Donne celebrates love's triumphs and puts even its

failures on a more personal footing. Similarly with the sermons, to regard them primarily as what sustain an ecclesiastical career and at last brings "the substantial rewards" of patronage is to submerge their substance and style in incidental social functions. See "John Donne and the Rewards of Patronage" in Guy Fitch Lytle and Stephen Orgel, eds., *Patronage in the Renaissance* (Princeton: Princeton University Press, 1981), pp. 207–34. John Carey makes similar reductions of several texts. See *John Donne,* pp. 43, 109, 155, e.g.

## CHAPTER SIX

1. Herrick "To Dean-Bourn, A rude River in Devon."

2. Robert Higbie explores Herbert's sense of place broadly in "Images of Enclosure in George Herbert's *The Temple,*" *TSLL* 15 (1974):627–38. See also Sara William Hanley, CSJ, "Temples in *The Temple:* George Herbert's Study of the Church," *SEL* 8 (1968):121–35.

3. Quotations from Herbert are taken from *The Works,* ed. F. E. Hutchinson (Clarendon: Oxford University Press, 1941).

4. "Though I am clean forgot" could be read as a consequence of the final line as well as a lingering recognition that the speaker expects no change in God's policy toward him. See Barbara Leah Harman, "George Herbert's 'Affliction (I)': The Limits of Representation," *ELH* 44 (1977):267–85. It seems more likely, however, that the speaker means "even though you persist in neglecting me, let me love anyway." See also Bill Smithson, "Herbert's 'Affliction' Poems," *SEL* 15 (1975):125–40, and Anne C. Fowler, "'With Care and Courage': Herbert's *'Affliction'* Poems," in *"Too Rich to Clothe the Sunne": Essays on George Herbert,* eds. Claude J. Summers and Ted-Larry Pebworth (Pittsburgh: University of Pittsburgh Press, 1980), pp. 129–46.

5. Opposite to "Temper I" in its discomfort with great spaces is "Content," in which the poet admonishes his "mutt'ring thoughts" to keep quiet and stay at home. There too the soul reaches to the ends of the cosmos, but it does so quietly:

> This soul doth span the world, and hang content
> From either pole unto the centre:
> Where in each room of the well-furnisht tent
> He lies warm, and without adventure.

The "discoursing soul" seeks "gentle measure" in place of "nourisht fame."

6. St. Augustine, *On Christian Doctrine,* trans. D. W. Robertson, Jr. (Indianapolis: Bobbs-Merrill, 1958), p. 38.

## CHAPTER SEVEN

1. Some of Herrick's images of kingship appear to be carry-overs from Tudor mythmaking; some of them come from King Solomon. See Heather Asals, "King Solomon in the Land of the *Hesperides,*" *TSLL* 18 (1976):362–80.

2. See K. M. Briggs, *The Anatomy of Puck* (London: Routledge and Kegan Paul, 1959), *The Fairies* (Chicago: University of Chicago Press, 1967), and *The Vanishing People* (London: B. T. Batsford, 1978); Daniel H. Woodward, "Herrick's Oberon Poems," *JEGP* 64 (1965):270–84; and Peter Schwinger, "Herrick's Fairy State," *ELH* 46 (1979):35–55.

3. Several critics have questioned the order and arrangement both of the items of "The Argument" and the collection, *Hesperides.* See John L. Kimmey, "Order and Form in Herrick's *Hesperides,*" *JEGP* 70 (1971):255–68; Richard L. Capwell, "Herrick and the Aesthetic Principle of Variety and Contrast," *South Atlantic Quarterly* 71 (1972):488–95; Leo Spitzer, "Herrick's 'Delight in Disorder,'" *MLN* 76 (1961):209–14; Roger B. Rollin, *Robert Herrick* (New York: Twayne Publishers, 1966). Rollin

stresses the unity of Herrick's conception of himself and the thematic order of the poems. I find the variety of the volume more impressive than any principle of order yet attributed to it, as does Austin Warren in "Herrick Revisited," *Michigan Quarterly Review* 15 (1976):245–67, and Gordon Braden, "Herrick's Classical Quotations," in *"Trust to Good Verses": Herrick Tercentenary Essays*, eds. Roger B. Rollin and J. Max Patrick (Pittsburgh: University of Pittsburgh Press, 1978), pp. 127–248. See also Paul R. Jenkins, "Rethinking What Moderation Means to Robert Herrick," *ELH* 39 (1972):49–65, who frames Herrick's classicism partly in terms of the change and difference that *Hesperides* reveals and its Dionysian temper.

4. Robert Harbison, *Eccentric Spaces* (New York: Alfred A. Knopf, 1977), p. 81.

5. Quotations are taken from *The Poetical Works*, ed. L. C. Martin (Clarendon: Oxford University Press, 1956). I have omitted italics and cited poems by the numbers of J. Max Patrick's edition, *The Complete Poetry* (New York: W. W. Norton, 1968), which I have used for "Master Herrick's Farewell unto Poetry" and "The Apparition."

6. Thomas Carlyle, *Sartor Resartus* (London: Dent, 1908), p. 25.

7. Ben Jonson, "On English Monsieur" from Epigrams, in *Poems*, ed. Ian Donaldson (London: Oxford University Press, 1975).

8. Harvest and festivity are the two most commented upon aspects of Herrick's poetry. See Robert H. Deming, *Ceremony and Art* (The Hague and Paris: Mouton Press, 1974); A. Leigh Deneef, *"This Poetick Liturgie": Robert Herrick's Ceremonial Mode* (Durham, N.C.: Duke University Press, 1974); Jay A. Gertzman, "Robert Herrick's Recreative Pastoral," *Genre* 7 (1974):183–95; Richard E. Hughes, "Herrick's 'Hock Cart,' Companion Piece to 'Corinna's going A-Maying,'" *College English* 27 (1966):420–22; Thomas R. Whitaker, "Herrick and the Fruits of the Garden," *ELH* 22 (1955):16–33; James S. Tillman, "Herrick's Georgic Encomia" in *Tercentenary Essays*, pp. 149–58. See also Josef Pieper, *In Tune with the World: A Theory of Festivity* (New York: Harcourt Brace and World, 1965) and Harvey Cox, *The Feast of Fools* (Cambridge: Harvard University Press, 1969).

9. Gordon Braden, *The Classics and English Renaissance Poetry* (New Haven and London: Yale University Press, 1978), p. 160.

10. Herrick's fondness for biblical reference and under certain circumstances even for hieroglyphics—despite his avoidance of them on occasions when they would seem natural—has been noted by A. B. Chambers in "Herrick, Corinna, Canticles, and Catullus," *SP* 74 (1977):216–27, and "Herrick and the Trans-shifting of Time," *SP* 72 (1975):85–114; Ronald Berman, "Herrick's Secular Poetry," *English Studies* 52 (1971):20–30.

11. James Turner, *The Politics of Landscape* (Cambridge: Harvard University Press, 1979), pp. 150–51. Herrick's alliance with the court and sympathy with cavalier verse are examined by a number of critics. As Joseph Summers points out, Herrick "seems to have wished very much to be a courtier," and the poems abound with indications of that wish, although he is not bothered by the sixteenth-century courtly poet's need to moralize or make poems of service to the state. See *The Heirs of Donne and Jonson* (London: Chatto & Windus, 1970), p. 52. See also F. W. Moorman, *Robert Herrick* (New York: Russell and Russell, 1962); George Walton Scott, *Robert Herrick* (London: Sidgwick Jackson, 1974); Rose Macaulay, *The Shadow Flies* (New York and London: Harper & Brothers, 1932).

CHAPTER EIGHT

1. For representative treatments of schemes a century apart, see Richard Sherry, *A Treatise of Schemes and Tropes* [1550] (facsimile from the Huntington Library) and John Smith, *The Mysterie of Rhetorique Unvail'd* (London, 1657). Smith cites similar tropes and figures but illustrates partly from the Bible.

2. Geoffrey H. Hartman describes a similar line of romance in "False Themes and Gentle Minds," which I have found suggestive and useful. See *Beyond Formalism* (New Haven: Yale University Press, 1970), pp. 283–97. See also George Geckle, "Miltonic Idealism: 'L'Allegro' and 'Il Penseroso,'" *TSLL* 9 (1968):455–73; Leslie Brisman, *Milton's Poetry of Choice and Its Romantic Heirs* (Ithaca: Cornell University Press, 1973); David M. Miller, "From Delusion to Illumination: A Larger Structure for *L'Allegro-Il Penseroso*," *PMLA* 86 (1971):32–39.

3. See Roland Mushat Frye's reproductions in *Milton's Imagery and the Visual Arts* (Princeton: Princeton University Press, 1978).

4. Appleton, *The Experience of Landscape* (Chicester, New York: John Wiley and Sons, 1975); Bert O. States, "Standing on the Extreme Verge in *King Lear* and Other High Places," *Georgia Review* 36 (1982):417–25.

5. P. 425. The quotation from Heidegger comes from *Being and Time*, trans. John Macquarrie and Edward Robinson (New York: Harper & Row, 1962), p. 140.

6. Henry Vaughan, *The Works*, ed. L. C. Martin (Clarendon: Oxford University Press, 1957), p. 403.

## CHAPTER NINE

1. John Bunyan, *The Pilgrim's Progress* (London: J. M. Dent, 1907), pp. 116–19. On topographical places and elements of homily and argument, see U. Milo Kaufmann, *The Pilgrim's Progress and Traditions in Puritan Meditation* (New Haven: Yale University Press, 1966), especially "Puritan Hermeneutics," pp. 25–60. Kaufmann also reads characters as intermediate between idea and event, p. 80. See also Henri A. Talon, "Space and the Hero in *The Pilgrim's Progress*," *Études anglaise* 14 (1961):124–30, reprinted in *The Pilgrim's Progress: A Casebook*, ed. Roger Sharrock (London: Macmillan, 1976), 158–68.

2. Critics have interpreted Bunyan's topography in basically psychological, social, and doctrinal ways. It is these and more, but I find the landscape-as-argument, with theses reaching into each of these areas, more encompassing. All views are ably represented in *The Pilgrim's Progress: Critical and Historical Views*, ed. Vincent Newey. See especially Newey, "Bunyan and the Confines of the Mind" for (to my mind) an overly psychological reading; and James Turner, "Bunyan's Sense of Place."

3. Henry Vaughan, *The Works*, ed. L. C. Martin (Clarendon: Oxford University Press, 1957).

4. The primrose path is familiar from the Canticles, for instance, as Barbara Lewalski points out, and the Mount of Olives may be implicated in the fountain of stanza seven, the church in the grove. See *Protestant Poetics and the Seventeenth-Century Religious Lyric* (Princeton: Princeton University Press, 1979), p. 106, and Jonathan F. S. Post, *Henry Vaughan: The Unfolding Vision* (Princeton: Princeton University Press, 1982), p. 196.

5. Thomas Traherne, *Centuries, Poems and Thanksgivings*, ed. H. M. Margoliouth, vol. 1 (Clarendon: Oxford University Press, 1958):110–11.

6. See R. A. Durr, *On the Mystical Poetry of Henry Vaughan* (Cambridge: Harvard University Press, 1962); Kenneth Friedenreich, *Henry Vaughan* (Boston: Twayne, 1978); Ross Garner, *Henry Vaughan: Experience and the Tradition* (Chicago: University of Chicago Press, 1959); Patrick Grant, "Hermetic Philosophy and the Naturae of Man in Vaughan's *Silex Scintillans*," *JEGP* 67 (1968):406–22; Elizabeth Holmes, *Henry Vaughan and the Hermetic Philosophy* (New York: Russell & Russell, 1932); H. J. Oliver, "The Mysticism of Henry Vaughan: A Reply," *JEGP* 53 (1954):352–60; Jonathan F. S. Post, "Vaughan's 'The Night' and his 'late and dusky' Age," *SEL* 19 (1979):127–41; Bain Tate Stewart, "Hermetic Symbolism in Henry Vaughan's 'The Night'," *PQ* 29 (1950):417–22; A. J. Smith, "Henry Vaughan's Ceremony of Innocence," *Essays and Studies*, n.s. 26 (1973):35–52; Rachel Trickett, "Henry Vaughan

and the Poetry of Vision," *Essays and Studies,* n.s. 34 (1981):88–104; A. W. Rudrum, "Vaughan's 'The Night': Some Hermetic Notes," *MLR* 64 (1969):11–19, "The Influence of Alchemy in the Poems of Henry Vaughan," *PQ* 49 (1970):469–80, and "An Aspect of Vaughan's Hermeticism: The Doctrine of Cosmic Sympathy," *SEL* 14 (1974):129–38; James D. Simmonds, *Masques of God: Form and Theme in the Poetry of Henry Vaughan* (Pittsburgh: University of Pittsburgh Press, 1972).

Several critics have commented on the pilgrimage figure in Vaughan. See Isabel G. MacCaffrey, "The Meditative Paradigm," *ELH* 32 (1965):388–407; Louis L. Martz, *The Poetry of Meditation* (New Haven: Yale University Press, 1954), pp. 61–67, 86–90; Barbara Lewalski on seventeenth-century symbols in general and Vaughan's dominant symbolic mode, in *Literary Uses of Typology from the Late Middle Ages to the Present,* ed. Earl Miner (Princeton: Princeton University Press, 1977), p. 96; Cleanth Brooks, "Henry Vaughan; Quietism and Mysticism," in *Essays in Honor of Esmond Linworth Marilla,* eds. Thomas Austin Kirby and William John Olive (Baton Rouge: Louisiana State University Press, 1970), pp. 3–26; A. W. Rudrum, "Henry Vaughan and the Theme of Transfiguration," *Southern Review* 1 (1963):54–67 (Australia); Donald R. Howard, *Writers and Pilgrims: Medieval Pilgrimage Narratives and Their Posterity* (Berkeley: University of California Press, 1980), pp. 111 ff.

7. Concerning the ring and the bridegroom figures, see Leland H. Chambers, "Vaughan's 'The World': The Limits of Extrinsic Criticism," *SEL* 8 (1968):137–50.

CHAPTER TEN

1. On the unity and structure of the poem, see David Evett, "'Paradice's Only Map': The Topos of the *Locus Amoenus* and the Structure of Marvell's *Upon Appleton House,*" *PMLA* 85 (1970):504–13; Rosalie L. Colie, *"My Ecchoing Song": Andrew Marvell's Poetry of Criticism* (Princeton: Princeton University Press, 1970), pp. 181–294; Frederic H. Roth, Jr., "Marvell's 'Upon Appleton House': A Study in Perspective," *TSLL* 14 (1972):269–81. For the garden elements and rural estate background, see William A. McClung, *The Country House in English Renaissance Poetry* (Berkeley: University of California Press, 1977), pp. 147–65; John Dixon Hunt, "'Loose Nature' and the 'Garden Square': the gardenist background for Marvell's poetry," in *Approaches to Marvell,* ed. C. A. Patrides (London: Routledge & Kegan Paul, 1978), pp. 331–51; Terry Comito, *The Idea of the Garden in the Renaissance* (New Brunswick: Rutgers University Press, 1978); Dale Herron, "Marvell's 'Garden' and the Landscape of Poetry," *JEGP* 73 (1974):328–37. Structural units in the work are discussed by Isabel MacCaffrey, "The Scope of Imagination in *Upon Appleton House,*" in *Tercentenary Essays in Honor of Andrew Marvell,* ed. Kenneth Friedenreich (Hamden, Conn.: The Shoe String Press, 1977), pp. 224–44, and in the same collection, Maren-Sophie Røstvig, "Circular Structure in 'The Unfortunate Lover' and *Upon Appleton House,*" pp. 245–67. See also my review article, "The Critical Reprocessing of Andrew Marvell," *ELH* 47 (1980):189–92, and comments on fitness of expressive forms in "Marvell's Songs and Pictorial Exhibits," *Tercentenary Essays,* pp. 105–20. Marvell citations are from *The Poems and Letters,* ed. H. M. Margoliouth (Clarendon: Oxford University Press, 1952).

2. See James Edward Seemon, "Art and Argument in Marvell's 'Horatian Ode Upon Cromwell's Return from Ireland,'" *Neuphilogische Mitteilungen* 73 (1972):823–35; Thomas R. Edwards, *Imagination and Power: A Study of Poetry on Public Themes* (New York: Oxford University Press, 1971), pp. 66–82.

3. A. R. Ammons, "Gravely Run" in *Collected Poems 1951–1971* (New York: W. W. Norton, 1972), p. 56.

# INDEX

Alpers, Paul, 55–59
Ammons, A. R., 3–5, 9, 10, 13, 14, 20, 21, 30, 230
Apostrophe, 3–11, 29–33, 39–40, 44–47, 145, 181, 183, 190, 203. *See also* Celebration; Crossing; Lyric object
Appleton, Jay, 173, 177
Appropriation. *See* Possession
Augustine, Saint, 142
Authority, 10–11, 29–33, 53–64, 69, 127–29, 130, 271. *See also* Orphic poet
Awakening, 29–32

Barnfield, Richard, 19–21, 22
Beaurline, L. A., 87
Bible, 46, 126, 142–43, 186, 191, 198
Birds, 2–9, 30–31, 198–99, 209, 223
Blake, William, 12, 85, 204
Bloom, Harold, 7
Braden, Gordon, 162
Bunyan, John, 57, 102, 166, 186–88, 190–91, 195, 200–201, 204, 207
Burke, Kenneth, 53–54, 56

Camden, William, 85–86, 87, 88, 92, 93
Carew, Thomas, 76, 89, 93, 226
Carey, John, 117
Carlyle, Thomas, 152, 154
Catullus, 161
Cavaliers, 54, 68, 107, 226. *See also* Herrick; Jonson

Celebration, 3, 7–9, 23–25, 33, 37–40, 65, 67, 74, 86, 89, 109, 110, 113, 143, 248, 205, 227. *See also* Apostrophe
Chaos, 34–36, 117–20, 180–82. *See also* Disorder
Charles I, 215–18
Clothes, 152–58
Coleridge, Samuel, 19, 191
Colman, Henry, 185
Comito, Terry, 36
Commonplaces. *See* Topics
Country house poem, 75, 77, 88–90, 129, 164, 180–81, 207–13, 218–24
Courtly poetry, 19–29, 97, 126, 177, 226, 229
Crashaw, Richard, 48, 89, 143, 185
Cromwell, Oliver, 213–18
Crossing, 7, 39, 42, 45–46, 121, 126, 190, 218. *See also* Apostrophe; Lyric object; Pilgrimage; Presence

Decorum, 65–66, 88, 155, 219–24
Derrida, Jacques, 49
Dickinson, Emily, 15–16, 20
Disorder, 14–17, 88, 151, 152, 164, 165, 181, 210. *See also* Chaos
Displacement, 40, 111, 117–18, 139–40, 225–26
Donaldson, Ian, 74
Donne, John, 19, 21, 23, 30–32, 54, 55, 66, 68, 69, 71–72, 77, 84, 92, 93, 94–121, 125, 126, 145, 147, 155, 169, 191, 192, 204, 226, 229, 239n.9

Drayton, Michael, 20, 68, 69, 84, 93, 159, 161, 237n.9
Dryden, John, 68, 226–29
Dyer, Edward, 80, 238n.8

Eliot, T. S., x, 62, 230
Elizabeth, Queen, 20, 126
Emblem, 17–24, 39, 43, 106, 108, 110, 114, 116, 129, 188, 202
Emerson, Ralph Waldo, 2, 9
Empson, William, 56
*England's Helicon*, 19–21, 22, 93

Fairfax, Maria, 207–10, 213, 214, 218, 222, 223, 225
Fairfax, Thomas, 208, 213, 221, 225
Falling, 168, 172–83, 193, 201–3
Fraser, Russell, 67
Frost, Robert, 4, 9, 230
Frye, Northrop, 234n.16

Gascoigne, George, 67, 93, 239n.9
Genius of place, 208, 235n.4
Genre, 64–69, 185, 208, 229
Greville, Fulke, 26–27

Hardy, Thomas, 9
Hartman, Geoffrey H., 242n.2
Harvey, Christopher, 185
Hawkes, Jacquetta, 4
Hegel, William, 14, 230
Heidegger, Martin, 2, 13, 15, 17, 30, 49
Helgerson, Richard, 67, 237n.8
Herbert, George, 20, 23–24, 26, 27, 29, 48, 54, 55, 68, 84, 107, 108, 124–45, 147, 149, 162–63, 169, 173, 177, 178–79, 185, 186, 189, 191, 192, 193, 194, 196–97, 198, 205, 207, 226, 229, 231, 240n.3
Herrick, Robert, 14, 76, 93, 128–29, 145, 146–65, 211, 226
Hobbes, Thomas, 64–66, 69
Hollander, John, 88
Holmes, Oliver Wendell, 99–100
Homer, 53, 66, 161, 168
Hopkins, Gerard Manley, 202
Horace, 78, 163, 215, 217
Hough, Graham, 18–19
Howell, James, 75

Javitch, Daniel, 67
Johnson, Samuel, 55
Jonson, Ben, 14, 46, 69, 70–93, 95, 99, 103, 104, 105, 125, 145, 146, 147, 148, 153, 154, 155, 158, 159, 161, 162, 163, 169, 204, 207, 213, 229

Kay, W. D., 87
Keats, John, 14, 144, 162, 191
Knevet, Ralph, 107–8, 185

Literary history, 53–54, 56, 63–64, 68–69, 71, 93, 185, 226–231
Love poetry, 19–29, 33, 38, 83, 105–120, 130–36, 144–45, 153, 164–65, 225
Lyric object, 7–17, 23, 29, 30, 39–41, 54, 114, 116–17, 119, 148–150, 154–55, 157–160, 167, 196–97, 208–210. *See also* Apostrophe; Celebration; Crossing; Presence; Substance

MacCaffrey, Isabel, 61

Marotti, Arthur, 26, 78, 82
Marvell, Andrew, 11, 12, 22, 31, 35, 36, 46, 48, 52, 54, 55, 64, 67, 69, 90, 107, 125, 128, 142, 147, 150, 154, 165, 169, 172, 179–182, 205, 206–27, 229
Mazzaro, Jerome, 18–19
Metaphysicals, 185
Milton, John, 22, 29, 30, 31, 33, 64, 66, 84, 90, 125, 129, 145, 147, 162, 167–72, 173, 177, 185, 195, 207, 213, 214, 217, 218, 224, 226, 229, 230, 231; "L'Allegro" and "Il Penseroso," 42, 60, 61, 65, 150, 165, 170–71; "Lycidas," 42, 48, 55–64, 65, 67, 68, 128, 170; *Paradise Lost*, 23, 24, 29–30, 33, 35–49, 54, 62–63, 65, 68, 171, 182–83, 218, 229; *Paradise Regained*, 57, 183
Moore, Marianne, 148, 165
Music, 17–24, 30, 82, 83, 92, 139

Nature. *See* Lyric object; Substance

Orphic poet, 10, 55, 67. *See also* Authority; Genius of place
Ovid, 161

Paradise, 33, 47, 120–21, 130, 137, 162, 183, 188, 194, 209–10, 213–14, 221–22, 227. *See also* Milton; *Paradise Lost*
Pastoral, 9–10, 19–21, 55–64, 65, 67, 68, 75, 92, 167–68, 225. *See also* Milton: "Lycidas"; Theocritus; Virgil
Peckham, Morse, 14
Peterson, Richard S., 88
Petrarch, 28, 32, 107
Pilgrimage, 177, 184–205. *See also* Bunyan; Vaughan

Pope, Alexander, 96–98
Possession, 2–17, 19, 20–30, 33, 35, 39–41, 64, 67, 74, 86, 88, 108–11, 114–15, 145, 148, 175, 205, 233–34n1. *See also* Address; Celebration; Crossing; Lyric object
Post, Jonathan, 198
Presence, 29–43, 45–46, 115–21, 129–30, 138, 140–41, 144–45. *See also* Apostrophe; Lyric object
Provincialism, viii, 9–10. *See also* Country house poem
Puttenham, George, 55

Raleigh, Sir Walter, 72, 93, 167
Ransom, John Crowe, 5–6, 16–17, 22, 53
Rhetoric, 7, 12, 18, 20, 55, 125, 167–70, 185–86
Riffaterre, Michael, 12–13

Satire, 94–105, 110, 155, 204–5, 228–29
Scripture. *See* Bible
Shakespeare, William, 7–8, 19, 24–26, 27, 28, 29, 46, 47–48, 69, 84, 168, 173–77, 231
Shelley, Percy, 8–9, 14, 144
Shepard, Paul, 4
Sherry, Richard, 169
Sidney, Sir Philip, 11–12, 17–18, 29, 55, 60, 67, 68, 69, 72, 92, 93, 125, 167, 177, 229
Spenser, Edmund, 10, 18, 21, 28, 29, 46, 54, 55, 59, 60, 61, 63, 67, 68, 69, 74, 77, 84, 92, 93, 105, 167–68, 177, 191, 199, 229, 230
States, Bert O., 173, 174
Stein, Arnold, 43
Stevens, Wallace, 16, 30–31, 230
Substance, 7, 11–17, 22, 35, 53–54, 64, 80, 110, 116, 121, 201, 208–9. *See also* Lyric object
Swift, Jonathan, 152

Theocritus, 53, 55, 63, 64
Topics, 4, 10, 13, 20, 53, 88, 107, 116, 125, 136, 143, 169, 185–88, 191. *See also* Emblem; Rhetoric
Traherne, Thomas, 177, 195, 198
Turner, James, 64, 164
Tuve, Rosamond, 125–26

Vaughan, Henry, 36, 46, 48, 55, 67, 84, 89, 107, 108, 125, 128, 145, 147, 149, 169, 172, 177, 179, 184–205, 207, 213, 214, 226
Virgil, 9–10, 14, 46, 53, 55, 60, 62, 63, 64, 76, 161, 168

Williams, Raymond, 64
Williams, William Carlos, 148, 165, 230
Wilson, Edmund, 88
Wordsworth, William, 6–7, 8, 14, 144
Wyatt, Thomas, 19, 20, 21, 23, 26, 27–29, 54, 93, 177, 179, 239n.4

Yeats, W. B., 85, 162